D0753138

Marx, Engels, and the Poets

Marx, Engels, and the Poets

Origins of Marxist Literary Criticism

By

Peter Demetz

Revised and enlarged by the author and
translated by Jeffrey L. Sammons

The University of Chicago Press

Chicago & London

This book is based upon the author's *Marx, Engels und die Dichter* (Stuttgart: Deutsche Verlags-Anstalt GmbH., 1959) © 1959 by Deutsche Verlags-Anstalt GmbH.

Library of Congress Catalog Card Number: 66–23685

THE UNIVERSITY OF CHICAGO PRESS, CHICAGO & LONDON
The University of Toronto Press, Toronto 5, Canada

73858

Preface

The present volume discusses the origins and formation of Marxist literary doctrine, which attempts to derive artistic achievements from economic and social elements. My investigation is primarily concerned to show the dependence of Marxist literary theory upon German nineteenth-century radicalism and its incipient articulation in the scattered writings of Karl Marx and Friedrich Engels; in later chapters I turn to the more modern Marxist critics, such as G. V. Plekhanov, Franz Mehring, and Georg Lukács, and briefly indicate the most recent developments in the work of Theodor W. Adorno, Hans Mayer, and Lucien Goldmann. I touch upon a number of questions that have provoked more than one generation of commentators to continual discussion and controversy, and inevitably concern myself with problems that have been treated by far more qualified critics before me. Nevertheless, my study differs from Edmund Wilson's *To the Finland Station* (1940) and Ludwig Marcuse's scattered but basic essays on the problem of Young Germany and Marxist aesthetics by what is perhaps a more systematic procedure; and from Auguste Cornu (Paris), Paul Reimann (Prague), Hans Koch (East Berlin), and other official apologists by what I hope is a more flexible as well as a more skeptical way of testing source materials for the theoretical validity of the arguments they put forward.

It is true that such an effort (which tries to encompass developments of more than a century and a half in a few chapters) must pay for such certainties as it may offer with a methodological compromise. I have attempted, on the one hand, to describe the historical filiation of ideas by referring to persons, documents, and texts; on the other, I have been concerned to fulfil the obligations of critical scholarship by inquiring about the validity of the ideas described. Fundamentally, I am trying to follow the example of my teacher René Wellek; if I have succeeded in avoiding the imaginative flights of German *Geistesgeschichte* as well as the descent into mere description, all the credit is due to Professor Wellek; where I have departed from the straight and narrow path, I am myself responsible.

I had the welcome opportunity to work out the basic arguments of the present study in my dissertation (Department of Comparative Literature, Yale University, 1956), which I then published at the invitation of the Deutsche Verlags-Anstalt under the title *Marx, Engels und die Dichter* (Stuttgart, 1959) in my own translation. But since then I have changed my opinion on many points, and much new material, for example, on the aesthetic implications of the *Economic-Philosophical Manuscripts*, on Heinrich Heine, on the recent writings of Lukács, and on intellectual trends after the Hungarian revolution, has been added. Whoever occupies himself with the fascinating history of nineteenth-century ideas cannot easily remove himself from the changing history of his own age, and finally finds himself writing a new book instead of merely revising the old manuscript. Preliminary studies for some of the chapters appeared in *Merkur* (Munich), *German Life and Letters* (Oxford), and *The Germanic Review;* and I wish to thank most cordially the editors for publishing my preliminary analyses, which subsequently underwent considerable revision.

I owe a particular debt of gratitude to Mr. Jeffrey L. Sammons, who resolutely shouldered the burden of this second translation, thus permitting me to devote my sabbatical year to an investigation of new questions, and to Miss Gudrun Schiller, who was particularly helpful in consolidating the growing bibliography. My sincere thanks are due also to those of my teachers who furthered my work with encouragement and justified skepticism, above all

Professors André von Gronicka, Maynard Mack, Konstantin Reichardt, and Hermann J. Weigand, and to Hans Egon Holthusen, who in his essays and letters never wearied of reminding me of the legitimate tasks of literary scholarship. *Docti indocti scribimus passim.*

P. D.

Lausanne, Switzerland

Contents

Introduction   1

1. *Young Friedrich Engels as a Critic*
   A LITERARY MODEL: KARL GUTZKOW   9
   THE POLITICAL PERSPECTIVE: LUDWIG BÖRNE   16
   PHILOSOPHICAL RADICALISM: THE YOUNG
       HEGELIANS   23

2. *Economics and Intellect: Thomas Carlyle*
   FRIEDRICH ENGELS AS CARLYLE'S TRANSLATOR   34
   THE "FILM" OF LITERATURE   40

3. *On the Way to Economic Determinism:*
   Karl Marx
   THE YOUNG POET   47
   VISIONS AND THEORIES (1844)   59
   DOUBTS AND DOGMAS (1857–59)   67

4. *Conflicts and Discussions*
   PERSONAL CONTACTS: MARX, ENGELS, AND HEINE   74
   GEORG HERWEGH   82
   FERDINAND FREILIGRATH   90
   KARL MARX'S COMMENTARY ON EUGÈNE SUE'S
       Les mystères de Paris   102
   MARX'S AND ENGELS' CRITICISM OF FERDINAND
       LASSALLE'S *Franz von Sickingen*   107

5. *The Later Engels as a Critic of Marxist*
   Literary Doctrine

   A DIFFERENT TASTE   116
   A THEORY OF SOCIALIST REALISM?   127
   ENGELS AS A REVISIONIST?   138

6. *Three Interpretations: Shakespeare,*
   Goethe, Balzac

   SHAKESPEARE   152
   GOETHE   159
   BALZAC   169

7. *The First Disciples*

   A SURVEY OF DEVELOPMENTS   178
   FRANZ MEHRING (1846–1919)   181
   GEORGY VALENTINOVICH PLEKHANOV
      (1857–1918)   189

8. *Georg Lukács as a Theoretician of Literature*   199

   THE HEIDELBERG PERIOD   200
   THE DOCTRINAIRE PERIOD   205
   IDEALIST AND DOCTRINAIRE: SOME CONTINUITIES   214
   THE OCTOGENARIAN LUKÁCS: ON THE WAY TO
      ARISTOTLE   217

9. *Marxist Criticism: Past and Present*   228

   Notes   237

   Bibliography   257

   Index   273

Introduction

Beginning with the French Revolution, private destinies came to depend more visibly than ever before on all-encompassing public events. The Jacobin celebrations on the Champs du Mars, with masses of people marching in close-order drill, symbolically anticipated the future regimentation of the individual by detached and calculating rulers; the total mobilization of the French nation against the intervening armies of the aristocratic coalition put an end to localized gentlemen's wars; in the Napoleonic conflicts all Europe was drawn into the maelstrom of popular revolts, fateful changes of government, strategic troop movements, and surprise invasions. After the artillery engagement of Valmy (September, 1792), Goethe predicted a new era of world history; and in the spring of 1813, when he fled to Teplitz from the noise of war at Weimar, he was inclined to admit that an age was dawning in which politics would be an all-pervasive force. The sons of his Dresden friends had hurried to the colors of the Prussian volunteers; in the colonnade at Teplitz the Russian princesses, sipping mineral water from delicate glasses, spoke of nothing but the war. Even in the heart of old Europe it had become impossible to escape the political demands of the moment.

The restoration attempted in vain to put an end to the continuing unrest. Metternich and the great powers formed their system of alliances in order to lull Europe once again away from politics into a passive slumber that they sought to maintain with bayonets and investigating commissions. They were unable to extinguish the fires that continued to smolder under the surface. Although the restoration tried to discourage general political interest, the result was, paradoxically, that spheres of life that up to

1

then had been self-contained now became increasingly involved
with politics. In this regard the intellectual development of the
German territories under Metternich runs parallel to that of Russia under the tsars in the nineteenth century; whenever the political spokesmen of the nation have no opportunity to criticize openly, all criticism—including that of literature—becomes political.
Instead of remaining legitimate and concrete subjects operating
in their own proper spheres, literature, aesthetics, and philosophy
become inextricably entangled with questions of power.

The young men who had carried the Prussian colors to Paris in
the wars of liberation and returned, disappointed, to an illiberal
homeland formed themselves into a resistance movement to carry
the passions of politics into the everyday drabness of the Biedermeier age. The disillusion of the veterans crystallized into the
Burschenschaft (1815); of the eleven charter members, nine had
served in the volunteer corps. But the young men lacked definite
goals and competent leaders; they lost themselves in raptures
about pan-Germany, the *Volkskaisertum* of the Middle Ages, gym-
nastics, and a future constitution, and were unable to formulate
tangible political goals. After the assassination of the popular
playwright August Kotzebue for his activities as a Russian agent
(March 23, 1819), the restoration went on the offensive with the
Carlsbad Decrees; liberal students and professors were jailed, and
witch-hunts were organized that found some of their victims even
among the clergy.

With such means it was, of course, impossible to prevent the
political unrest from spilling over into literature and literary
criticism. The patriotic German reader escaped, to an ever increasing degree, into a literature that spoke of beauty but meant
liberty. Wolfgang Menzel's book *Die deutsche Literatur* (1828),
which discussed the most current political questions beneath a
thin disguise of literary concerns, was an immediate success. Menzel had fought at Waterloo and had been a member of the
Burschenschaft before he chose journalism as his profession. The
message of this bulky work on the development of German literature was not hard to grasp. Germany had produced books long

enough; it was high time, in Menzel's opinion, to turn the virile energy that had been squandered on belles-lettres to historically meaningful actions. "Nothing is more common," wrote Menzel, "than the error of valuing the word, especially the printed word, more than free ideas, and books more than men. . . . The spirit grows flabby among books. . . . One learns the words by heart and feels relieved of the trouble of doing one's own thinking. . . . There is no easier way to make a stupid herd of sheep out of free men than to make readers of them." (1836 ed; I, 12.)

It is hardly surprising that the patriot Menzel, who only in later years was revealed as a chauvinist, agreed on literary matters with Madame de Staël, a resolute admirer of German forests and German Romantics. In her study *De la littérature considérée dans ses rapports avec les institutions sociales* (1800), she called attention to those questions that arise from the intimate connection between national history and literature. She by no means neglected the ideas of virtue and *gloire* as expressed in the lean rhetoric of the eighteenth century, but she also argued, with more modern intensity, that no attempt had been made to examine the moral and political motives that modify the spirit of literature ("il me semble que l'on n'a pas suffisamment analysé les causes morales et politiques, qui modifient l'esprit de la littérature" [2d ed., 1801; I, 27]). To be sure, Madame de Staël must share the credit of having opened the modern sociological discussion of literature with Louis-Gabriel-Ambroise de Bonald (1754–1840), who, as H. F. Fuegen points out, as early as 1796 in his *Théorie du pouvoir politique et religieux dans la société civile* investigated the influence of politics upon art and literature, and began his later treatise *Du style et de la littérature* (1806) with the assertion that literature is an expression of society. Without realizing it, he had formulated one of the most persistent clichés of modern sociology of literature.

Neither Menzel nor his French predecessors were the first to raise such questions. The interaction and antithesis of intellect and society had occupied the attention of philosophers and critics since Plato, Aristotle, and Horace. With its own peculiar optimism, ancient poetics trusted in the immanent power and theoretical knowledge of the creative intellect; the poet created a work out of an inborn harmony of talent and practical mastery of rhetorical principles. Even if Plato and Aristotle did admit that a poetic work of a special kind might derive from superhuman inspiration, it is nevertheless clear that the idea of divine inspiration, depreciating the human achievement as it does, appeared highly suspect to the *clarté* of the ancient mind. Even Plato occasionally referred to divine inspiration only in order to place the poet—irresponsible, confused, and obscure—beneath the precise and rigorous philosopher in his scale of values. In early aesthetics, the poet appeared as a peculiarly gifted being with a strange power of contributing to the refinement of society. Whether the poet appeared as "maker" (Aristotle), as the guardian of tradition (Horace), or as a courtly teacher and singer (Sidney), the assumption always obtained that society was his audience and that his poetic works were intended to affect it. Strangely enough, it did not occur to the ancient mind to inquire more closely into the possible effects of a society refined in this way upon rhetoric and the poets themselves.

This did not happen until the time when ancient poetic doctrine collapsed. In the second half of the eighteenth century there was a tendency to see the once independent poet as subordinate to the external forces around him, to belittle his creative autonomy, and finally to "explain" him as a mere product of historical forces. The new perspective of historicism, which began to push normative aesthetics into the background, became less and less interested in the work of art itself; it turned to the development of the artist and, beyond him, to those determining elements of history that forced from the artist causally explicable works. At first, the collapse of the ancient normative theories, as Meinecke pointed out, promised to open up a magnificent epoch of joyful discovery of the individual, the nation, and the many voices of humanity. But as early as 1725, Giovanni Battista Vico in his *Scienza nuova* declared that the typical individual is determined by the cyclical movement of the total historical process. Voltaire's *Essai sur les mœurs et l'esprit des nations* (1756) pointed to government combined with religion as the most decisive factors in the formation of cultures; in Germany, Winckelmann insisted that the character of artistic achievement is determined by the degree of freedom granted to the individual. With Johann Gottfried Herder (1744–1803), who embraced the ideas of his English and German predecessors with enormous enthusiasm, the possible dangers of historicism emerge for the first time: the joy of discovering the matchless radiance of the unique historical figure was coupled with the tendency to dissolve the individual into the stream of history or of the *Volksgeist*. Herder enthusiastically sensed the individuality of the artist, only to dissolve it again in the onrushing flood of the historical process. For the sake of history, of the *Volksgeist*, of the nation, the possibility of a genuinely independent artistic achievement was denied. Historicism, which began with the discovery of the unique, developed among the later disciples of Herder—among whom were Madame de Staël and Menzel—into a theory of causality, of determination, of individual subjugation.

In the era of Metternich, literary historicism had effects of the most convincing kind; as soon as politics became everyone's fate, the idea of historical change dominated every theoretical effort. This situation was made more melancholy by the fact that the German readers of Madame de Staël and Wolfgang Menzel were still condemned to perpetual inactivity. Only a few continued the work of the *Burschenschaft* in increasingly radical meetings; most preferred to derive solace from the noise of revolution far beyond Germany's borders, sympathizing with the heroic Greeks and the brave Poles. The Paris revolution of July, 1830, and its echo in Poland brought no basic change in the German situation. Heine and Börne traveled to Paris in order to observe the victory of the cause on the spot; other writers contented themselves with reading the moderately liberal Augsburg *Allgemeine Zeitung* and filled their chatty writings and multilayered novels with a

vague feeling of apathetic discomfort and despair at German
sterility. The north German philologist Ludolf Wienbarg gave the
name of "Young Germany" to the generation that began anew
in the early thirties to stress the close connections between the
creative intellect and society. He was thinking above all of his
friend Karl Gutzkow and a circle of ambitious young writers who
had chosen Heine and Börne as their models. Young Germany,
however, hardly had an opportunity to constitute itself as a compact intellectual and political resistance group in the manner of
Young Italy. Metternich was much too alert not to sense potential
opponents among the young intellectuals. Under pressure from
Metternich, the German Diet published on December 10, 1835,
a decree which condemned the unorganized group known as
Young Germany as an immoral and seditious body, and threatened to imprison any bookseller who might sell the works of its
adherents. The Young Germans, declared the decree, directed
their attacks against the Christian religion; they were contemptu-
ous of the existing social order and were determined to destroy
public morals and the discipline of the state. This parliamentary
decree was sufficient to wreck whatever solidarity there might
have been among the young writers. Gutzkow went to north
Germany; others of his colleagues took refuge in politically safe
family magazines or professorships for older German literature.

Nevertheless, there remained an unusual way in which to discuss political questions right under the eyes of the watchful
German governments. Under existing law, books of more than
320 pages (twenty signatures) were not subject to obligatory
censorship. Thus it was possible, under certain conditions, to
present current political questions in the guise of voluminous
literary and philosophical studies. In the same year as the Diet
denounced the Young Germans, there appeared the first volume
of Georg Gottfried Gervinus' *History of the Poetic National Literature of the Germans* (*Geschichte der poetischen National-
literatur der Deutschen* [1835–42]), which was read widely as a
political document of the growing German liberalism. Gervinus,

too, demanded that political action should be substituted for belles-lettres; with the death of Goethe, German literature belonged to the past; the future called for a struggle with other than literary weapons. In the famous epilogue to his literary history, Gervinus wrote:

> We do not want to believe that this nation has been able to produce the greatest achievements in arts, religion, and science, yet can accomplish nothing at all in statecraft. . . . It is up to us whether we understand the signs of the times, cease splintering our activity, and direct our efforts to the point that has become the object of our most intense desires. Competition in art is over; now we should set ourselves the other goal that as yet none of our marksmen has hit, to see whether Apollo will grant us here, too, the fame he did not deny us elsewhere. (V, 735.)

After the muzzling of the *Burschenschaft* (1819) and of Young Germany (1835), the radical philosophers appeared on the scene in the third attempt to change the status quo. Inspired by Hegel's idea of continuing dialectical change, the Young Hegelians began by seeking help from Frederick William IV, who at first did not appear averse to certain reforms. But the alliance between the philosophers and the Prussian king was of short duration: Frederick William IV became increasingly orthodox and was prepared to take decisive action against any young philosophers who exercised rational thought too publicly. For a short time, the Young Hegelian opposition was able to resist pressure from the Prussian administration by moving the editorial offices of its *Hallische Jahrbücher* from Prussia to Saxony. But Prussian pressure increased and Saxony yielded; Arnold Ruge, the editor-in-chief of the *Jahrbücher*, was finally forced to cease publication of the periodical in January, 1843. The *Jahrbücher* had not withstood the move into Saxony without considerable losses; most of the contributors were, as professors, officials of the Prussian crown, and as soon as they had to choose between furthering either the *Jahrbücher* or their own academic careers, they made the understandable choice. Ruge had to rely more and more on those members of the Young Hegelian circle who did not have tenure positions in the Prussian civil service. Even though he hesitated to ally himself with the extremists, in the end his desire to carry on the fight against the new royal obscurantism won out. Ruge came into closer contact with two young men who had not yet been numbered among the leading minds of the Young Hegelians. One of them was a certain Dr. Karl Heinrich Marx from Trier, the other a young, self-educated philosopher named Friedrich Engels from Barmen-Elberfeld. Arnold Ruge considered making use of their help—at least temporarily.

1

Young Friedrich Engels
as a Critic

A Literary Model: Karl Gutzkow

In March, 1839, there appeared in Karl Gutzkow's opposition
newspaper *Telegraph für Deutschland* a series of satirical and
critical reports on the religious and cultural life of Barmen-
Elberfeld, the center of the rapidly-developing west German textile industry. The first of the "Letters from the Wuppertal"[1]
appeared without any indication of authorship; not until a later
letter "From Elberfeld" (November, 1839) was the author of the
series identified as a certain "S. Oswald," who soon admitted his
real first name, Friedrich. It was apparent that here was a very
young writer addressing a larger audience for the first time. The
"Letters from the Wuppertal" were one of the innumerable imitations of Heine's famous reports to the Augsburger *Allgemeine
Zeitung* that filled the German newspapers at this time with
"Salons," "Travel Pictures," "Characters," and "Conditions."
The author was unable to resist the temptation to sneak in a
blunt but ironic advertisement for himself in his melodramatic
description of the situation in the Wuppertal:[2] Among the intellectual lights of the area, he pointed out, there was a keen-witted
writer who hoped to surprise the German public with his brilliant
works as soon as he could find a publisher for them. "[I] must
yet mention a clever young man," he wrote, ". . . it is to be hoped

9

that German literature will soon be enriched with some of his *Novellen,* which are not inferior to the best; the only failings with which he can be charged are triteness of plot, hasty conception, and sloppy style. I would gladly give an excerpt of one of them if decency did not forbid it; but perhaps a book dealer will soon . . . be merciful and publish these *Novellen.*"[3]

Even though he failed to find such a publisher, "Friedrich Oswald" had undergone his initiation into journalism with his "Letters from the Wuppertal," and he soon became a regular and industrious reporter for the *Telegraph.* In the period from November, 1839, to April, 1841, more than twenty contributions from his pen appeared: scornful epigrams, whimsical *entrefilets,* belligerent poems, and thorough analyses of the latest developments in German literature. Only Gutzkow knew that "Friedrich Oswald" was the pseudonym of a young clerk who was determined to earn his laurels as a "clerk and poet to boot." This young man was Friedrich Engels.[4] To be sure, Gutzkow was none too impressed with the emotional outpourings and critical meditations of his new protégé, for he soon realized that Engels' contributions often only repeated with verbose enthusiasm what had already appeared in the *Telegraph* and elsewhere.

Friedrich Engels (b. November 28, 1820) was forced to find his way to literature and criticism against the will of his parents and the religious beliefs of his early youth. In Barmen-Elberfeld, which he was to denounce in his first article, he grew up in an atmosphere conditioned by Protestant orthodoxy and the price of cotton. Engels senior, a well-to-do factory owner, was one of the pillars of the Pietist community. Like his Puritan competitors in England, the elder Engels believed in religious and industrial discipline and thought of the world beyond the pew and the spinning frame as full of devilish temptation. Young Engels at first lived and wrote in the inherited faith of his Pietist ancestors; some of his early poems follow closely in rhythm and metaphor the traditional German Protestant hymn.[5] But as soon as he left the circle of his family, his religious certainty crumbled. Unfortunately, his three years at the Gymnasium were all the formal

education he had. His teachers called his Greek and Latin satisfactory and designated his early enthusiasm for German literature
as "very praiseworthy."[6] His parents undoubtedly wished him
to have a practical education in international trade, for which
neither Horace nor Goethe seemed pertinent. But the boy persisted in his literary studies, driven on by his own stubbornness
and helped by circumstances: during his last school year he discovered to his surprise and delight that none other than the poet
Ferdinand Freiligrath (b. 1810), for whom the Berlin papers
were just then full of praise, was earning his living in a Wuppertal office as a clerk. Only a few years later, in one of his "Letters
from the Wuppertal" (April, 1839), Engels admitted that Pietism and Philistinism had surrounded him at home like an ocean,
with Ferdinand Freiligrath appearing to him as "a shipwrecked
sailor" on the provincial rocks and sandbars.[7] Following swiftly
in Freiligrath's footsteps, Engels rejected the religious attitudes
of his earliest poems and turned to more fashionable motifs:
Arabs and harems, moors and wildernesses, distant Florida and
the noble Indian. One of these Freiligrath imitations was even
accepted for publication, to the understandable joy of the author,
and appeared in the *Bremisches Conversationsblatt* on September
16, 1838,[8] a quaint prelude to a passionate, lifelong journalistic
career.

The elder Engels insisted that his son should serve his appren-
ticeship with a north German business firm. Engels was glad to go
to Bremen, where he worked under the guidance of Consul Heinrich Leupold, a personal friend of his father. For Engels, this
period in Bremen was marked by an insatiable urge for freedom.
For the first time in his life he was able to obtain all literary
publications immediately, as well as to find enough leisure to
write his own verses and *Novellen* along with his literary correspondence. Engels was still looking toward the example of
Freiligrath: what that poet had achieved, young Engels hoped
to do also.

Nevertheless, Freiligrath's luster quickly faded before that of
a new model.[9] It was hardly surprising that Engels chose Karl

Gutzkow, whom Metternich himself had just declared the arch-enemy of the existing order, as his new hero. Engels had already heard of Gutzkow and the Young Germans while he was still at home; the Wuppertal textile merchants believed, wrote Engels, that Young Germany was a secret society led by the conspirators Heine, Weinbarg, and Gutzkow. It was no wonder that Engels used his freedom in Bremen to read Gutzkow's most recent works and to seek encouragement and counsel in his novels and critical writings.

The young malcontents of that prerevolutionary period rightly saw Karl Gutzkow (1811–78) as a fascinating character whose destinies seemed, at that time, to rule the literary scene in Germany. Gutzkow was born in the servants' quarters of the Berlin Court; he studied theology before he decided to preach freedom in the daily papers. He himself told a story suggesting the motives behind his change of mind: in July, 1830, when he was about to receive an academic award for his essay *De diis fatalibus* from Hegel himself, at that time rector of the University of Berlin, he had only one wish—to escape to the Café Stehely and bury himself in the latest newspapers with their exciting reports of the Paris revolution. Five years later Gutzkow was the center of a literary scandal of the first order: his novel *Wally the Skeptic* (*Wally, die Zweiflerin* [1835]) was praised by the liberals as a brilliant document of Saint-Simonianism, while the conservatives condemned it as pornographic. His attempt to found a *Deutsche Revue* as a critical organ for the younger generation was quickly suppressed by the censor; after the Diet had accused him of immorality and conspiracy and had imprisoned him for a time, Gutzkow found himself poorer by many an illusion and many a cautious friend. He moved to Hamburg in order to edit his *Telegraph;* nevertheless it seemed as though he had already wasted the decisive moments of his life. In a time of increasing political and social tension, it was both Gutzkow's virtue and failing that he believed both in rational political deeds *and* the dignity of art. Inevitably, the dogmatic radicals accused him of being an aesthete, while his literary colleagues distrusted him as a regrettable revolutionary. Although in his time he enriched the theater with several well-made plays and considerably expanded the technique of the German social novel, he ended his life in a strange twilight. When he died in 1878, embittered and completely abandoned, it was uncertain whether or not he had died by his own hand.

In 1838, Gutzkow's persecution and imprisonment appeared as almost symbolic to the restless younger generation. Friedrich Engels did not hesitate to make this martyr his first guide into the complex field of contemporary literature. First he read, as was to be expected, *Wally the Skeptic*.[10] Soon he obtained a copy of Campe's *Jahrbuch der Literatur* (1839),[11] and concentrated primarily on Gutzkow's contribution, a critical essay entitled "Past and Present" ("Vergangenheit und Gegenwart"), which analyzed the literary tradition and revolution in Germany. Engels probably also read Gutzkow's collection of essays *Gods, Heroes, Don Quixote* (*Götter, Helden, Don Quichote* [1838]); at least he mentions Gutzkow's arguments at various points in his correspondence at that time. Whether or not Engels read the publications of the other Young Germans or Gutzkow's early collaborators with equal zeal seems highly doubtful; he does mention Heinrich Laube's *Travel Stories* (*Reisenovellen* [1834–37]), Theodor Mundt's *Madonna* (1835), and Kühne's *Quarantined in the Madhouse* (*Eine Quarantäne im Irrenhause* [1835]) in his correspondence, but it is quite possible that Engels drew his knowledge of these works from Gutzkow's reviews without reading them thoroughly himself. This is true with one important exception. Later writings indicate that the young Engels studied the essays of Ludolf Wienbarg (1802–72) with particular interest and close agreement.

Engels' devotion was probably one of the reasons that induced Gutzkow to publish the numerous contributions that poured from Bremen into the Hamburg office of the *Telegraph*. Toward Engels, Gutzkow exercized patient and unusual tolerance. Perhaps it was not unpleasant for this lonely man to see his critical judgments echoed in the writings of a young disciple, even if in an unsophisticated and muddled way; it provided at least an illusion of communication and response. Friedrich Engels' essay on the Rhenish poet Karl Leberecht Immermann (1796–1840) may serve as a typical example in this regard. Gutzkow stated in *Gods, Heroes, Don Quixote* that the younger generation was turning to Immermann in increasing numbers because they found in his works a realistic view of contemporary problems; at the same time he characterized Immermann as a writer with dual loyalty, who looked to the past rather than to the future.[12] Engels repeated Gutzkow's commentary point for point. Neither in his essay on Volume I (1840) of Immermann's *Memorabilia*[13] nor in his poem on Immermann's funeral (October 10, 1843)[14] does a single idea appear that can be termed original. Engels, too, speaks of "Immermann's well-known dualism" and alludes in both prose and poem to the fact that Immermann's memory was becoming a common inspiration for the younger generation.

Engels' discipleship was manifested even more clearly when he attempted to follow Gutzkow's changes of mind. In his study "Past and Present," Gutzkow praised the Hungarian-German poet Karl Beck (1817–79)—whose mixture of pathetic rhetoric on freedom and empty melancholy had misled many observers—as a figure of importance in German literature. He even expressed the hope that Beck might one day mature into Germany's Byron. Engels followed this judgment and spoke in detailed letters to his friend Graeber of Beck's "enormous talent."[15] Fortunately Gutzkow was prepared to revise his earlier judgment; surprisingly enough, however, he indicated his change of mind through a contribution by his young correspondent in Bremen. In March, 1839, there appeared on the front page of the *Telegraph* a discussion by Engels of recent poems and dramatic fragments from Beck's pen. Engels now called them "absurdities" that quite embarrassingly recalled those "expectations Herr Beck no longer seems able to fulfil."[16]

Engels' close agreement with the ideas of Gutzkow and the Young Germans was no less apparent in his readiness to regard himself—with ironic tardiness—as a member of that ill-defined group which was given its cohesion by the collective condemna-

tion of the German Diet rather than by common ideas or solidarity of action. Engels began to sign his letters as "a Young German" and to explain at length why he was enthusiastic about
Young Germany. "It will probably do the cause of freedom no
harm," he wrote to his friend in humorous dog-Latin, "if I feel
attracted to Young Germany (*ad juvenilem germaniam*). . . .
This group of writers (*haec . . . classis scriptorum*) is trying . . .
to infuse the flesh and blood of the German nation with the ideas
of our century: the emancipation of Jews and the slaves, universal constitutionalism. . . . Their ideas are not unlike the direction
of my own mind; therefore why should I remain aloof?"[17]

Karl Gutzkow did not respond very eagerly to this somewhat
delayed enthusiasm for the ideas of Young Germany and for himself. Fundamentally he never rated the critical and literary
achievements of his Bremen correspondent very highly. On the
contrary, in a letter that was only discovered and deciphered a
generation later by H. H. Houben,[18] he called Engels a "Young
German shopkeeper's clerk" and he harshly criticized Engels'
contributions from Bremen as "a critic's first vomitings."
To be sure, objective judgment in this case was not unaffected
by personal motives. Gutzkow noted with some mistrust that
Engels on an excursion to Münster had met the poetess Annette von Droste-Hülshoff (1797–1845) and her friend Levin
Schücking (1814–83), and had unexpectedly compared Droste's
poems with those of Shelley, the idol of the revolutionary youth
of the time. Even if the comparison was not very good, young
Engels showed, at least in this isolated case, a deeper insight into
the values of poetry than his master. This was only Engels' first,
hesitating step out of Gutzkow's circle; other more important ones
were to follow. It was Gutzkow himself who bore a good part of
the responsibility for Engels' progress to radicalism; his essay
"Past and Present" had most expressly referred the young man
to one of the teachers of the Young German generation. Following Gutzkow's hint, Engels quickly became an ardent admirer
of the Robespierre of German literary criticism, Ludwig Börne.

The Political Perspective: Ludwig Börne

Of all the writings of Gutzkow that young Engels studied eagerly in Bremen, the essay "Past and Present" (1839) remained of the greatest importance for his intellectual development. In his essay, Gutzkow had adumbrated Börne's importance with somewhat glaring metaphors, behind which lurked a number of reservations. Börne had not only, Gutzkow declared, torn to pieces the veil of history to reveal its naked framework; he was also the "yeast" that would leaven the bread of revolution in the future heat of conflict.[19] Engels was prepared to share Gutzkow's respect for Börne's sharp eye and inflexible character. But it escaped him that Gutzkow was not among Börne's blind admirers—Gutzkow did not hesitate to mention the external causes that had driven Börne to literature and accused him of speaking of Goethe and Schiller when he actually meant Metternich and Montesquieu.[20] Engels, on the other hand, just at the moment when he was stepping out of the confines of his circle, was delighted to find a stubbornly political personality in German literature.

Ludwig Börne (1796–1837) was regarded by the liberals of the late thirties as the venerable prophet who had anticipated their battles long before and had hurled his denunciations against the German princes from Paris. As part of the reaction at the time of the Congress of Vienna (1815), the city of Frankfurt rescinded the civil rights that Napoleon had granted to the Jews, and Börne was removed from his municipal post; thus he had his own personal reasons for making war upon the restoration that was robbing him both of his personal rights and of the rights of men in general. But in the era of Metternich political demands could not be made in a correspondingly political form. Börne was forced to express his demands behind the veil, not to say the allegorical disguise, of biting dramatic criticism. Perhaps it was the pressure of his times that forced him into predominantly political interests; perhaps the inner urge of the instinctive revolutionary unerringly made contact through art with the political elements. Whatever the reason, Börne became a tribune of the people, though without a people, and in a paradoxical and inimitable way, created a rapier-like critical language: flexible, pure, tense, and of unsurpassed strength. Like other German patriots of that time, Börne chose voluntary exile. After the July Revolution (1830), he hurried to Paris and wrote reports for the German reader about the new, symptomatic problems of French politics. In the same year in which young Engels left his home town, Börne's long fight with tuberculosis ended with an attack of influenza and he was buried in Père Lachaise Cemetery (1837).

Börne's concept of literature, indeed, of art itself, was grounded in a single-minded equation of art forms with the destinies of nations. He declared in his widely read *Dramaturgical Leaflets* (*Dramaturgische Blätter* [1835]) that drama is a mirror of society; the critic ought to occupy himself with the reflected image, not with the complex facets of the glass. "I saw in drama the mirror-image of life," he admitted, "and when I didn't like the image, I struck the mirror, and when it disgusted me, I smashed it."[21] Like Madame de Staël and her pupils in France and Germany, Börne also believed that the artistic reflection of reality remains substantially tied to the social problems of the nation; in the age of Kleist, Büchner, and Grillparzer, he could assert that Germany was incapable of producing great drama because it lacked a heroic and independent society of truly free individuals. "A people that is made into a people only by being herded into a sheepfold . . . , such a people will have no drama, in every foreign drama it will only be the chorus making wise observations, it will never itself be the hero."[22]

Obviously such a perspective seeks its central focus outside the work of art in the non-artistic field of politics. When art is effective as a stimulus or spur in the fight against the aristocracy, the reactionaries, or the tyranny of the status quo, it receives Börne's highest praise; when it fails to strengthen the liberal movement, his judgment is merciless. Börne necessarily concludes that all critics who endeavor to examine the immanent structure of a work of art are to be condemned out of hand: they lack, as Börne and his later followers suppose, political "direction" or are guilty of escapism. Those critics who insist upon analysis of artistic structures Börne calls, not without a bitter glance at his archenemy Goethe, "godless Chinese."[23] According to Börne, the only art that belongs to the future is that which demands universal equality, constitutionalism, independence for citizens; meanwhile our judgment of the art of the past must be revised before this glorious future can emerge. Racine, as the representative of monarchical France, is devalued in favor of the partisans of freedom, Shakespeare and Calderon; only among the readers of these, asserts Börne in notable contrast to the beliefs of Friedrich and August Wilhelm Schlegel, are the "really dangerous democrats" to be found.[24]

Engels read Börne's *Dramaturgical Leaflets* in the spring of 1838. Without hesitation he abandoned Gutzkow's faith in a loose and subtle balance of art and society in favor of a dogmatic and political view of aesthetic problems such as Börne had formulated. What Engels learned from Börne is shown by a comparison of Engels' first contributions to the *Telegraph für Deutschland* (March–April, 1839) with his later ones. "The Letters from the Wuppertal" were an innocent attempt to imitate Heine and the Young German *feuilleton;* although they are written in a clearly aggressive tone and from a liberal mood, they do not display a profound knowledge of the actual political situation. The contrast revealed by these letters between rationalistic ideas and the mystical fervor of Pietism, reflects Engels' private conflict with his parents, home, and church—it is not yet a matter of politics. But in November, 1839, the first indications of a basic change appear: Engels' essay on "The German Chapbooks" ("Die deutschen Volksbücher")[25] in Gutzkow's *Telegraph* clearly proves how openly he was beginning to use political criteria in his judgment of literature.

It is the function of literature, asserts Engels in November, 1839, to strengthen the peasant, the laborer, and the apprentice:

"to make his ethical feeling clearer, to make him conscious of his power, his rights, his freedom, to awaken his courage and his patriotism."[26] Engels insists that from now on literature must "lend a hand to the less educated."[27] In the spirit of Börne, Engels measures the tales of the chapbooks, *Faust* as well as *Till Eulenspiegel*, with the yardstick of liberalism and tries to explain these venerable stories as political allegories that conceal, behind their medieval façade, a timely message for the oppressed. Above all, Engels praises the story of *The Children of Haimon* because to him it represents "unrestrained pleasure in opposition."[28] Figures like Genoveva and Griselda, on the other hand, are relegated to the rubbish heap of the past because they symbolize base submissiveness. "For heaven's sake, what does the German people care about all that today?" asks Engels without considering at all the literary value of the chapbooks. "Griselda . . . reads to me like a petition to the high German Diet for the emancipation of women. . . . The people have played the parts of Griselda and Genoveva long enough; now it is time to play Siegfried and Reinald as well."[29] In the name of the "less educated," Engels demands a new censorship that will proscribe mercilessly any art that does not serve directly the interests of the people. The stories of *Helena* and *Emperor Octavianus* especially provoked Engels' immature thirst for liberty. He complained that they propagated the myth of the aristocracy's blue blood and should therefore be condemned without regard for their poetic quality. "How often do we not find this idea [of blue blood] among the people themselves! . . . When I consider that *that* idea must first be rooted out before the constitutional institutions can develop— let the book be as poetic as it may be, *censeo Carthaginem esse delendam*."[30] These words, undisciplined as they are, strike an ominous note for the future: while Metternich's censors are still at work, young Engels demands, in the name of the "less educated," a censorship in the interests of freedom. The circular arguments of political terror appear here like a dark cloud on the horizon.

After Engels had studied the *Dramaturgical Leaflets* in the winter of 1839, he turned to Campe's complete edition of Börne's

works and at once began to study intensively the polemical essay
Menzel the French-Eater (Menzel der Franzosenfresser [1836]).
There is no doubt that he greatly overestimated this polemic:
Börne scored many a critical point against his former comrade
Menzel, who had sacrificed his liberal ideas to a new obscurantism, but as a whole the essay was a tiresome attack protracted by
long digressions upon Prince Pückler-Muskau. Once again Börne
characterized Germany as the "ghetto of Europe";[31] once again
he conjured up his basic notion of the intimate relationship between political conditions and intellectual power. "Freedom is
everywhere or nowhere," he wrote perceptively, "it either needs
no asylum or finds none. You will look in vain in Germany for an
area of life, a science, an art, a trade in which you can enjoy both
peace and the confidence of peace. . . . If there are still narrow
areas of life in which you have remained master without restriction, it is merely because your overlords have not yet perceived
the point at which those areas intersect with their own. Let it
once become accidentally known that there is a mathematician
among the Spanish Jacobins, and the Diet will immediately forbid logarithms."[32] Börne contrasts the submissiveness of Germany
with the pride of Spain: in Spain, he asserts, they would condemn
the informers, the compromisers, and the political sluggards with
a single quotation from the *Cid: Lengua sin manos, cuemo osas
fablar?* ("Tongue without hands, how dare you to speak?").

This attack upon Menzel's form of nationalism seemed to
Engels a most important piece of contemporary literature. "I
would like it best of all if you could get hold of Börne's *Menzel
the French-Eater,*" wrote Engels to a friend. "This work is without doubt the best we have in German prose with respect to style
as well as in power and richness of ideas; it is magnificent, and
anyone who is not acquainted with it would not believe that our
language possesses such power."[33] But by recommending Börne
to his friend in this way, Engels betrayed his lack of interest in
genuine literary discussions; increasingly he transformed Börne
into a political hero. Börne, said Engels, repeating the favorite
quotation of his master, "came to the Germans with the words of

the *Cid: Lengua sin manos, cuemo osas fablar?* The glory of action has never been described by anyone as it has by Börne."[34]

Engels' new desire was to become politically active; after a few weeks of reading Börne he felt compelled to take part in underground politics. To be sure, his first contribution was extremely modest: he decided to smuggle the most important volumes of Campe's edition of Börne's works from Bremen into those Prussian territories closer to home in which the censor, in collaboration with the police, prevented the distribution of Börne's writings. A new pride in conspiracy began to fill Engels' letters: "I am now a colossal carrier of forbidden books into Prussian lands; Börne's *French-Eater* in four copies, the *Letters from Paris* by the same author . . . are ready for shipment to Barmen."[35] Nevertheless, young Engels seemed to feel that smuggling books was not enough. Should he not take more risks? Was it not his duty to follow in Börne's footsteps as a writer? Finally his old confidence in the poetic word regained the upper hand; Engels set about writing a hymn to Börne (and to the latter's favorite writer, Calderon). He actually hoped it would draw the younger generation, whose apathy Börne had condemned, into political action.

Engels' hymn to Börne—entitled, innocuously enough, *An Evening (Ein Abend)*[36]—appeared in August, 1840, in the *Telegraph für Deutschland*. It is a work of rhetorical enthusiasm, not of poetic intensity; in its clichés, its artistic incompetence, and its mixed metaphors, it represents the third-rate poetry of the prerevolutionary youth movement. Politically it was inadvisable to jump into the subject head over heels; the poem begins, probably to conceal the radical point, as a meditation upon the falling shadows of twilight and the weary return home:

Im Garten sitz' ich—eben ist gesunken
Des alten Tages Sonne in die Fluten
Und, die von ihr beherrscht, verborgen ruhten,
Sprüh'n lustig jetzt der Abendröte Funken.
Die Blumen steh'n und schau'n sich an so trübe,
Dass ihnen schwand der Sonne heit'res Leuchten,
Die Vögel aber auf den unerreichten

Baumgipfeln singen froh ihr Lied der Liebe.
Die Schiffe ruhen auf des Stromes Rücken,
Die sonst den weiten Ozean durchfahren,
Und fernherüber dröhnt das Holz der Brücken,
Drauf heimwärts ziehn der Menschen müde Scharen.[37]

[In my garden I sit—the sun of the old day | has just sunk
into the waves, | and the glowing sparks of the sunset, |
which lay hidden when ruled by the sun, | now flash joy-
fully. | The flowers stand and look at each other so sadly |
because the cheerful rays of the sun have vanished from
them, | but the birds on the unattained treetops | sing hap-
pily their song of love. | The ships which otherwise traverse
the wide sea | rest upon the river's back, | and from far away
resounds the wood of the bridges | on which the tired crowds
of men wend their way homeward.]

But Engels cannot long conceal his political message: night and
day are allegories for tyranny and freedom; the birds singing on
the highest branches of the German oaks, catching sight of the
dawn before the poor people in the valley, are none other than the
revolutionary poets who can sense freedom behind the political
clouds. At this point Engels finally speaks of his most intimate
concern:

Und ich bin einer auch der freien Sänger;
Die Eiche *Börne* ist's, an deren Ästen
Ich aufgeklommen, wenn im Tal die Dränger
Um Deutschland enger ihre Ketten pressten.
Ja, einer bin ich von den kecken Vögeln,
Die in dem Äthermeer der Freiheit segeln;
Und wär ich Sperling lieber unter ihnen
Als Nachtigall, sollt' ich im Käfig liegen,
Und mit dem Liede einem Fürsten dienen.[38]

[And I too am one of the free bards; | it is the oak *Börne*
upon whose branches | I have climbed, when in the valley
the oppressors | have pulled their chains still more tightly
around Germany; | yes, I am one of the bold birds | who
sail on the ethereal sea of freedom, | and I would rather be
a sparrow among them | than a nightingale, were I obliged
to lie in a cage | and serve a prince with my song.]

The ornithological allusions would have been clear to the politically sensitive reader. Engels, like Börne, was content to be a politically conscious if somewhat homely revolutionary sparrow rather than to "serve a prince" as a politically indifferent nightingale. In other words, young poets should imitate the sharp sounds of Börne, not the sweet melodies of the caged Goethe, whom Börne himself, misapplying a line from Schiller's *Don Carlos*, had called a mere courtier. Börne was, after all, as Engels stressed, the only writer who had pointed the way into that age of freedom that would accompany a glorious new age of literature. Engels was probably thinking of himself when he described the ideal poet of that freer future as a new Calderon and outlined with enthusiasm his probable deeds:

Und dann ersteht ein Calderon, ein neuer,
Ein Perlenfischer in dem Meer der Dichtung,
Von Bildern flammt sein Lied, die Opferfeuer
Von duft'ger Zedernblöcke hoher Schichtung;
Es rauscht sein Sang, es rauscht die gold'ne Leier
Von des Tyrannen blutiger Vernichtung![39]

[And then will appear a Calderon, a new one, | a pearl fisher in the sea of poetry, | his song, the sacrificial fires from high stacks of aromatic cedar, | will flame with images, his song, his golden lyre | will roar about the bloody destruction of the tyrant!]

Philosophical Radicalism: The Young Hegelians

Engels did not only admire Börne's sharp intellect and political inflexibility. Engels would hardly have chosen him as his heroic model had he not concluded that Börne represented the same principles in politics as those realized by Hegel in his philosophy. In Bremen, Engels had not only been able to procure the new literary publications but had also had enough free time to pursue philosophical studies. As a self-educated young man, he was inclined to turn first to the most recent developments. In the spring of 1839 he read David Friedrich Strauss's *Life of Jesus* (*Das*

Leben Jesu [1835]); in the winter of 1840 he had already discovered Hegel. "[I] am studying Hegel's philosophy of history,"
he confessed to his friend, "a tremendous work. I read some of it
religiously every evening; the immense ideas thrill me frightfully."[40] From that winter on he occupied himself with Hegel's philosophy to the exclusion of all else. He soon became interested in
the internal conflicts of Hegel's disciples and delved into the involved pamphleteering of that philosophically excited age. Engels
did not feel the least annoyance when he was called in 1841 to
perform his military service in Berlin; at the University of Berlin,
he remarked with surprising perspicacity, battles were raging that
would decide the future of Germany. Engels scarcely complained
about the harsh discipline of the Prussian army; he seems to have
participated with pleasure in the drill of his artillery unit so that
after hours he might have time to play the young philosopher,
auditing courses at the university, regularly reading the Young
Hegelian *Hallische Jahrbücher* and sitting together with his new
friends in a noisy club proudly calling itself "The Free Men."

Nonetheless, Engels had come to Berlin too late to experience
the massive triumph and absolute sovereignty of Hegel's philosophy. The power and brilliance of Hegelianism was already beginning to show signs of decay in the forties. Not only did internal
battles weaken the common cause of the Hegelians, but the Prussian state itself, which at first had raised Hegel's philosophy to its
position of power, began to seek its salvation in religious orthodoxy and mystical irrationality. Frederick William IV himself had
summoned Schelling to the university in order to break the
hegemony of the Hegelians and thoroughly undermine their opposition, which had become too well articulated.

Twenty years before Engels arrived in Berlin to perform his
military service, Hegel's philosophy, officially supported by the
minister of culture, Baron Karl Altenstein (1770–1840), had
been in undisputed control of intellectual life in Prussia. Almost
all the important professorial chairs in the country were occupied
by friends and pupils of Hegel; the *Jahrbücher für wissenschaftliche Kritik,* which proposed to regulate the intellectual life of

Prussia and all Germany according to the ideas of the master, appeared for the first time in 1827. But the latent conflicts among Hegel's disciples became more and more obvious after 1835. Strauss's Bible criticism inspired the younger generation, which quickly set about using selected elements of the Hegelian system for their own interpretations of history and contemporary problems. Soon there was open fighting among the Hegelian factions: on the one hand, the Old Hegelians remained steadfastly loyal to the idea of the absolute spirit as the highest being and supported Protestant orthodoxy with concepts of Hegelian metaphysics; on the other, the generation of Young Hegelians began to dismantle the total meaning of Hegelian philosophy and to regard the dialectical method, the principle of fruitful historical development, as their actual heritage. Only a few of Hegel's pupils, such as K. L. Michelet (1801–93) and Karl Rosenkranz (1805–79) insisted upon the indispensable unity of his system and attempted in vain to bridge the growing gap between the two groups. The speed with which this controversy developed can be seen from the fact that Arnold Ruge (1803–80), the most articulate and stubborn of the Young Hegelians, had preceded Engels only by a few years in his study of Hegelian philosophy. Ruge was sentenced to fifteen years in prison (of which he served six) for complicity in the conspiratorial activities of Karl Follen (1795–1840), later professor of Germanic languages and literatures at Harvard. After his release, Ruge taught aesthetics at the University of Halle, where his colleagues Rosenkranz and Vatke (1806–82) introduced him to Hegelian philosophy. He was one of the many who interpreted Hegel in a personal way: his bitter anger and thirst for freedom combined with Hegel's terminology to give keen expression to his concept of liberty. Ruge found an equally impatient ally in Theodor Echtermeyer (1805–44), a colleague who possessed a broad literary education and a particular interest in older German poetry. After the two academic colleagues had discovered the harmony of their ideas, they decided to found a literary organ which, in strict opposition to the Old Hegelian *Jahrbücher für wissenschaftliche Kritik,* would pass judgment on intellectual developments and events in Germany from the standpoint of the Young Hegelians.

The first issue of the new *Hallische Jahrbücher für Wissenschaft und Kunst* appeared on January 1, 1838, under the co-editorship of Ruge and Echtermeyer. The editorial prologue proudly announced that the new *Jahrbücher* would not only observe the new spirit of the times but also, in critiques and studies, directly represent it.[41] A number of features quickly transformed the *Hallische Jahrbücher* into one of the most important organs of literary criticism in prerevolutionary Germany.[42] Theodor Echtermeyer regarded himself as a dedicated Germanic scholar by profession and preferred to occupy himself, much to Ruge's regret, with Middle High German literature than with contemporary politics; many of the other contributors as well, for example. the radical poet Robert Prutz (1816–72), the writer Adolf Stahr (1805–72), and particularly the young Friedrich Theodor Vischer (1807–87) were more interested in problems of cultural criticism than in actual politics or abstract philosophical ontology. The *Hallische Jahrbücher* presented the educated reader with an almost impenetrable thicket of Hegelian antitheses and triads; nevertheless few of its contributors seem to have studied Hegel's *Lectures on Aesthetics* seriously and systematically. It is probable that among Ruge's contributors only Rosenkranz, Hegel's loyal biographer, and Friedrich Theodor Vischer proceeded from a penetrating study of Hegel's aesthetic system.

The theoretical criteria of the *Hallische Jahrbücher* were based upon the nearly boundless use of Hegel's fashionable terminology and on a few ideas from his philosophy of history. But ultimately the Young Hegelians insisted upon their own interpretation. Hegel viewed history as a progressive self-realization of the *Weltgeist*, the essence of which was freedom and spontaneity; the Young Hegelians felt obliged to interpret progression as progress and spontaneity of the *Weltgeist* as the political independence of the Prussian citizen. They substituted political relevance for metaphysical depth. In an age that was already beginning to feel the convulsions of revolution and modern industry, they contented themselves with a superficial sociological analysis of problems, and a problem was of interest to them only if it was of immediate social significance. It followed, therefore, that the decisive criterion of genuine literature was whether or not it took the side of the *Zeitgeist*, which had replaced what Hegel meant by *Weltgeist*. In a further oversimplification, the "spirit of the times" was mechanically equated with the impatience of the young liberals, and writers were charged with taking the side of civil progress. Thus the Young Hegelians, in their own way, arrived at the critical hypotheses of Ludwig Börne, who had formulated them, twenty years before Ruge, purely on the basis of his republican enthusiasms and fanatical belief in the European legacy of the Enlightenment. Young Engels was by no means unjustified in thinking that Börne was, in practice, the herald and immediate predecessor of Young Hegelian literary criticism.

To have degraded Hegel's *Weltgeist* to the *Zeitgeist* was not the only doubtful achievement of the Young Hegelians. Ruge and his circle of friends preferred to misunderstand the Hegelian idea of a hierarchically ordered self-realization of the spirit in the ascending spheres of religion, art, and philosophy. The Young Hegelians declared that art was only one of the elements within the superordinate, sovereign, determining movement of history. Hegel himself had developed philosophical motifs that were not without their dangers: in his system, art was nothing more than one—the intermediate one—of three possible manifestations of intellectual spontaneity. As soon as art, following upon religion, had exhausted its possibilities, its function was at an end; its tasks were taken over by the higher and purer processes of philosophy, in which the free spirit no longer needed to alienate itself into the material element. The Hegelian devaluation of literature was mercilessly pursued by the Young Hegelians and debased into a political slogan. Once profaned into a dependent element of the totality of political development, literature in and of itself could no longer be appreciated as a world and structure that was self-sustaining. The *Hallische Jahrbücher* steadfastly persisted in the idea of the undifferentiated unity of literary and historical developments: "The interests and conditions of our modern literature are too inextricably intertwined, too complicated, too calculated as an interaction of all tendencies to be in a position to demand an isolation of individual areas."[43] Friedrich Engels formulated the same Young Hegelian thought when he asserted that the writer as a single individual had lost all importance. "In literature," claimed Engels, "each can be assessed . . . only by his relationship to the whole."[44]

The critical attacks of the *Hallische Jahrbücher* were directed first of all against those writers whom the Young Hegelians called "Romantics" in the widest sense of the word. Echtermeyer had formulated the theoretical basis of these attacks; Ruge popularized them in a series of essays entitled "Romanticism and Protestantism" ("Die Romantik und der Protestantismus" [1839]).[45] Germany, Ruge wrote, had reached the first peak of its spiritual development in the Reformation; contemporary literature was nothing other than a significant retreat from the advanced positions of the Reformation and the Enlightenment. According to the Young Hegelian view, the cardinal sin of the Romantics was a hopeless philosophical dualism. The Romantics had paid far too much homage to the empty cult of the Fichtean ego. In their inability to grasp the idea of the single self-development of the substantial spirit, the Romantics had stumbled into the poisoned net of subjective reflection and remained, as Ruge claimed, prisoners of their blindness and frivolous immorality. Since the Romantic writer lacked any firm ethical moorings, he had no choice but to place himself under the protection of political restoration and, forced into shameful service, abandon the possibility of dialectical growth. Ruge wrote in a surprisingly modern way of the evil fixation of the Romantic intellect upon orthodoxy and restoration; he never tired of pointing to the disastrous consequences that resulted from the alliance of the Romantic intellectual with traditional religion and the Prussian bureaucracy. Recently, Young Germany, too, had entered into the inheritance of the Romantic fixation; there was a slight difference because of the touch of French perfume with which the Young Germans scented their works. Young Germany was guilty also of other Romantic sins. Even Gutzkow and his friends were incapable of recognizing the redeeming and beneficial power of the Hegelian dialectic, of rising to the unified perspective of a total philosophical conception of reality, of calling a halt to the increasing moral decay and frivolity.

With these basic ideas, the *Hallische Jahrbücher* found it necessary to defend Börne, the politician, against Gutzkow's faint praise[46] and the objections of his Young German friends. Basically, to be sure, Young Germans and Young Hegelians were of one mind about the primarily political character of Börne's cultural criticism; what separated the two groups was a radical difference in values. Gutzkow distrusted Börne's lack of aesthetic sensitivity; the Young Hegelians felt that this deficiency—the sacrifice Börne made to the *Zeitgeist*—was more than compensated for by his abundance of political passion. Adolf Stahr, in his review of Gutzkow's *Life of Börne*,[47] as well as Karl Biedermann (1812–1901) in an open attack upon Gutzkow,[48] praised political perspicacity as the highest virtue. Stahr condemned those "aesthetes" who were incapable of comprehending Börne's greatness: "He was not a poet by profession," declared Stahr with an obvious glance at Gutzkow, but "[he was] quite a different sort of poet than the professionals."[49] Probably none of the Young Hegelian converts took up these ideas more willingly than Friedrich Engels. The more he inclined toward political radicalism, the more unrelentingly he had to revise his critical ideas, taking the *Hallische Jahrbücher* as his model.

The first thing to be done was to separate his exemplar, Börne, from his false Young German followers and to place him closer to Hegel and the new philosophical movement. Politics was the common denominator to which he reduced philosophers and critics: ". . . Who will reproach Börne," asked Engels, referring ironically to Young German judgments, "for looking at 'life only from the standpoint of politics'? Does not Hegel do the same? Does he not also believe that in the transition of the state into world history, that is, in the relationship between internal and external politics, the concrete reality of the absolute spirit lies?"[50] In the work of Hegel and Börne, Engels thought he had found a new basis from which important insights into contemporary problems could be gained. Börne represented the political experience of the present, Hegel had discovered the dialectical approach to the future. Engels therefore set himself the task of "digging out the blocked paths of ideas between Hegel and Börne"[51] and thus of preparing the synthesis of system and action, of spirit and deed.

From this new point of view gained from the *Hallische Jahrbücher*, Engels reviewed his modest literary past and prepared to revise a number of his basic literary ideas. He realized that his literary development represented the various stages of growth of a radical German from the literary irresponsibilities of Young Germany to the philosophical seriousness of Young Hegelianism. "There are many who . . . placed some hope for a while in recent literature," admitted Engels. "No doubt anyone who has passed through the most recent developmental stages of the German spirit in his own consciousness will at one time have looked with approval upon the works of Mundt, Laube, or Gutzkow. But the progress beyond this movement has meanwhile been made much too obvious, and the emptiness of most of the Young Germans has become terribly apparent."[52] But Engels came only slowly to specific criticism of the Young Germans. The first signs of growing alienation are to be found in a review in the Bremen *Morgenblatt für gebildete Leser*, on July 30, 1840, in which Engels discussed Gutzkow's play *Richard Savage*,[53] which had just been performed in Bremen. Engels hardly bothered with the details of the play, since the play had been, as he said, exhaustively analyzed in the *Hallische Jahrbücher*.[54] Although Engels did not fall into the rude tone of the *Jahrbücher* (nevertheless he expressly referred to the *Jahrbücher*'s biting criticism of Gutzkow), he was very outspoken about the weak dramatic plot. Engels was still ready to admit that Gutzkow possessed an unusual dramatic talent, even if it did not appear in its most advantageous light in *Richard Savage*.

Two more years went by before Engels repudiated Gutzkow and the Young German generation. Here, too, like many of his

Young Hegelian friends, he used an indirect method that quickly turned into an abrupt attack upon Young Germany. The occasion was a late defense of Young German literature which Engels reviewed for Ruge. Although it appeared at first glance that Engels was primarily concerned with Alexander Jung's *Lectures on the Modern Literature of the Germans* (*Vorlesungen über die moderne Literatur der Deutschen* [Danzig, 1842]), the attentive reader could hardly fail to grasp the true object of his energetic and angry attacks.

Alexander Jung (1779–1884)[55] still possessed enough critical discrimination to distinguish carefully between aesthetic and political problems. "We are threatened with a political poetry, a political philosophy," he declared, "indeed, even with the anarchy of a political prose."[56] Jung saw clearly that the emphasis on social bias demanded by the Young Hegelians would necessarily lead to a new dictatorship in the name of freedom and to sterility of the poetic imagination. The new demand for the subordination of literature to politics caused the friend of beauty to worry, said Jung, that "all the mystery, all the freshness, as it were all the forest primeval of our being . . . might disappear, which then really would bring forth a stagnation of forces, a crudeness in the spiritual atmosphere. . . . Meanwhile let us be on our guard lest the *political* forces, no matter how liberal they may be, put our writing and thinking and speaking in new chains."[57]

In his review, Engels hardly found it necessary to grapple with Jung's pertinent arguments. With his new dogmatism it seemed necessary only to condemn this late defense of Young Germany in principle; oversimplifying, he brutally calls Jung's statements a "bucketful of vague, uncritical claims, confused judgments, hollow platitudes, and ridiculously narrow-minded views."[58] For Engels, Young Germany had already been absorbed [*aufgehoben*], in the Hegelian sense of the word, in the work of the Young Hegelians. It was not sufficient to dismiss Alexander Jung as a defender of Young Germany; Engels had to proceed immediately to a direct attack upon Young Germany itself. "Young Germany is over and done with," he declared categorically, ". . . the *Jahr-*

bücher have attracted everyone's attention, the battle for principles is in full flower, it is a matter of life and death, Christianity
is at stake, the political movement is accomplishing everything,
and the good Jung is still of the naïve opinion that 'the nation' has
nothing better to do than wait impatiently . . . for a new play by
Gutzkow."[59] But even here Engels hesitates to launch a final
attack upon the man who had introduced him to literature; even
here Engels still concedes to Gutzkow considerable literary talent.
Nevertheless he argues that if Gutzkow wishes to fulfil the true
mission of a modern writer, he must radically transform his literary work. Engels demands that Gutzkow should stress the ideological element in his plays more resolutely; furthermore, in his
prose he should pay closer attention to the development of "the
great movement of the times."[60] The ultimatum the pupil presents
to his quondam master is unmistakable: if Gutzkow did not model
his works upon Young Hegelian standards, he would be excluded
from the important German writers.

The *Deutsche Jahrbücher* (1841–43), published by Ruge in
the more tolerant Saxony in place of the *Hallische Jahrbücher,*
which had been expelled from Prussia, were eagerly read by the
prerevolutionary intellectuals, and as a result Engels' brutal attack
on Young Germany and its late apologists quickly came to the
attention of Gutzkow and Jung. Gutzkow well remembered Friedrich Engels—or "Friedrich Oswald." Perhaps he regretted that he
had taken the young critic so unhesitatingly under his protection.
In a letter of December 6, 1842, he confessed to Professor Jung
that he felt no small responsibility for the unfortunate utterances
of Engels in the *Deutsche Jahrbücher.* "The sad honor of having
introduced *E.* [*sic*] *Oswald* to literature unfortunately belongs to
me," wrote Gutzkow to his friend in Königsberg. "Years ago a
shop clerk named *Engels* sent me letters from Barmen about the
Wuppertal. I corrected them, deleted personal attacks that were
too harsh, and printed them. After that he sent a number of
things that I regularly had to rework. Suddenly he refused to accept these corrections, studied *Hegel* . . . and transferred to other
publications. . . . Almost all of these neophytes are like this. They

owe it to us that they know how to think and write, and their first act is intellectual patricide."[61]

Engels knew nothing of this melancholy letter, nor was he any longer in a mood to pay much attention to Gutzkow's admonishments. Gutzkow had permanently lost all fascination for him; a decisive and momentous change had taken place in Engels' intellectual development and in his relationship to the literary work of art. Gutzkow was the first and last German writer who could have led Engels to the core of art, who could have taught him instinctive respect for the essence of literature. As soon as Engels renounced Gutzkow's leadership and trusted himself to the guidance of Börne and the Young Hegelians, he found himself inevitably in opposition to any art not obligated to society. With every step he moved away more and more from the sphere of literature and turned, with growing intolerance, to the facts of society and economics soon to come strongly to his attention in England.

2

Economics and Intellect:
Thomas Carlyle

Friedrich Engels as Carlyle's Translator

In the late fall of 1842 Engels returned from Berlin to his home town, but he did not stay there very long. His father, who distrusted Engels' philosophical adventures in Berlin, wanted to establish him as quickly as possible in middle-class respectability and therefore sent him to Manchester, where an English branch of his firm had been opened. Friedrich Engels obeyed his father's orders without a moment's hesitation—although their motives were certainly not identical. If Engels senior had really known his son's reasons, he probably would have kept him in Barmen-Elberfeld, for young Engels had come to the opinion that England would shortly be the scene of a great social upheaval in which he hoped to be able to play an active part.

The twenty-two-year-old Engels clung obstinately to the notion of the coming revolution in England. During his last weeks in Berlin he studied thoroughly Moses Hess's fascinating pamphlet, *The European Triarchy* (*Die Europäische Triarchie* [1841]), which prophesied, under the fashionable disguise of Hegelian terminology, a social tumult and chose England as the place for it. The author of *The European Triarchy* (whom Engels met personally) supposed that human history, which he equated with the evolution of the Hegelian Idea, proceeded within a metaphysical trinity of great European powers. Germany in its Reformation had taken the lead over other countries with a "socio-spiritual" revolution; France in its Revolution had completed the "socio-moral" transformation; finally, Hess concluded, it was England's task to fill out the Hegelian scheme with a final "socio-political" upheaval. England was after all—and here Hess began to combine the purity of the Hegelian system with elements of modern sociology —the only country in which the dangerous tension between rich and poor had reached explosive intensity. Young Engels kept these doctrines well in mind. Hardly had he set foot on English soil than he began to write a series of political newspaper articles in which he clearly sacrificed his first concrete observations to the idea of immediate revolution.

It is worth noting that these were not the first reports on England presented by Engels to German readers. Two years earlier, he had described an imaginary trip to England in a short article in Gutzkow's *Telegraph für Deutschland,* which appeared under the title "Landscapes" ("Landschaften" [July, 1840]).[1] The style of this first "English" report was still under the influence of those pieces by Heine and the Young Germans that enlivened the otherwise rather stagnant liberal press. For the rest, "Landscapes" represented a journalistic caprice hardly corresponding to biographical reality. Although—or rather, just because—this report describes a purely imaginary England, it provides an interesting glimpse into the imaginative powers of the writer, then only twenty years old, who, still far removed from political and economic realities, preferred the rather frivolous mode of the *feuilleton.*

"In England, one sees," wrote Engels, "nothing of dazzling beauty, no colossal mountain masses, but a land full of gently rolling hills. . . . Far below lie the cities and towns, the forests and fields, between which the river meanders; to the right and left are mountains fading into the background, and above the charming valley and enchanting light, half-mist, half-sunshine. . . . Oh, there is a rich poetry in the provinces of Britannia! Often one imagines one's self to be back in the *golden days of merry Eng-*

*land,** seeing Shakespeare slip behind the hedge with his blunder-
buss . . . or one is surprised not to see one of his divine comedies
actually taking place on this green meadow."[2]

Two years later, not the slightest trace of this frivolity remained. Engels published his first political article in the *Rheinische Zeitung* on April 12, 1842;[3] in November, 1842, only a
few days after his arrival in London, he became exclusively absorbed with social problems and promptly fired off articles to
the *Rheinische Zeitung,* the editorship of which had been taken
over by Dr. Karl Heinrich Marx, and to the *Schweizer Republikaner.*[4] Moonlight, meadows, and Shakespeare were gone and
forgotten; an excited reporter whose perspective was concentrated exclusively on the political scene now wrote about Whigs
and Tories, Corn Laws and Reform Bills, the revolts of 1832 and
the condition of the working classes.

In December, 1842, young Engels entered the office of his
father's firm in Manchester. During the day, Engels, who only a
few months before had defended Hegel's doctrines against Schelling's followers, worked at the calico and cotton business. In the
evenings he devoted his energy to radical politics and to investigating the slums, where he found not only unimaginable misery,
but an unexpected attraction in the person of a simple working
girl, Mary Burns, who was to share his life. It would be quite
mistaken to doubt in the least the violent outrage of the young
man as he was suddenly faced with the indescribably wretched
existence of workingmen in industrial Lancashire. Even his experiences in the west German textile-producing area could not
have prepared him for such degradation. Having been accustomed up to now to regard all problems from the perspective of
Hegelian philosophy and a purely academic liberalism, Engels
found himself faced here with a stupefying and terrible new
world that must have seemed as strange to him as the landscape
of the moon. The people whom he met in the working-class sections of Manchester were reduced to a bare animal existence by
alcohol and robbed of their humanity by endemic diseases. He

* In English in Engels' text.—TRANSLATOR.

was by no means the only observer who was shaken by the misery of the English industrial quarters. At that time there was hardly a sensitive traveler who did not send home wrathful and despairing letters from Manchester and Liverpool—whether the traveler was a conservative historian like Friedrich von Raumer (1781–1873), who was outraged by the mass of beggar children, clothed in rags under his hotel balcony;[5] or a foreigner such as Herman Melville (1819–91), who as a poor sailor on shore leave in the summer of 1839 saw so many starving and dying mothers and children[6] that he was tormented for years by the memory until he freed himself from it in *Mardi* (1848) and *Redburn* (1850).

Engels' outrage was all the more intense and fruitful because he saw the English industrial situation, as did Melville later, through the eyes of Thomas Carlyle (1795–1881). Engels arrived in Lancashire at the end of December, 1842; he mentioned Carlyle's name for the first time on May 16, 1843, in an article in the *Schweizer Republikaner*.[7] After he had read Carlyle's book *Chartism* (1839), he turned immediately to the recently published work *Past and Present* (1843), which occupied him for nearly a year. He realized that in Carlyle's merciless denunciation of early Victorian England he had discovered an important document of social criticism, and he felt it necessary to make the book accessible to his radical friends in Germany as soon as possible. This plan was soon carried out. A year later, the *Deutsch-Französische Jahrbücher* (1844) appeared under the editorship of Marx and Ruge; it was the last manifesto that the liberal and radical wings of the German opposition were to produce as a joint effort. As well as Engels' economic studies it contained his contribution entitled "The Situation of England" ("Die Lage Englands").[8] Engels did not conceal from his readers that this report on the English social situation was largely made up of extensive translations from Carlyle's *Past and Present*; as his own material the translator added a short introduction, some commentary, and a few factual explanations.

The selection Engels laid before the German public in "The Situation of England" reveals a good deal about his viewpoint;

those chapters to which he gave prominence are no less revealing of his polemic intent than those he silently suppressed. Engels begins his translation of Carlyle, systematically enough, with the first three chapters of the Proem, in which Carlyle sketches the new economic problems and recalls the bloody revolts that had just shaken England. But Engels had no intention of presenting the text unaltered. Instead he subjects Carlyle's ideas to a continual ideological censorship, thus reducing the translation to a political pamphlet. For Engels completely conceals from his German readers Carlyle's second book, the religious core of the work. In Engels' translation there remains not a single word of Carlyle's portrait of the righteous abbot of St. Edmundsbury and the harmonious, well-ordered, and secure world he represents. Engels' antipathy for praise of the Middle Ages may have had literary as well as philosophical and political grounds. As a pupil of the anti-Romantic Young Germans and Young Hegelians, he shared the inclinations of the younger generation and could not join in Carlyle's celebration of the age of priests and knights. To be sure, Engels failed to see that Carlyle's description of times gone by, in its concrete soberness and bitter humor, had nothing at all in common with the saccharine Romanticism of such a writer as De la Motte-Fouqué (1777–1843). Engels was simply alienated by Carlyle's medieval gospel and did not trouble to reproduce the pithy language with which Carlyle draws a thoroughly hardheaded picture of medieval England.

Engels concentrated his entire ideological and interpretive interest upon the second chapter of the third book, entitled the "Gospel of Mammonism." It is the chapter in which Carlyle's bitter anger against the greed of the new industrial society is most clearly expressed. Like Melville, Engels was profoundly impressed by Carlyle's indictment of the new spirit of trade that substitutes for the certainties of an organically ordered life the bare, metallic fact of "cash-payment" as the single bond between men. Here Carlyle reaches the high point of his social criticism, and as soon as Engels had mastered this passage in his translation, he simply gave up any systematic attempt to follow Carlyle's train of thought any farther. He adds—no doubt with the German reader particularly in mind—a few of Carlyle's remarks upon Goethe; for the rest he hurries to the end of his translation. Thereby he cheats his readers of the closing argument, the great finale of Carlyle's sermon, for Carlyle closes his social criticism with a call to the new captains of industry and the old country nobility to grasp the reins of power once more, to invigorate the secular order once again with religious spirit, and to rule England according to God's laws. But of this there is not a word to be found in Engels' translation.

In the translations of these passages the arrangement and distribution of stresses and values clearly indicate the insoluble dilemma in which Engels finds himself vis-à-vis Carlyle. In order to satisfy his polemic intent, Engels must completely separate Carlyle the cultural critic from Carlyle the religious philosopher and thus destroy a unified complex of ideas. While he gladly seizes upon Carlyle's anticapitalistic *j'accuse* and translates it for his radical German friends, he throws Carlyle's whole metaphysical concept overboard as obsolete and superfluous. Engels' Carlyle criticism (in which Marx was to follow him only a little later) is characterized essentially by a radical secularization of concepts. Engels destroys the theological heart of Carlyle's vision of God and universal order, and uses the scattered socio-critical splinters, robbed of their ontological context, for his own purposes. Basically, in his quarrel with Carlyle, Engels set him up as a straw man, accusing the rigorous Calvinist, who believed in a single God-Creator separated from his creation, of a vague pantheism of the German type, fusing God and nature; he takes a zealous stand against this pantheism and thus attacks his own, highly subjective image of Carlyle's religion. This he does with weapons borrowed from Feuerbach's arsenal, chiefly from the *Principles of the Philosophy of the Future* (*Grundsätze der Philosophie der Zukunft* [1843]). Engels thought Carlyle mistaken in believing that new substance could be given to the empty universe through religion; it was, after all, religion itself, as Feuerbach had shown, that had transformed the world into a desert.[9]

Carlyle, demanded Engels, should read Feuerbach and other radical writers like Bruno Bauer if he really wanted to learn "whence the immorality that poisons all our circumstances comes."[10] Carlyle's philosophy would continue to present a distorted picture of the world as long as he could not bring himself to replace the absurdities of traditional theology with Feuerbach's view of the proud, true, and autonomous human being.

However, this metaphysical truncation of Carlyle is not the only problem created by Engels' essay. There is also a second, no less decisive misinterpretation. Engels separates Carlyle all too successfully from his British soil and Scottish tradition in order to celebrate him, in a void as it were, as the herald of German liberalism. To be sure, Engels admits from time to time that many of Carlyle's ideas were occasionally to be found in the ideology of the English Tories;[11] yet he remains incapable of seeing Carlyle as a product of the British conservative tradition. It is true that a detached evaluation of Carlyle was difficult for Engels because, like other German observers, Engels was so fascinated by Carlyle's interest in the German intellectual that he forgot the British premises upon which Carlyle worked.

Engels ignored Carlyle's Scottish background to his own disadvantage. Whether he did not want to see Carlyle in context, or whether, with his limited knowledge of English intellectual history, he could not see him so, his recommendation of Carlyle as it appears in the *Deutsch-Französische Jahrbücher* rests upon a dual paradox. Not only did he recommend to his liberal friends an arch-Tory as a politically exemplary figure, but he felt obliged to present the Scottish preacher as a "German-Englishman"[12] who had been converted into a critic of society by German philosophy.

The "Film" of Literature

In Carlyle's work Engels found his own radical change from literature to political concerns not only confirmed but prefigured. Carlyle and Engels shared a common experience in the restless intellectual movement of that age; both deserted the realm of poetry and, as modern followers of Plato and Hegel, turned their attention to society and its concrete problems. In the second third of the nineteenth century this tendency became apparent in both East and West: the bourgeois progressives who criticized the politically "useless" literature in the *Westminster Review*, were, although they could hardly have been aware of it, of one mind with radicals such as Vissarion Belinsky (1811–48), the first important literary critic of tsarist Russia. Whether they had studied Hegel as Engels did or acquired knowledge of him at second and third hand like Belinsky, whether they despised literature with Old Testament zeal as did Carlyle or, like Carlyle's utilitarian opponents, rejected socially irrelevant literature, in both Russia and England intellectuals took pride in turning their backs on a literature that seemed to be alienated from the spirit of the times. They assigned to poetry a new position, either as a subordinate pedagogical aid or, ultimately, as the handmaiden of morality, politics, or the state.[13]

In his early critical essays, Thomas Carlyle spoke enthusiastically and without reservation of the special dignity of literature.[14] Referring to his German models, he insisted that literature must be judged from within according to its own criteria. Praising the new criticism of Germany in 1827, Carlyle declared that the main problem of literature was "properly and ultimately a question on the essence and peculiar life of the poetry itself."[15] Far from condemning pure literature, he insisted, in dramatic contrast to the contemporary utilitarian criticism in Great Britain, upon the independent and innate value of poetry. "Art is to be loved," he declared, ". . . not because it is useful for spiritual pleasure, or even for moral culture, but because it is Art, and the highest in man, and the soul of all Beauty."[16]

Nevertheless, Carlyle's criticism quickly reveals a developing preference for the silent doer above the wordy writer. Hardly a year after he had praised the inner value of literature, he wrote in his essay on Goethe (1828) that poetry was to be found in action as well as words.[17] In his study of Robert Burns (1828)

he carried the devaluation of literature a step farther; in a highly
moralistic judgment he insisted that Burns's "acted" works were
far more interesting than his written ones. Burns's written poems,
added Carlyle, were only "little rhymed fragments, scattered here
and there in the grand unrhymed Romance of his earthly existence."[18]

By the forties, Carlyle, the lover of literature, had turned into
an angry prophet who had lost all interest in the autonomy of
literature. Literature was now subordinate to homiletics, if not
to pastoral theology. In his book *Past and Present* (III, 5),
Carlyle praised the gift of silence; he conceded to the wordless
"doers" the ability to write the chronicle of their lives in immutable, flaming letters on the sky itself. "Great honour to him,"
he cried, "whose Epic is a melodious hexameter Iliad; not a
jingling Sham-Iliad, nothing true in it but the hexameters and
forms merely. But still greater honour, if his Epic be a mighty
Empire slowly built together, a mighty Series of Heroic Deeds.
. . . Deeds are greater than Words."[19] Carlyle was suspicious of
literature because of its element of illusion, which he called a lie;
the poet as a creator with words gave way to the poet who created for the sake of creation though without any specific literary
achievement. This Romantic confusion of life and literature, deed
and word, which had been anticipated by Friedrich Schlegel,
Schelling, and Coleridge, finally forced Carlyle to condemn literature as the mere art of words and to praise the "poetic" meaning of even a totally inarticulated deed. The silent ones, as long
as they excelled in their activity, were more to be praised as
poietai (in the non-literary sense) than those who had nothing but
shallow words. The laurel for the most beautiful poem went to
the greatest deed.

Engels' literary progress from the traditional Protestant hymn
to Freiligrath, Gutzkow, Börne, and the *Hallische Jahrbücher* also
led, although in a far less complicated pattern, from enthusiasm
for literature to admiration for political action. As early as the
summer of 1842, before Engels was even thinking of a trip to
England, he condemned contemporary literature as empty and

useless and avoided critical discussions that dealt with literature
alone. "The . . . belletristic journals . . . ," he wrote at that time,
"[are] neither fish nor fowl. . . . Their day is past, they are
gradually being reduced to political newspapers that can easily
deal with what little literature there is."[20] Carlyle and Engels
came to share this devaluation of literature, although from widely
differing premises; Carlyle made his decisions on the basis of
theological and moral considerations, while those of Engels derived from an increasingly intense political dogmatism. But the
differing sources led to the same end: literature had long since
ceased to be the highest achievement of man. It was only one of
many methods of impressing upon men messages that they could
also receive from other sources, perhaps in purer and less adul-
terated form. But even on this subordinate plane to which they
relegated literature there were true and false accomplishments.
Whenever the writer tried to press the essential message upon the
reader as clearly as possible and without decorative embellish-
ments, he was sure of serious acclaim; but whenever he attempted
to dress up his message with pretentious ornaments, or worse,
with inessential themes, his achievement had to be rejected as
specious and "fashionable." Carlyle had earlier defined his concept of "fashionable literature" more precisely in *Sartor Resartus*
(1836). Professor Teufelsdröckh, the hero of the book, did not
spare his sarcastic and disparaging comments about contemporary best-sellers such as the novels of Bulwer-Lytton. Shortly
afterward Carlyle abandoned the disguise of the German meta-
physician Teufelsdröckh from Weissnichtswo and expressed in
his own person his deep aversion to the popular novel. In *Past and
Present* he condemned out of hand whole periods of English literature because they failed to praise the divine core of the universe.
"Our most melodious Singers," he declared categorically, "have
sung as from the throat outwards: from the inner Heart of Men,
from the great Heart of Nature, through no Popes or Philips has
there come any tone. The Oracles have been dumb."[21]

As soon as Engels read Carlyle's *Past and Present*, he took hold
of the idea of "fashionable literature" and used it for his own

purposes. "All fashionable literature," he asserted, referring to the English literature of the forties, "revolves in an eternal circle and is just as tedious and sterile as the jaded and hollow fashionable society."[22] More consistent than Carlyle, he ascribed a definite class character to fashionable literature. Only the upper strata of society admired it, while the poor and oppressed, showing much better taste, were eager to hear the more substantial message of philosophy: ". . . The workers of Manchester, Birmingham, and London constituted the only audience for [David Friedrich] Strauss in England."[23] Only the exploited classes read the literature of true progress; only they loyally followed the revolutionary writers of the time. "Shelley," emphasized Engels, "the prophetic genius, and Byron, with his sensual heat and his bitter satire upon prevailing society, have most of their readers among the workers; the bourgeois own only castrated 'family editions' that are bowdlerized according to today's hypocritical morality."[24] The unsuspecting German reader who was not in a position to assess the English situation with any great accuracy could hardly know that Engels had distorted the extremely complex and paradoxical conflicts within the English publishing trade into a gross piece of propaganda.[25]

Fortunately Engels was by no means determined to follow Carlyle slavishly in his every literary judgment. In contrast to him, Engels remained loyal to the English social novel that had been imitated by the Young Germans and justly praised by the Young Hegelians as a progressive new departure in literature. Above all, Engels departed from Carlyle's judgment on Charles Dickens (1812–70). Carlyle reported Dickens' triumphal tour through the United States (1843) with biting commentaries. Although he appreciated Dickens' achievement, he spoke with great irony in *Past and Present* of the popular successes of the "small good 'Schnüspel the distinguished novelist,' "[26] who was celebrated in America with "blazing torches, dinner invitations, universal hep-hep-hurrah!"[27] To Carlyle's irritation, however, the Anglo-Saxons did not appear to be in a mood to pay enthusiastic tribute to "a hero-martyr and great true Son of Heaven." Engels did not at all agree with such deprecating remarks; for him Dickens' growing work represented a literary event of the first order that had triggered publishers' wars and innumerable pirated printings and translations in Germany.[28] Perhaps he still remembered the enthusiastic reviews with which the Young Germans and Young Hegelians—such as Heinrich Laube and Robert Prutz—had greeted the great array of Dickens translations.[29] Engels gladly remained devoted to the liberal German enthusiasm for Charles Dickens. When he reported on the problems of the young European communism in the *New Moral World*, a publication of Robert Owen, he also mentioned Dickens, who together with George Sand (1804–76) and Eugène Sue (1804–57) had brought about almost a social revolution in continental literature. This new class of novelists had dethroned the kings and princes and finally elevated the poor, the "despised class," to a suitable subject for literature.[30] Eleven years later Karl Marx was to say similar things about Dickens. Marx wrote in the *New York Daily Tribune* on August 1, 1854, about "the splendid brotherhood of fiction writers in England, whose graphic and eloquent pages have issued to the world more political and social truths than have been uttered by all the professional politicians, publicists and moralists put together."[31] Marx's particular praise went to Thackeray, Charlotte Brontë, Elizabeth Gaskell, and above all to Charles Dickens. Marx, however, hardly added anything new to the usual Young Hegelian commentaries on Dickens when he called the novelist a painter who had drawn an accurate picture of the affected, ignorant, and tyrannical bourgeoisie.

Of more decisive importance than possible agreements or discrepancies in literary value judgments is the more subtle legacy that the cultural critic Carlyle left with young Engels. Although Engels had come to England as, to quote Carlyle, a "speculative radical . . . of the very darkest tinge,"[32] after a few weeks he began to develop a growing feeling for that force of history that he was to identify as economic. It is true that he joked from time to time about the inability of the all too practical Britons to recognize the essential meaning of the Hegelian idea, but this skepticism was short-lived. As soon as he had completed his first analyses of the political and economic situation of England, he admitted without hesitation that the English political parties were identical with social interest groups and that the epoch of modern English history bore the imprint of the steam engine and the spinning jenny. His thinking began to concern itself with the economic element; like Carlyle, he was also of the opinion that the world had "been terribly inattentive to that question of work and wages."[33]

From now on it was clear to Engels that these concrete problems had to be solved before all others; the questions of politics, philosophy, and aesthetics followed at a considerable distance. But here too Carlyle had given the young man advice that was not free of pitfalls. The "speakable," Carlyle declared, was nothing more than a superficial "film" that "lies atop" the world, nothing more than an "outer skin"—only the deed, the doable, really "reaches down into the World's centre."[34] It was not long before Engels, together with his friend Marx, would be ready to believe that literature is nothing other than an epiphenomenon on the upper surface of the universe; the wordless deed alone reaches into the economic heart of existence.

3

On the Way to Economic
Determinism: Karl Marx

The Young Poet

Karl Marx (b. May 5, 1818) came from a Jewish middle-class family of civil servants in Trier; if time, place, and heredity indeed had the importance the nineteenth century so devoutly ascribed to them, Marx would have been destined for a career as a liberal-minded and efficient Prussian civil servant. At the venerable Friedrich-Wilhelms-Gymnasium in Trier he received an excellent education in Latin and Greek that was to affect his literary sympathies for the rest of his life. In contrast to Engels, who concerned himself primarily with the most recent developments in literature and liked to boast of his little Greek, young Marx studied the ancients thoroughly. His school certificate (*Reifezeugnis*, September 24, 1835), speaks with old-fashioned detail of his knowledge of the classics. Young Marx, it reads, showed in his essays on the Latin authors "a richness of ideas and a deep penetration into the subject";[1] in Greek as well he showed "almost as much knowledge and ability . . . as in Latin."[2] Nevertheless, Marx did not pass his final Greek examination with highest honors: his teacher remarked somewhat dryly that he had translated the required passage from Sophocles' *Women of Trachis* (11. 140–76) quite tolerably but added the critical comment that from time to time he had followed neither the author nor the sense of the lines.[3]

Marx's early intellectual development was advanced and directed by Ludwig von Westphalen (1770–1842),[4] a leading official of the Prussian administration in Trier. This widely traveled, learned, and worldly-wise benefactor, whose daughter Jenny was later to follow Marx through all the tragic paths of his life, was for him an attractive symbol of the great world. The Westphalen family had a tradition for outstanding careers and great successes. Ludwig's father, Philipp Westphalen (1724–92), went into service as a young commoner with the Duke of Brunswick and executed diplomatic negotiations for his master with German princes, Prussian generals, and British army officers during the Seven Years' War. At one of these military conferences, Philipp became acquainted with a certain Miss Jenny Wishart from Edinburgh, whose family tree allegedly reached back to the Duke of Argyle; Philipp fell in love with her and promptly married her. As the youngest daughter of an Edinburgh minister, Jenny had enjoyed a solid education in the best eighteenth-century Scottish tradition. Into her new German household she brought not only her select private library but above all her girlish enthusiasm for the epics of Homer and the theater of Shakespeare. In the course of events, the literary inclinations of the young Scotswoman turned out to be decisive for the cultural horizons of young Marx. Jenny Wishart raised her son, Ludwig von Westphalen, to admire Homer and Shakespeare; he, in turn, transmitted this admiration to young Marx, to whom he recited epic poetry and dramatic scenes in German, Greek, and English while on long walks. It is questionable whether Ludwig von Westphalen succeeded equally in passing this enthusiasm on to his own son Georg, who was to conduct the affairs of Prussia as minister of the interior during the period of the most stifling reaction (1850–58).

During Marx's first year at the University of Bonn (1835–36), the genuine vehemence of his passionate temperament was concealed behind the fashionable mask of the restless student whom the university had to punish for drunkenness and illegal possession of weapons. Marx devoted his time in Bonn to his own poems, which he transmitted to his fiancée Jenny and to his father in beautifully written copies. Marx was not the only would-be poet among his fellow students; he found like-minded friends who also preferred literary endeavor to attending lectures, and he became a member of a poets' club that met for readings in the taverns of Bonn. It was a diverse group in every sense of the word.[5] There was a young student named Karl Grün (1817–87), who later on as the leader of the German Proudhonists had to fight many a battle with his former companion, and also a north German student, Emanuel Geibel (1815–84), who appears to have taken part in the meetings from time to time—he later became the poet laureate of the Bavarian court. Heinrich Marx admitted in his letters to his son that he did not know much about poetry, but he was not sorry to hear about the poets' club; he thought his son to be in good company at last. "Your little circle," he wrote unsuspectingly from Trier to Bonn at the beginning of 1836, "pleases me . . . better than the tavern. Young people who find pleasure in such a gathering are necessarily educated men and have a better sense of their worth as future good citizens."[6] Since Karl Marx had put together his first collection of poems, he hoped that his father would bear the cost of publication; fortunately Marx *père* remained somewhat skeptical. He advised his son to wait a little with the publication of his poems until he could really compete with the important authors of the age. "A poet, a writer," wrote Heinrich Marx, "must these days know that he has something sound to offer if he wants to appear in public. . . . I will tell you frankly that I am delighted by your talents . . . but I would grieve to see you appear before the public as a common poetaster. . . . Only an outstanding man has the right to lay claim to the attention of a pampered world. . . ."[7]

How much time and intellectual effort young Marx gave to the six lecture courses of the winter semester of 1835–36 and to the five more of the summer semester of 1836 is difficult to ascertain. His university records testify that he was far more interested in aesthetic problems than in those legal questions his father put to him in nearly every letter. Although he registered for the required courses in the faculty of law, he seems to have been zealously occupied with Greek art and mythology. As the university officials testified, he followed Friedrich Gottlieb Welcker's (1774–1868) famous lectures on Greek and Latin mythology "with outstanding industry and attention" and also attended Eduard d'Alton's (1772–1840) course in art history.[8] He went to two of August Wilhelm Schlegel's (1767–1855) popular lecture courses: to the winter semester course on Homer, and the summer semester one on the *Elegies* of Propertius. It would probably be fruitless to seek a definite influence of August Wilhelm Schlegel on young Marx's thinking, yet his choice of Schlegel's lectures shows that in Bonn he continued as before to pursue those classical studies that his patron, Ludwig von Westphalen, had urged upon him.

Heinrich Marx was soon quite disastisfied with "the wild rampaging in Bonn."[9] For his son there was, of course, no question of any career other than one as a lawyer or judge. He hoped that a change of scene from Bonn to Berlin would lead his son back to the straight and narrow path of legal studies. But he was mistaken. In Berlin Karl found himself only more cruelly separated from his distant Jenny and his poet friends in Bonn, and he poured the melancholy of his impatient heart into another copybook of poems. Soon even the poems no longer sufficed; the young student considered trying his literary luck with a novel and a tragedy.

Marx's early poems and ballads[10] are not artistically significant, but they are indicative of his personal motivations. They reveal much about his reading, his taste, and the development of his literary inclinations. Young Marx did not write contemporary poetry; between the style of his youthful works and the important poetry of that day there is a gap of at least one generation. Whether his youthful work suffered from the cultural lag of the Trier ghetto, or whether Ludwig von Westphalen's distinctly classicist tastes turned him to already obsolete forms—Marx's poems were curious anachronisms. Although there are some traces of Heine, Marx's youthful poetry was based principally on Goethe, Schiller, Bürger (1747–94), and Hölty (1748–76). The philosophical pieces, which Marx's father called "abstract idealizing,"[11] clearly betrayed their source in the abstract youthful poetry of Schiller; the influence of Bürger's famous ballad *Lenore* (1774) is found in more than one poem. The overwhelming majority of Marx's early poems followed the tradition of Goethe's ballads, above all *Der König in Thule*, the rhythms of which Marx was able to imitate very exactly. It can hardly come as a surprise that Marx was unsuccessful in getting these poems published as a group. Like many other young writers, he submitted examples of his poems to the tolerant judgment of Adalbert Chamisso (1781–1838), editor of the annual *Deutscher Musenalmanach*, but Chamisso politely refused to print them. Marx quoted a few lines of Chamisso's answer in a letter to his father (November 10, 1837): Chamisso had informed him on a "highly unimpressive scrap of paper" that the *Musenalmanach* was "long since printed,"[12] and the poems could not be included in it. "I swallowed [the note] out of fury," added Marx,[13] somewhat overdramatizing his suffering. But he was yet to gain some consolation. Long after he had laid his youthful poems aside, two of them, "Der Spielmann" ("The Minstrel") and "Nachtliebe" ("Night Love") were printed in the Berlin *Athenäum* on January 23, 1841. They were the first and last of his poems to reach a wider public during his lifetime.

Of particular interest are Marx's sarcastic epigrams in the tradition of Goethe's and Schiller's *Xenien* (1797). Particularly in the epigrams directed against Hegel, he shows effectiveness and skill in the most compressed of all verse forms: in the pairing of the rising hexameter and the falling pentameter, in the sudden break between them, Marx found an effective method of representing with surprising accuracy the central dialectic of Hegelian philosophy. The dialectical tension of the verse form itself conveyed ironically and aptly Hegel's form of thinking.

Hegel: Epigramme

1.

Weil ich das Höchste entdeckt und die Tiefe sinnend gefunden,
Bin ich grob, wie ein Gott, hüll' mich in Dunkel, wie er.

Lange forscht' ich und trieb auf dem wogenden Meer der
   Gedanken,
Und da fand ich das Wort, halt' am Gefundenen fest.

[Because I have discovered the highest of things, and, medi-
tating, found the deep, | I am crude as a god, cloak myself
in darkness as he does. | Long I inquired and sailed on the
wavy sea of thought, | and there I found the word, and hang
on firmly to what I have found.]

2.

Worte lehr' ich, gemischt in dämonisch verwirrtem Getriebe,
Jeder denke sich dann, was ihm zu denken beliebt.
Wenigstens ist er nimmer geengt durch fesselnde Schranken,
Denn wie aus brausender Flut, stürzend vom ragenden Fels,
Sich der Dichter ersinnt der Geliebten Wort und Gedanken.
Und was er sinnet, erkennt, und was er fühlet, ersinnt,
Kann ein jeder sich saugen der Weisheit labenden Nektar,
Alles sag' ich euch ja, weil ich ein Nichts euch gesagt.[14]

[Words I teach in a demoniacally confused to-do, | and every-
one may then think what he chooses. | At least he will never
more be restricted by limiting fetters, | for as out of a roar-
ing flood pouring from a projecting rock, | the poet invents
the words and thoughts of his beloved, | and perceives what
he thinks and thinks what he feels; | everyone can sip the
refreshing nectar of wisdom; | after all, I am telling you
everything because I have told you nothing.]

In Marx's fragment of a novel, "Skorpion und Felix,"[15] written at about the same time (1837), there is none of this arch and
clever gaiety. The crude jokes, the forced literary associations,
the whole chaotic wilderness of puns, hardly justify the subtitle,
"A Humorous Novel," that Marx gave it. The dilettante was attempting too much. Since he was trying to imitate all the virtues
of Sterne, Jean Paul, Hippel, and E. T. A. Hoffmann in a single
work, his effort necessarily remained without order, force, or
effect.

The failure of this novel—he finished only a few chapters—
convinced Marx that he had to prove his talent in a different

literary genre. With the ease of the true literary amateur, he turned to tragedy. He reported his new plan, as usual, to his father, who for his part offered modest encouragement; nevertheless, he urged Karl to produce a literary work that would ultimately be of use to him in his future official career. "You have taken up the drama, and there is certainly much of truth in it," wrote Heinrich Marx from Trier to Berlin on March 2, 1837, "but connected with its importance, with its great public notoriety, there is the danger of failure."[16] In his fatherly concern for the future welfare of his son, Heinrich Marx immediately sketched a plan to aid Karl in writing a literary work while still convincing the Prussian state, his future employer, of his patriotism. He advised Karl to select a subject from Prussian history in order to prove to the state, at least in a literary way, that he was inclined to all those ideals he would later represent in the administration. As the most suitable subject, Heinrich Marx recommended one of those moments of Prussian history that proved the timelessness of the Hohenzollern ideals; an important emphasis should be put on the genius of the monarchy, personified by Queen Louise. The most serviceable event, Heinrich Marx felt, would be the Battle of Waterloo; if Karl would only select this battle as the subject or at least as the background of a new work, he would surely make a name for himself. Even if he could not make up his mind to write a tragedy, a great patriotic ode would probably be sufficient to assure the gratitude of the House of Hohenzollern: ". . . Patriotic and sentimental, and worked out with German temperament, such an ode would by itself be sufficient to found a reputation, to consolidate your name."[17]

Unfortunately, this exhortation came too late. Without waiting for fatherly advice, young Marx had already completed the first scenes of a new tragedy called "Oulanem." Much to his father's regret, there was nowhere in the manuscript the slightest trace of enthusiasm for the Prussian state.[18]

Since only the first act of the draft has survived for posterity, the plot and the actual intention of the tragedy can only be reconstructed approximately. However, such an approximation is

made easier by the fact that the author of "Oulanem," as can
clearly be seen in the first scenes, followed closely the conventions
of the contemporary Gothic thriller. The first scene brings Oulanem, a somewhat mysterious German traveler, along with his
young companion, Lucindo, into an Italian city, where both are
warmly greeted by Pertini, one of the citizens. But Oulanem, an
aging poet, is incapable of any real joy; as soon as he finds himself alone in his room, he is overcome by secret despair, which is
enhanced by a premonition of an inescapable disaster:

> Verfall'n! Die Stunde, sie ist abgelaufen,
> Die Horen stehn, der Zwergbau stürzt zusammen!
> Bald press' ich Ewigkeit ans Herz und heule
> Der Menschheit Riesenfluch in sie hinein!
> Ha, Ewigkeit! Das ist ein ew'ger Schmerz,
> Ein unaussprechlich unermess'ner Tod!
> Schnöd' Kunstwerk, uns zum Hohn ersonnen,
> Wir Uhrwerk, blindmechanisch aufgezogen,
> Des Zeitenraums Kalendernarr zu sein,
> Zu sein, damit doch irgendwas geschieht,
> Zerfall'n, damit doch irgendwas zerfällt! ...
> Die Welten fassen's und sie roll'n dahin.
> Und heulen ewig ihren eig'nen Totensang,
> Und wir, wir Affen eines kalten Gottes,
> Wir hegen noch die Natter üppig warm
> Mit toller Müh an voller Liebesbrust. ...
> Jetzt schnell—das Los geworfen—alles fertig,
> Zerstört, was Lügendichtung nur ersann,
> Mit Fluch vollendet, was der Fluch begann![19]

[Lost! The hour has run out, | the Horae stand still, the
house of dwarfs caves in! | Soon I will press eternity to my
bosom and howl | the giant curse of humanity into it. | Ha,
eternity! That is an eternal pain, | an unspeakably immeas-
urable death! | Vile artifice, invented to our scorn, | We are
clockwork, blindly and mechanically wound up, | to be the
fool of time, | to be, just so that something happens, | de-
cayed, just so that something decays! | ... The planets
understand it and they roll on, | eternally howling their own

death-dirge, | and we, we monkeys of a cold God, | we still
cherish the viper, luxurious and warm, | at our love-filled
breast with furious effort. . . . Now quickly—let the die be cast
—let everything be finished, | destroyed, that ever lying po-
etry devised, let be completed with a curse what the curse
began!]

Not only Oulanem, but his companion Lucindo, is also surrounded by mysteries. Only Pertini seems to know of the past of
both of them and confesses in an extensive monologue his desire
to make destructive use of his knowledge:

> Mein Plan ist fertig, seine tiefste Seele,
> Sein Leben bist Du selber, Oulanem!
> Willst du das Schicksal ziehn, wie eine Puppe?
> Den Kalkulator mit dem Himmel spielen?
> Aus deinen morschen Lenden Götter drechseln?
> Mein kleiner Gott, bet' deine Rolle ab . . . ![20]

[My plan is finished; you yourself, | Oulanem, are its deepest
soul, its life! | Do you want to pull the strings of destiny like
those of a marionette? | To play the calculator with heav-
en? | To form gods out of your rotten loins? | My little god,
recite your role to the end!]

In order to fulfil his unrevealed objective, Pertini first brings
Lucindo to the young and beautiful Beatrice, in order perhaps to
tempt the youth with her charms. For Beatrice also destiny seems
both unknown and ominous. Like Lucindo, she is of German
origin and suffers like an alien flower in the quiet heat of the
southern city. Lucindo and Beatrice are quickly attracted to one
another, but their union suggests connections reaching far and
cruelly beyond the feelings of the impassioned youth and the
delicate girl. A last sign ("My foreboding heart!"), uttered by
Beatrice before the curtain falls, may suggest that perhaps her
beloved Lucindo is her own brother and that both may stand in a
secret family relationship to Oulanem.

There can be no doubt but that this fragment is in essence derived from the conventions of the tragedy of fate (*Schicksalstra-*

* gödie*), which had already passed the peak of its popularity in the thirties. In his tragedy Marx implies most of the motifs from which Zacharias Werner (1768–1823) and Adolf Müllner (1774–1829) regularly constructed their thrillers: destiny ruled by the calendar and by monotonous curses, the return of the apparently unknown but secretly recognized stranger, the threat of incest between brother and sister, the fate of fathers and sons who fall victim to an increasing emotional confusion. However, Marx added to the tradition of the popular tragedy of fate a number of elements that reveal his enthusiasm for Goethe's *Faust*. In Oulanem he produced nothing more than a very shadowy copy of the aging Faust; the urgent longings of the rejuvenated Faust appear in Lucindo. Pertini is a weak imitation of Mephistopheles: in his consistently ironic, even nihilistic attitude he appears as Marx's embodiment of the spirit "who always denies" (*Faust*, I, 1. 1338). For this reason, he is, however, the only interesting character in the draft. Pertini goes so far as to mention Goethe's theme explicitly ("You are thinking of Mephistopheles and Faust?").[21] He also tempts Lucindo with a charming piece of woman-flesh[22] and insists, in the manner of Mephisto, upon calling his protagonist a "little god." Reminiscences of Goethe are also evident in the verse structure. Instead of using the fashionable tetrameters of the tragedies of fate as Werner and even Grillparzer did, Marx uses the madrigal verse over long passages. Marx's enthusiasm for Goethe's *Faust*, a performance of which in Berlin with Carl Seydelmann (1793–1843) as Mephisto impressed itself ineradicably upon his memory as a young student, appears also in later years. For example, Mark's criticism of Hegel in the *Deutsch-Französische Jahrbücher* (1844) begins with a paragraph woven around the two key words *Unmensch* ("subhuman," "monster") and *Übermensch* ("superman") as they appear in the first part of *Faust* (I. 11. 3349, 490).[23] The German Social Democrat Karl Liebknecht reports that Marx, even as an old man in exile in London, recited the role of Mephisto and greatly enjoyed imitating the skilful performance of Seydelmann.[24]

This fragment of the tragedy seems to have thoroughly disappointed Marx's own hopes. He explained to his father that he now planned to publish a critical magazine dealing mainly with the theater, and he once again asked Heinrich Marx for active material support. But his father insisted, more strictly and stubbornly than ever, that Karl should at last devote himself to his prescribed legal studies and no longer waste his time with literature. "With regard to your plan for dramatic criticism," wrote Heinrich Marx, "I must first of all confess that I am not competent with respect to the subject itself. . . . Such a labor might be one of the most useful in our time so far as its effect on art is concerned . . . but how will it be taken? I think, with more hostility than favor; and good, learned Lessing did not lie much in a bed of roses, so far as I know, but lived and died as a poor librarian."[25] Heinrich Marx had come to the end of his patience: "I can only address one wish to heaven, that somehow or other you will get as quickly as possible to your true goal."[26]

Karl Marx himself felt that his numerous intellectual and literary efforts had remained without visible effect. It is true that in Berlin he had listened to law lectures by Eduard Gans (1798–1839), the editor of Hegel's *Philosophy of Right* (*Philosophie des Rechts*), but literature and aesthetic studies had still been in the foreground. Marx had read Lessing's *Laokoon* (1766) and extensively excerpted Solger's *Erwin* (1815) and Winckelmann's *History of Ancient Art* (*Geschichte der Kunst des Altertums,* 1764); to train his style he had translated passages from Ovid's *Tristia* and, somewhat later, a few from Aristotle's *Rhetorics*.[27] But he felt he had not achieved power or order in these works, either. Finally the constitution of the young student, weakened by this intellectual crisis, gave way; Marx fell into a severe illness accompanied by violent attacks of fever.

The crisis in Marx's health in the early summer of 1837 was the first turning point in his intellectual development. During the first days of his convalescence he decided to occupy himself with contemporary philosophy before all other interests; philosophy appeared as the new, healing force in which he began to place his whole trust. Although earlier he had ridiculed Hegel's philosophy and laughed at the "grotesque melody of the rocks" (*groteske Felsenmelodie*)[28] of the philosopher, he now felt as though annihilated by the force of the Hegelian system. Hardly had he begun to read Hegel than he wrote his first philosophical dialogue—only to be obliged to admit that the final conclusions of the dialogue were, as he put it, the first word of the Hegelian philosophy. Half against his will, he yielded to the philosophy of objective idealism and was carried into the hostile arms of Hegel by his youthful spirit "as by a false Siren."[29] Marx never returned to a systematic study of aesthetics; although from time to time he concerned himself with concrete aesthetic problems, he did so more for external than internal reasons. As late as the spring and early summer of 1842 he considered writing an analytic essay on "Religion and Art" for Ruge's opposition publications, in which he wanted to show that the neo-Christian art that had become fashionable in the reign of Frederick William IV had in reality quite pagan roots. As usual, Marx copied long excerpts from works which Hegel had cited with praise, including some from C. F. Ruhmor's *Italian Studies (Italienische Forschungen* [1827]),[30] but political developments prevented him from carrying out his plan. Fifteen years later he turned once again, this time at the behest of an American friend, to the problem of a systematic aesthetics. His patron Charles Anderson Dana (1819–97) asked him to write a few pages on the aesthetician and humanist Friedrich Theodor Vischer (1807–87) for the *New American Cyclopedia*. Although Marx made fun of this journalistic commission, he started work on it for pressing financial reasons in May and June of 1857 and filled his notebooks with excerpts from Vischer.[31] The required Vischer article was never finished, but particular motifs from Vischer's aesthetics were to turn up quite surprisingly in Marx's drafts of that time.

The fragmentary character of these later efforts shows even more clearly the importance of the crisis in the early summer of 1837. In Marx's development it occupies a place similar to Engels' arrival in England. It is as though Marx had personally experienced one of the essential postulates of Hegelian aesthetics:

the young student from Trier had left behind the golden days of poetry, and, like Engels only a few years later, had entered upon the epoch of prose, of the more substantial interests of mankind.

Visions and Theories (1844)

Following his own inclinations and temperament, the young philosopher Marx moved toward the radical wing of the Berlin Young Hegelians, who met in a club called "The Free Men." In both his doctoral dissertation and his notes for it Marx almost instinctively confessed that he and his friends felt themselves to be reluctant heirs to Hegel's theories. Aristotle had triumphed in Greek philosophy and had condemned the Epicureans, the Stoics, and the Skeptics to present a "feeble conclusion";[32] people in Marx's time were living, after Hegel, in an "iron age."[33] But it was up to the heirs to make a decision. They could be satisfied with poor repetitions, like those artists in "centuries that limped behind great artistic epochs" who occupied themselves only with "copying in wax, plaster, and copper what had burst forth in Carraran marble, just like Pallas Athena from the brow of the godfather Zeus,"[34] or they could undertake new titanic struggles and understand that Prometheus (the hero of Marx's doctoral dissertation) was the incarnation of the true essence of philosophical activity. Like Prometheus, "philosophy, which has expanded itself to the world, turns also toward the world of appearances";[35] and even the iron age was "like a storm that follows a great, a worldwide philosophy."[36] With Ludwig Feuerbach's *Essence of Christianity* (*Wesen des Christentums* [1841]), which young Marx studied no less attentively than the rest of his generation, the titanic philosophical struggle of the transformation of Hegelian philosophy into the material and the practical element began. In Feuerbach's vision the human periphery of the Hegelian *Weltgeist* had become the center of the universe; religion was revealed as the fatal self-projection of mankind, for mankind through its concept of God had alienated itself from its own essence (as with

Hegel the spirit had alienated itself into the world). No longer was the world ruled by the distant spirit but, as Marx said a little later (1844), by "the real, the sensory, the existent, the finite, the particular";[37] man was no longer seen as an unknown abstract but "as a corporeal, living, real being, naturally impelled and sensorially present."[38] Without renouncing Hegelianism, Marx turned Feuerbach's method against Hegel and, in a critical commentary to Hegel's view of civil law drew the necessary conclusion (summer, 1843): Feuerbach had discovered man as the creator of religion; Marx confirmed man as the creator of the state. In place of Hegel's "state-formalism"[39] appeared the "real man";[40] the "logical, pantheistic mysticism"[41] yielded to a sketch of a political anthropology. "Hegel starts from the state," wrote Marx, "and makes man into a subjectified state; democracy starts with man and makes the state into an objectified man. Just as religion does not make men, but men religion, so the constitution does not make the people, but the people the constitution."[42]

But the titanic struggles had just begun. The first step that led Marx to the "real man" was soon followed by the next one that caused him to confront man, as a real being, with economics and to force him into a fateful constellation of objects, commodities, greed, and money. It is difficult to tell whence the philosophical impulses came and how, around the turn of the year from 1843 to 1844, they began to unite in the changed thought of the young philosopher. Feuerbach and Moses Hess (b. 1812) had their part in it, as did also the young Friedrich Engels, who had gone ahead of Marx in concrete economic observations. Feuerbach was the first to declare real man to be the creator who is unthinkable without a created object: "man is nothing without object . . . the object is his revealed essence, his true objective ego."[43] In Feuerbach, too, are to be found the arguments that the Jewish faith is "egoism in the form of religion,"[44] which were to occupy Marx in his fragments *On the Jewish Question* (1843–January, 1844).

It was Moses Hess who drew a clearer analogy between religion and economics and projected Feuerbach's idea that man alienates himself in religion into the realm of commodities. Man creates the world of religion *and* the world of commodities, and alienates himself from his true and free essence as much in the one way as the other; therefore it is necessary to study economic relationships as the most oppressive form of human alienation, and to seek a revolutionary way that would correct the alienation of man in a new world of togetherness (which Hess called the communist world). Moses Hess believed that *all* mankind should bear the responsibility for destroying this alienation; Marx, who had just read the interesting study of the Prussian conservative (and police agent) Lorenz von Stein on *Sozialismus und Kommunismus in Frankreich* (1842),[45] assigned the liberating role to the proletariat, which alone was the representative of oppressed mankind. Philosophy, he stressed in January, 1844, was the head of the liberation, but the proletariat was its heart.[46]

Friedrich Engels, by his personal example, led Marx to a study of economic relationships. At the very time that Marx in Paris sought for a concrete definition of the relationship between man and society, he received as editor of the *Deutsch-Französische Jahrbücher* Engels' English essays, which, in Hess's sense, made the modern national economy and Carlyle's stress upon economic problems the center of radical theory. With the violent energy characteristic of him, Marx threw himself into theoretical economics, studied Ricardo, Say, and MacCulloch, the authorities whom Engels had recommended, and only months later did he return, with new insights, to his criticism of Hegel.

In the Heraclidan darkness of the *Economic-Philosophical Manuscripts* (1844), which were not published until 1932 and thus remained unknown to the older generations of Marxists, Marx picked up the various strands of his criticism of Hegel and fitted them, along with his newly gained insights into economic life, into a highly romantic myth of the alienated human being in industrial society. Man appears, as in Feuerbach's work, as a fundamentally productive being who has lost his true purpose. Instead of being a free individual engaged in spontaneous activity (*Selbsttätigkeit*), man is degraded to forced labor (*Zwangsarbeit*); and the more he creates, the more inimically he is faced with the "evermore" of his work. The process of self-alienation into the religious object (as sketched by Feuerbach), has given way, following Moses Hess, to the process of self-alienation into commodities, that is, into the industrial object: "the more the worker achieves, the more powerful the alien, objective world that he creates over against himself becomes, the poorer he becomes himself, the less his inner world belongs to him. It is the same in religion. The more man stakes in God, the less he retains within himself."[47] The metaphysical vice of greed drives man ever deeper into alienation by creating private property; money, as Marx tried to prove from his favorite reading, Goethe's *Faust* and Shakespeare's *Timon of Athens* (cf. below, chap. vi, pp. 154–57, becomes the perverse god that tears self and being asunder and turns all human relations into absurdity. The laboring man (that is, the proletarian as a symbol of mankind) is subject to a triple alienation: first, he alienates himself into the object he produces, which glares at him coldly, hostilely, and strangely; second, he alienates himself through the act of production itself, for labor "belongs only externally to the worker," that is, it "does not belong to his essence";[48] finally—and this idea remains obscure—he alienates himself from the human race, for whatever advantage he has over the animals as a conscious producer becomes a degrading handicap. Young Marx says nothing about the technique of revolution that is to remove this alienation; it seems to be more of a capacity to change one's destiny through thought than a specific set of political measures with economic consequences. He differentiates, however, very sharply between a first stage, *raw* communism,[49] which as "only one manifestation of the vileness of private property"[50] yet further intensifies chaos, discord, and degradation, and the actual goal of human history, perfected *humanism*, which he defines "as the complete conscious return of man, developed within the whole richness of previous evolution, for his own sake as a social, that is, a *human* human being";[51] and indeed Marx did not even require this reference to the return of man in order to unveil the idea that when alienation is overcome, in a religious sense, there is hope for a Paradise Regained. It would be difficult to ignore the exact analogy to the idea of *t'shuvah* that, in Hebrew theology, suggests the return of the man alienated from God to his true destiny.

The end of alienation is a beautiful and glorious celebration of integration. The once dissociated ways of human production (religion, family, state, law, morals, science, art, and so on)[52] "fall," as Marx says, "under a general law";[53] and man returns out of "religion, family, state, and so on"[54] into the indivisible wholeness of his existence. Even the objects, which once stood over and against him coldly and hostilely as something "other," are now transformed into an "objectification of his being,"[55] confirming and realizing him. They are now of his being, though not his possession: "how they become his depends upon the nature of the objects and the nature of their corresponding intrinsic forces."[56] In Feuerbach's world the happy man celebrates "theoretical festivals of the sense of sight (*Augenfeste*)";[57] in the paradise without alienation postulated by young Marx the *Augenfest* expands into a festival of all the senses, which, as it were, evolve beyond themselves. In the state of alienation man is "so stupid and one-sided"[58] that he becomes aware of objects only in terms of their use, that is whether they are "possessed, eaten, drunk, worn, inhabited."[59] The age that follows alienation brings with it "the complete emancipation of all human senses and qualities."[60] Eye and ear, and all other senses, become "human"[61] because they relate to an object for the sake of the object and do not attempt to achieve its possession; pleasure will have lost its "egotistical nature," Nature its "mere usefulness."[62] Marx does not doubt that the senses of the liberated human being will change, intensify, become refined; "the senses of social man," he suggests, "are other senses than those of non-social [that is, alienated] man."[63] "The needy, worried man has no sense of the finest drama; the mineral merchant sees only the mercantile value but not the . . . particular beauty of the mineral."[64] Only in the age after the destruction of alienation "will the wealth of subjective *human* sensuality, a musical ear, an eye for the beauty of form, in short, senses capable of human pleasures . . . be partly . . . developed, partly

. . . engendered."[65] It is remarkable to see the lifelong Puritan, Marx, in his romantic vision of the world, draw the future human being, as it were, as a divine being who enjoys pleasure without care and with infinite finesse. It is difficult to say whether this image of man is closer to the Plotinian creative spirit in the *Enneads,* who blissfully contemplates himself in the mirror of creation, or to the artist who finds himself in his work of art.

Be that as it may, corruption and "contemplation stained with egotism" (as Feuerbach characterized it)[66] are things of the past, and in their place there appears in the moment of redemption the purity of "joyful, self-contained, blissful beholding"[67] that reveals all existence to be "wonderfully glorious, like a diamond" and "transparent like a rock crystal."[68]

It is evidence of the inner disparities of Marxism that the romantic vision of the oppressed situation and ultimate liberation of alienated man no longer radiated through the discussions that followed the *Economic-Philosophical Manuscripts.* Only isolated passages, for example, Engels' reference to the great artists of the Renaissance "who were not yet enslaved by the division of labor" (1875–76),[69] suggest perhaps the spirit of Marx's early vision. As though Marx's speculative furor had exhausted itself, the vision of man yielded to an interest in society as a whole, and the tone began to become drier and more didactic. Marx and Engels met in Paris in the summer of 1844 and established their agreement "in all areas";[70] without hesitation they set about giving firm polemical expression to their common principles (including some schematic ideas about the connection between matter and intellect). Their pamphlet *Die deutsche Ideologie* (1844) was aimed at those philosophical friends among the Young Hegelians who had not comprehended the hegemony of economics in human affairs. But as Marx and Engels worked out their standpoint in sharp polemic against their former friends, the pamphlet, which found no publisher during the lifetime of its authors, grew into a first fundamental declaration of their main ideas about man and the development of his mind in religion, art, and philosophy.

Marx and Engels described the relationships between the material and spiritual elements of human existence in the following way:

> The production of ideas, concepts, and the consciousness is first of all directly interwoven with the material activity and the material intercourse of man, the language of real life. Conceiving, thinking, the spiritual intercourse of men, appear here as the direct efflux of men's material behavior. The same is true of intellectual production, as it appears in the language of the politics, the laws, the morals, the religion, the metaphysics, and so on, of a people. Human beings are the producers of these concepts, ideas, and so on, that is, real, functioning men, as they are determined by a particular development of their productive forces and of the intercourse corresponding to these forces in its highest forms.[71]

Feuerbach's idea of man as a producer threatens to lose a significant portion of its universal validity; indeed the industrial meaning of the image seems more relevant here. But Marx and Engels paraphrase the connections between matter and intellect in a series of analogies that permit a variety of interpretations. Either, Marx and Engels imply, the intellectual is "directly interwoven" with the material, that is, the two elements exist primarily as separate threads that are joined only in the fabric of a living, moving development; or, as a half-biological, half-medical analogy suggests, the intellect appears as a "direct efflux" (*Ausfluss*) of the material substances. Indeed, in such an image the intellect has lost all its purity and dignity, for it is identified, even if only unconsciously, with a slimy, repulsive form of matter. In contrast to these still wavering metaphors, which belong partly to economics, partly to biology, the position of man in the universe is sketched in far more precise language. Although man retains a modest field of activity, he is, as the producer of the intellect, fundamentally "determined" (the idea of causality is distinctly audible in the background) by a "particular development of . . . productive forces." The formative order of the economic realm takes precedence over all intellectual activity of man. The ruling center of human destiny lies outside his intellect, which helplessly subordinates itself to the material causal law working from without.

Marx and Engels were clearly the first to be dissatisfied with such definitions. The immediately following paragraph of the *Deutsche Ideologie* (5*b*) indicates that the authors kept trying to study and clarify from new perspectives the recalcitrant problem of matter and spirit, which in turn involves the premises for any possible aesthetics. It is obvious that they did not regard their results as unchangeable dogmas, but as provisional insights or temporary results that remained open to new modifications. This paragraph of the *Deutsche Ideologie* undertakes once more to define the relationship of spirit and matter by making the method of investigation, in a surprisingly modern way, itself the object of analysis:

> [That is,] we do not proceed from what men say, imagine, conceive, nor from men as described, thought of, imagined, conceived, in order to arrive at corporeal man; rather we proceed from the really active man, and it is out of this real process of life that the development of the ideological reflexes and echoes is described. Even the foggy phantasmagorias in the minds of men are necessary sublimates of their material life-processes, which can be empirically established and are connected to material premises. . . . They [morality, religion, and so on] have no history, they have no development, but rather men, developing their material production and their material intercourse, alter along with these also their thinking and the products of their thinking. Consciousness does not determine life; life determines consciousness.[72]

In these arguments the economic element has by no means a monopolizing power. Although Marx and Engels still insist that the life-process is "connected to material premises"; although they still stress that spiritual events have no autonomous history, nevertheless it is surprising how many new positive features the picture of man acquires. In the manner of Feuerbach, man appears again as "corporeal" and "really active"; his consciousness, as Marx and Engels point out, is not only formed by the economic element, but by the whole, comprehensive, all-pervading principle of "life," which must include, apart from the economic elements, an abundance of organic partial processes. We are almost in the neighborhood of a philosophy of vitalism. Marx and Engels speak here, unexpectedly enough, of an active man who develops his material production and his material communication simultaneously, and alters his way of thinking *along with* his way of production. The idea of a correspondence between matter and spirit appears; this mutual correspondence, as narrow as it may be, rescues some autonomy for the intellectual element.

The lack of consistency with which Marx and Engels are working here appears in their definition of the intellectual activity of man, which appears mercilessly limited. The results are of some consequence for the nature of the writer and poet. In their first statement (paragraph 5a) Marx and Engels, in an almost Hegelian manner, speak of an intellect that seems "directly interwoven" with matter; here, in their second significant formulation (paragraph 5b), thought and imagination are reduced to a series of psychological, acoustical, and chemical analogies, with the intellect appearing as a "reflex," as an "echo," as a "necessary sublimate." Though Marx and Engels may raise some hopes for a tolerant amplification of their determinism through their unexpected stress upon the "real life-process," these hopes are brutally disappointed again by their effort to rob the human spirit—and with it the poetic imagination—of any autonomous energy. Along with the image of man, the mind of the poet and writer is robbed of the element of freedom and is thereby degraded to an impersonal servant of the economic process.

Doubts and Dogmas (1857–59)

Marx was sensitive enough to feel the inadequacies of his dogmatic definitions. Above all, he was convinced of the unalterable greatness of Greek literature. He had never ceased to admire

Homer and Aeschylus, whose fame rested securely upon a time-less consensus of men in all ages, and he inevitably had to ask himself whether a consistent theory of the causal dependence of the work of art on the determining productive relationships was valid in the case of Greek literature. The first opportunity of discussing these inevitable doubts presented itself during the London exile, when Marx began to outline his future *Critique of Political Economy*, for his ill-defined aggregate of programmatic points and marginalia yet to be worked out allowed some room for skepticism.[73] Marx drafted the plans for the future book on August 23, 1857. With rare frankness he admitted the contradictions that necessarily resulted from an overly rigid application of his theory to the concrete wealth of art and literature. As early as the sixth point of his program there is an indication of a significant modification suggesting important consequences for his theory. "The concept of progress throughout," he admitted, "is not to be taken in the usual abstraction."[74] Between the material foundation and the intellectual superstructure a temporal gap may open up, and the tempo of development might differ; there was no other possibility than to postulate "the unequal relationship of the development of material production . . . to artistic production."[75] Marx considered Greek art the last significant example of such an "unequal relationship." Between Greek art and ancient Greek economics there was a palpable contradiction that required a theoretical explanation.

> In the case of art it is well known that certain flourishing periods by no means stand in a direct relationship to the general development of society, that is, to the material foundation, as it were, of the organizational skeleton. For example, the Greeks compared with the moderns or even with Shakespeare. With respect to certain forms of art—for example, the epic—it is even recognized that they can never be produced in their epoch-making classical form as soon as artistic production as such appears; that is, within the area of art itself, certain significant formations are only possible at an undeveloped stage of the development of art. If this is the case in the

relationships between the various genres of art within the field of art itself, it is less noticeable that it is also the case in the relationship of the whole field of art to the general development of society. The difficulty lies only in the general statement of these contradictions. No sooner are they specified than they are already explained.[76]

Such an attempt at interpreting the contradictions between the economic forms and the creative mind indicates an evident contradiction to the earlier explications of the *Deutsche Ideologie* (1845). There Marx and Engels had claimed that art changes in close correspondence to the economic foundation, concomitantly with the changing relationships in production. Here a radically different concept emerges: not only that there are periods of great artistic development that are completely removed from the effect and reach of productive relationships, but that aesthetic "formations" (that is, literary genres) exist in which art is able to develop to a state of highest perfection while productive relationships are at a crude and early stage. Demonstratively, Marx does not hesitate to admit a contradiction between high art and primitive economics; in a surprisingly idealistic turn, he hopes that the discrepancy of the facts can be "logically specified" and thus reconciled by a pure act of reflection. It is remarkable how much the materialist trusts the ontological power of creative thought.

Marx's fragment of August 23, 1857, is essentially a stubborn but hopeless attempt to pursue these ideas consistently and to clear factual contradictions from the path of future theories. He follows Hegel strictly and explains Greek art as the fruit of Greek myth. "Greek art," declares Marx, "assumes Greek mythology, that is, nature and the social form itself assimilated in an unconsciously artistic form by the popular imagination. This is its material. . . . Egyptian mythology could never be the ground or the womb of Greek art. Nevertheless, *some* mythology."[77] Greek art can never arise from a modern civilization that demands an imagination freed from and purified of myth. Achilles, Marx remarks somewhat sadly, could never coexist with lead and gunpowder; the *Iliad* is incompatible with the world of printing presses and steam hammers; Vulcan would have had no chance confronting the steel mills of Roberts and Company; Jupiter could not compete with the lightning rod, or Hermes with the *crédit mobilier*. "What becomes of [the goddess] Fama," asks Marx, "next to Printing House Square,"[78] where the London *Times* is published?

This unexpected elegy on the golden but irretrievably lost days of Greek myth and art only conceals the fact that Marx studiously avoids the real problem—the contradiction between his theory of the dependence of art upon economics and his personal faith in the timeless value of the Greek achievement. Marx knew that a theory of historical causality must be essentially free from value judgments; the productive relationships arising in particular epochs of art can be described, but an incisive value judgment can hardly be based upon mere descriptions of variable relationships. If in the case of Greece it should be true that a sophisticated art arises from rudimentary productive relationships, does it not follow that a highly organized economic form could correspond to rudimentary artistic achievement? And furthermore, if Greek art implies an immutable element, does this not point to the ultimate autonomy of the intellect? Marx attempts to defend himself against these pressing questions by insisting that "the difficulty does not lie in the fact . . . that Greek art and the epic are bound to certain forms of social development. The difficulty is that they still provide us with artistic pleasure and in a certain sense represent for us a norm and an unattainable standard."[79]

Marx extracts himself from this contradiction between dependent and independent intellect by suggesting, if not counterfeiting, a solution that makes use of the traditional image of the cyclical growth of cultural periods. In the hope of being able to "specify" the insoluble paradox, he identifies the enthusiastically admired Greek art with the childhood of mankind; it is not the glory of the artistic achievement itself that still charms later and more mature generations but the magic of childhood that continues to exercise its indestructible fascination even in later centuries.

A man cannot become a child again, or he will become childish. But does he not enjoy the naïveté of a child, and must he not himself strive to a higher stage in order to reproduce the child's truth, and is not the genuine character of the child [*Kindesnatur*] regenerated in every age in its natural truth? Why should not the social childhood of mankind, where it is most handsomely unfolded, exercise its charm as a never recurring stage? There are ill-bred children and precocious children. Many ancient peoples belong in these categories. The Greeks were normal children. The charm of their art for us does not stand in contradiction to the undeveloped social stage out of which it grew. It is rather a result, rather an inseparable connection, that the immature social conditions under which it arose and only could arise can never recur.[80]

This interpretation tries in vain to unite two different trains of thought; Marx, the friend of literature, finds himself here in open revolt against Marx, the theoretician. He insists upon his theory of economic causality and declares Greek art to be a necessary and inimitable product of early Greek productive relationships. At the same time, however, in order to justify the value judgments of his taste and German tradition, he combines the economic theory with the traditional metaphor of the cyclical growth of arts and cultures that arise, flourish, and mature in the same way as seeds, blossoms, and fruit. Economic thinking is here bound up with ideas that recall Vico's preindustrial theory of history, Herder's poetic visions of the development of art, and Hegel's systematic aesthetics. But the attempt at compounding and uniting such disparate elements cannot succeed: the essential oppositions remain unreconciled, and economic theory continues to clash with traditional value judgments. It is perhaps not without deeper significance that Marx's incomplete manuscript breaks off abruptly at this place; just at the point where Marx himself was willing for the first and last time to apply his theory to a concrete phenomenon of art, the theory proves to be completely incapable of encompassing the reality, and Marx's personal value judgment, his traditional admiration of the Greeks, wins the vic-

tory over the unsatisfying theory of economic determinism. Unfortunately Marx never again returned to the drafts of his fragment, which remained unknown to the first generation of his
disciples until Karl Kautsky edited the text and published it as a
hypothetical introduction to his edition of the *Critique of Political
Economy* (1902–3).[81]

In his London exile, Marx was not at all willing to allow the
political formulations he needed in the period of his most abrasive
ideological conflicts to be obscured by symptoms of lingering
doubts and potential inadequacies; he possibly feared to rob
them of their offensive force. Perhaps he had consciously thrust
all his doubts into a fragment that was not intended for the eyes
of a wider readership. Two years later, when he began to sketch
again the ideological motifs of his *Critique of Political Economy*
in a more programmatic Foreword (1859), all doubts seem to
have been allayed and the theory of economic causality frozen
into a consistent dogmatism. In striking contrast to the disquiet-
ing doubts of the fragment (1857), the Foreword of 1859 formulated the theory of economic causality in art with a radicalism
hardly to be outdone:

> In the social production of their lives men enter into specific,
> necessary relationships, independent of their wills, produc-
> tive relationships that correspond to a particular stage of
> development of their material means of production. The
> totality of these productive relationships forms the economic
> structure of society, the real basis upon which a juridical and
> political superstructure arises, and to which particular social
> forms of consciousness correspond. The manner of production
> of material life determines altogether the social, political, and
> intellectual life-process. It is not the consciousness of men
> that determines their being, but on the contrary their social
> being that determines their consciousness. . . . With a change
> in the economic basis the whole enormous superstructure is
> transformed with greater or less speed.[82]

In contrast to earlier expositions, this dogmatic formulation is
based not on the existence of the two spheres of economic and

intellectual development but speaks of four clearly separated levels. Upon the necessary basis of human existence rests, as the single, the uniquely efficient cause, the "stage of development of their material means of production"; thereupon develop "specific, necessary . . . productive relationships" as a third sphere of existence. Only as the fourth, ulterior, most dependent surface level does an intellectual "superstructure" appear in which all the possibilities of intellectual activity, whether philosophy or art, are thrown together helter-skelter without any differentiation. The second, economic level constitutes the *primum movens* that alone "determines" the connection between productive relationships and intellectual superstructure.

In the *Deutsche Ideologie* (1845), Marx and Engels still had spoken of the broad "life-process" to which intellectual events correspond; in the Foreword to the *Critique of Political Economy* (1859), Marx restricted the foundation of existence to an "economic" basis, to which intellectual processes no longer simply correspond, but which they follow in strict causality. In contrast to the preceding interpretations, the role of the creative human being appeared reduced to an all but absurd level. In the *Deutsche Ideologie* it was at least still a question whether and to what extent the active man could change the economic order and with it the corresponding forms of the intellect and the artistic imagination; in the Foreword man lost all significance as an individual. Here Marx spoke exclusively of economic foundations, productive relationships, and an intellectual superstructure; between the economic necessity and the shadowy chaos of the intellectual superstructure the creative intellect of individual man has hardly a chance. He cannot do more than take note of the distant tremors of the economic bedrock.

4

Conflicts and Discussions

Personal Contacts: Marx, Engels, and Heine

In their younger years, Marx and Engels often thought quite differently about Heine's work and character.[1] Young Engels was a convinced admirer of Börne; in a symptomatic conflict that broke out in the forties between Heine's supporters and the apologists of Börne, Engels privately and publicly supported the politically committed efforts of Börne and took a position against the irresponsible charm of Heine's art. In April, 1840, "Heine" and "servility" seemed to him to be almost synonymous.[2] Heine's polemical *Ludwig Börne: A Memorial* (1840) was "the most worthless thing ever written in the German language" (July, 1842).[3] This essentially Young Hegelian antipathy may have led Engels in his critical essays to call Heine "an old hedgehog (*einen alten Schweinigel*),"[4] a "modern Tannhäuser"[5] who gave himself up to enervating dissipations in the Parisian Venusberg. But it was the political issue that was decisive: after Marx had met Heine in 1843 and Engels was given the task of reporting to English friends on German radicalism, he found himself prepared to concede to Heine's poetry considerable political merit. Reporting in English in the radical *New Moral World* (1845), he named Karl Marx, Moses Hess, and himself as "the most active literary personalities of German Socialism,"[6] and added that even "Henry Heine, the most eminent of all living German poets,"[7] had joined this circle. As a characteristic example of Heine's art, which he described as "social literature,"[8] he offered his English readers "a prosaic translation" of the famous "Weavers' Song." "In its German original," he remarked modestly (for his translation lacks neither freshness nor force), "[it] is one of the most powerful poems I know of."[9]

Marx, on the other hand, undeviatingly took sides for Heine and against Börne from the beginning of his career. Marx met Heine personally for the first time in Paris in 1843, and after he had occasionally thanked Heine for sending him poems and had conveyed his greetings, a more personal letter, which he passed on to Heine by way of his Russian friend Annenkov (*ca.* April 5, 1846), spoke of his firm support for the poet and of his readiness to speak out publicly against Heine's opponents.[10] Marx had just come across a polemical compilation of passages from Börne's letters attacking Heine (put together by Börne's friend Jeanette Wohl in 1840 to revenge Heine's attacks);[11] he called this pamphlet "a little lampoon"[12] and condemned it as "insipid, petty, and tasteless."[13] In order to parry the attacks of Börne's supporters, among whom Engels was still to be numbered, Marx offered to write a positive review of Heine's book on Börne; in addition, he asked politely whether the poet would not pass on personal impressions and experiences that could be of use to him. From the letter of April, 1846, it appears clear that young Marx planned a frontal attack against those who scorned Heine's talents: Heine's merits were to be honored, his opponents, above all Karl Gutzkow and "his miserable twaddle,"[14] exposed in all their wretchedness.

Marx was twenty-five years old when he met Heine for the first time in 1843; a year later Engels joined in Marx's good opinion of Heine, although even in later years he did not overcome completely a continuing and often repressed skepticism. Young Marx could learn much from Heine, who had gone far ahead of him in the incisive recognition of political and economic realities. In 1843, Marx was only beginning to move forward from his private metaphysical war against Hegel's *Philosophy of Right;* Heine, on the other hand, had long been examining and interpreting the

concrete forms of French social conflicts. Since 1831, in his communications to the German public, Heine had not wearied of
pointing to the paradigmatic and dangerous social tensions in
France nor of sending his often ironically veiled warnings across
the Rhine. Modern society, he stressed, was based upon an order
of property, the inequity of which would necessarily unleash a
terrible duel between rich and poor.[15] Heine himself was, by reason of his poetic temperament as well as of his intellectual inclinations, completely unwilling to stand dogmatically with one faction
or the other and even less willing to be co-opted by either; he
stood on aesthetic ground and wavered first toward one position,
then another, provoking the fury of the German supporters of
Börne. The bourgeois world of luxury, wit, polite society, and
aesthetic nuance was the only atmosphere in which Heine could
breathe and thrive; nevertheless, he had no illusions about the
robust materialism of the new bourgeois civilization and about its
incapacity to defend itself against the storm of the inarticulate
masses. While gladly breathing the piquant bourgeois air, at the
same time he was fascinated by the strangely brutal power of the
proletariat, which in his eyes (as later in those of the brothers
Goncourt) possessed all the charm of the exotic; in one of his
earliest letters in the *Lutetia* (April 30, 1840), he supplied a
penetrating description of the Parisian ateliers, which he thought
he could characterize only with the key words "flame" and "passion."[16] But this exotic fascination contained also an essentially
repellent element: as a poet who cherished a "self-aware freedom
of the spirit"[17] above all things, Heine felt insulted by the brutality and massiveness of his newly discovered world. Its slum mixture of dirt, disrespect, and sweat was just as unbearable to him
as the orthodox faith in the equality of men as it was preached
by the spokesmen of the proletariat in the *faubourgs* of Saint-
Antoine and Marceau. Heine hated this "universal kitchen-equal-
ity"[18] as well as those "400,000 rough fists that are only waiting
for the signal to realize the idea of absolute equality brooding in
their rough heads."[19] In a polemic against Louis Blanc, whom he
called "the great man of the small,"[20] Heine spoke half-frivolously

of the autonomous dignity of the creative intellect, which he frankly declared to be his cause. "It is true," he quipped, "that we are all brothers, but I am the big brother, and you are the little brothers, and I am entitled to a more substantial portion."[21]

This ambivalence of attraction and repulsion that he felt when confronted with the growing mass of the industrial proletariat sharpened Heine's eye for the oblique connections leading from economic facts to the realm of art. Thus he wrote on May 7, 1843, of an "unparalleled discomfort" that overcame him on a walk around an exhibition of contemporary paintings in the Louvre; always anxious to find that "kindred characteristic by which the paintings are revealed as products of the present,"[22] he felt nothing but the effect of brutal commercialism and a base greed for money distorting all the efforts into meanness. In a scene of the scourging of Christ, the central figure, with his suffering countenance, reminded him of the "director of a bankrupt stock company";[23] similarly, paintings with historical themes recalled "retail shops, stock-market speculation, mercantilism, Philistinism."[24] But the new spirit of the bourgeoisie appeared to him at its most naked in the portraits, in which the worthies represented seemed to be filled with a material greed equaled only by the contempt and despair of the painters obliged to do such work. "Most of the [pictures] have such a pecuniary, selfish, peevish look that I can only explain it by assuming that the living original during the hours of the sitting was continually thinking of the money the portrait would cost him, while the painter constantly regretted the time he had to waste on this miserable servitude."[25]

There can be no doubt that in the year 1843 Heine had progressed much farther in the analysis of economics and the arts than the youthful Marx, who was still a prisoner of German metaphysics. It was not common ideas that brought Heine and Marx together, but the common fate of the Prussian exiles, the common bitterness against Frederick William IV and his circle, and the necessity of battling the same opponents: the new nationalists, the new obscurantists, the new state-supported mysticism. Heine, extremely angered, was gladly willing to join the most radical mind

of the Prussian opposition in order to give his cause added political emphasis; the exiled Marx, for his part, whose hope was to
publish the *Deutsch-Französische Jahrbücher,* not unreasonably
expected to further his project significantly through Heine's co-
operation. As Ludwig Marcuse points out in his study of Heine,[26]
both Marx and Heine were ready for a friendly approach to one
another because they needed each other in order to further their
most personal concerns.

Marx printed Heine's poems on King Ludwig of Bavaria[27] in
the *Deutsch-Französische Jahrbücher;* in return, Heine, with particular attentiveness, on September 21, 1844, sent Marx as a present the proofs of his long poem *Germany: A Winter's Tale* with
a friendly letter. "We need, after all, few tokens," Heine wrote
from Germany, "to understand one another."[28] From Heine's letter it appeared that he was stubbornly pursuing his personal goals.
"I am sending you the proofs [of the *Winter's Tale*] today," he
confessed to Marx, "for three reasons. Namely, first, that you may
amuse yourself; second, that you may immediately make arrange-
ments to boost the book in the German press, and third, that you
may be able, if you think it advisable, to have the first excerpts
from the new poem printed in the *Vorwärts.*"[29] At that time their
personal relations became very friendly, to which their respective
ladies also contributed. When Marx was expelled from Paris, he
wrote to Heine that "I would gladly pack you along";[30] in Brussels he regretted having left Heine, a real friend, behind in
Paris.[31]

To be sure, the succeeding correspondence between Brussels
and Paris returned without further ado to concrete problems;
Marx was thinking about his new *Rheinische Jahrbücher* and
asked Heine for suitable contributions, above all an article on the
question of the German fleet. Marx, and with him the Brussels
office of the Communist League, had obviously not given up hope
of making use of the poet for their own purposes. Engels and
Ewerbeck, both members of the League, paid visits to Heine in
Paris; Engels reported on Heine's state of health not only to Marx
personally but also to the Communist Committee of Correspond-

ence. "[I wish] finally to communicate to you," wrote Engels on September 16, 1846, to the Committee of Correspondence, "that Heine is here again and I visited him with E[werbeck] the day before yesterday. The poor devil has gone to the dogs horribly. He has become as thin as a skeleton. The softening of the brain is spreading, the paralysis of the face ditto. E[werbeck] says he could easily die at any time of a paralysis of the lungs or of some kind of paroxysm of the brain, but could also drag himself on for three to four years alternately better and worse. Naturally he is depressed, melancholy, and what is most characteristic, extremely benevolent (and seriously so) in his judgments. . . . Otherwise he has his full intellectual energy, but his appearance, made even more curious by a greying beard (he cannot be shaved around the mouth any more) suffices to put everyone who sees him in a highly lugubrious (*trauerklötig*) mood. It is most disagreeable to see such a splendid fellow die bit by bit."[32] But it was not enough that the friendly visitors wrote secret reports; Richard Reinhardt, one of Heine's private secretaries, was also a member of the League and reported directly to Marx.[33]

It was Heine's progressive illness and his return to the religion of his fathers that alienated him from Marx and his circle of radical friends in Paris, Brussels, and beyond the Rhine. In a letter to Engels, Marx spoke somewhat condescendingly of the "old dog" Heine;[34] after Heine's death (1856), he mocked in his ruthless way the poet's religious testament (November 13, 1851), not without sending Engels several incorrectly quoted fragments from its text.[35] Indeed, all the political plans that Marx and the Communist League had based upon Heine's popularity collapsed with his religious return. Heine's death in his "mattress-grave" was so wretched that it could not fail to have a touching, if somewhat grim, effect upon the disappointed former allies; even Engels, the one-time follower of Börne, willingly admitted that the "old hedgehog"[36] had after all been a likeable, if irritating, character. Ten years after Heine's death, when Engels reread Horace's epistles, he wrote to Marx that he was immediately reminded of Heine, who, like Horace, had known how to remove his poetry from the conflict of parties. "Old Horace," wrote Engels on December 21, 1866, "reminds me here and there of Heine, who learned a great deal from him, and also *au fond* was an equally common dog *politice*."[37] Like Horace, Engels claimed, Heine had also provoked the threatening eye of the tyrant (*vultus instantis tyranni*) and then "crawled up Augustus' rear."[38] Engels' analogy, as angry as it is vulgar, clearly betrays how successful Heine had been in his effort to save his poetry from political captivity.[39]

In Heine's relationship to contemporary communism his definite progression from an aesthetic repugnance to a more metaphysical opposition should not be overlooked. At first Heine the "Hellene" protested in the name of his sensitive Epicureanism and his delicate aversion to the ugly, massive, anticultural vulgarity of the proletariat, whose victory must mean the end of all differentiated art. Nowhere did Heine formulate his bitter prophecies of those future events more forcefully than in his famous *je crains* in the Preface to the French edition (1855) of his *Lutetia:* ". . . It is with fear and horror only that I think of that age when these sombre iconoclasts will come to power; with their calloused hands they will smash unmercifully all the marble statues of beauty, so dear to my heart; they will shatter all the fantastic baubles and bangles of art that the poet loves so well; they will destroy my forests of laurel and plant potatoes there . . . the nightingales, those useless singers, will be chased away, and alas! my *Book of Songs* will serve my grocer for paper bags into which he will pour coffee or snuff for the old ladies of posterity."[40]

Surprisingly enough, Heine admitted despite all these bitter warnings that it was just the brutal power of the masses and their cry for bread that exercised a charm on his soul against which he was powerless (". . . *exerce sur mon âme une charme dont je ne puis me défendre*").[41] This Epicurean protest, which was by no means without a certain aesthetic pleasure, was, however, not the last word Heine was to say about his relationship to contemporary communism. After he had renounced "philosophical pride"[42] while in his "mattress-grave" and had faithfully returned to the "only God, the eternal Creator of the world,"[43] he felt that his resistance against communism could not remain merely a matter of his insulted yet secretly charmed sensibilities. From subjective repugnance he proceeded to a more fundamental opposition, the principles of which he was able to formulate with metaphysical relevance. The late Heine—Ludwig Marcuse forgets to admit this —identified communism, *le plus terrible antagoniste*,[44] with atheism, with philosophical *superbia* in general; that man had dared to put himself in place of God seemed to him a confusion of thought deriving from Hegel: communism was no longer for him synonymous with anti-artistic brutality but with Satanic blasphemy. Heine left the politically excited world and his radical friends with a last piece of advice that he urged them to take to heart. He recommended that they read "the magnificent, grandiose Book of Daniel"[45] in the Old Testament—that book which reports the story of the Babylonian King Nebuchadnezzar, who thought he was God, but fell miserably from the heights of his arrogance, crawled on the earth like an animal and ate grass.[46] With the earnestness of a dying man, Heine believed that the warning of the Old Testament book was unmistakable.

> At the end of twelve months he walked in the palace of the kingdom of Babylon. The king spake, and said, Is not this great Babylon, that I have built for the house of the kingdom by the might of my power, and for the honor of my majesty? While the word was in the king's mouth, there fell a voice from heaven, saying, O king Nebuchadnezzar, to thee it is spoken: The kingdom is departed from thee. And they shall drive thee from men, and thy dwelling shall be with the beasts of the field: they shall make thee to eat grass as oxen, and seven times shall pass over thee, until thou know that the most High ruleth in the kingdom of men, and giveth it to whomsoever he will. The same hour was the thing fulfilled upon Nebuchadnezzar: and he was driven from men, and did eat grass as oxen, and his body was wet with the dew of heaven, till his hairs were grown like eagles' feathers, and his nails like bird claws (Dan. 4:29–33).

With undimmed intellect the paralyzed Heine urged this warning against the boundless pride of men upon his philosophizing friends, whom he characterized with fine insight as "godless self-gods."[47] Among the names he cited were not only Feuerbach, Bruno Bauer, and "the good Ruge";[48] in a last, touching, and friendly but penetrating gesture Heine recommended the Book of Daniel, with its story of the fall of the Babylonian king, to his "much more impenitent friend Marx."[49]

Georg Herwegh

Marx's personal contacts and correspondence with Georg Herwegh (1817–75) exhibit no urgent literary interests of any kind. From the beginning of their personal relations (1842), Marx was inclined to see in Herwegh a potential political confederate; as long as the least hope remained that Herwegh's popularity could be of value to the cause of the Communist League, Marx remained quite affable and courted the young poet, who liked to be courted, with extraordinary civility. To be sure, certain sharp tongues among the German prerevolutionary exiles turned out to be right when they asserted that "Marx had taken up [Herwegh] so warmly that he seemed to want something from him,"[50] for as soon as it became clear that Herwegh as a political confederate would only expose Marx and the League to ridicule and failure Marx brusquely dropped him. In 1844, Marx had been happy to publish a poem by Herwegh; fifteen years later he was furious that Herwegh's poem "The Clam-Galass Cuirassiers Riding through Munich" ("Kürassiere Clam-Galass, durch München reitend") had appeared without his knowledge in the newspaper *Das Volk* (London), which he was managing. Marx wanted nothing more to do with this "trashy poem" and its author.[51]

Georg Herwegh had studied in the famous Tübingen Theological Seminary (Tübinger Stift) before he threw in his lot with radical liberalism. Conflicts with the army forced him to seek asylum in Switzerland. There he published his *Poems of a Living*

Man (*Gedichte eines Lebendigen* [1841]), which quickly became a triumphant if momentary success. Inevitably Herwegh found himself among the contributors to the *Rheinische Zeitung* as well as the *Hallische Jahrbücher*, which competed with one another to print and comment upon Herwegh's famous poem, *Die Partei* (1842).[52] This poem was essentially conceived as an answer to Ferdinand Freiligrath, who in November, 1841, published an elegy entitled "From Spain" ("Aus Spanien") upon the execution of the Royalist general Don Diego Leon (1804–41). The liberals were evidently annoyed that Freiligrath had celebrated a conservative soldier:

> Schlank, hoch und herrlich trat er aus dem Wagen;
> Dann küss' er brünstig ein Marienbild.
> "In allen Schlachten hab' ich dich getragen:
> Was du vermochtest, hast du treu erfüllt!
> Die dich mir gab, mein Weib, hat dich gesegnet;
> Geh' zu ihr heim—getan ist meine Pflicht!
> Du lenkst die Kugeln, so die Walstatt regnet,
> Der Richtstatt Kugeln lenkst du nicht!"
>
> Dann, dass kein Blei an ihm vorüberpreife,
> Gab er den Schützen selber ihren Stand,
> Und wies sie an, und richtete die Läufe,
> Und riss sich auf sein blitzend Kriegsgewand;
> Gab Ring und Kreuz dem Freunde drauf:—"Du Treuer!
> Dies dem Regenten—meinem Weibe dies!
> Zerbrich mein Schwert! Was zaudert ihr? Gebt Feuer!"
>   . . . Exoriare aliquis![53]

[Slender, tall, and fine, he stepped out of the car; | then he passionately kissed a portrait of the Virgin. | "I have carried you in all my battles: you have loyally done what you could. | She who gave you to me, my wife, blessed you; | go home to her—my duty is done! | You guide the bullets that rain on the battlefield, | but not the bullets of the place of execution!" | Then, so that no lead would shoot past him, | he himself gave the firing squad its position, | guided them and aimed the gun barrels, and tore open his gleaming uniform; | gave ring and cross then to his friend: "Loyal friend! | This to the regent—to my wife, this! | Break my sword! Why do you hesitate? Fire!" | ... *Exoriare aliquis!*]

Freiligrath provoked the rage of his liberal readers above all with the following two stanzas, in which he demanded for the poet that vital freedom that rises above transitory and narrow party quarrels and discovers tragedy and heroism in world history as a whole:

> Die Salve fiel:—was wollt ihr weiter wissen?
> Die Salve fiel:—sein Auge zuckte nicht!
> "Legt an, gebt Feu'r!"—Zerschmettert und zerrissen
> Sank in den Staub sein edel Angesicht!—
> So war sein Tod; Ich heiss ihn einen schönen!
> Es war ein mut'ger, ritterlicher Fall,
> Und er verdient es, dass ihm Verse dröhnen,
> Dumpf, wie gedämpfter Trommeln Schall.
>
> Die ihr gehört—frei hab' ich sie verkündigt!
> Ob's jedem recht:—schiert ein Poet sich drum?
> Seit Priam's Tagen, weiss er, wird gesündigt,
> In Ilium und ausser Ilium!
> Er beugt sein Knie dem Helden Bonaparte,
> Und hört mit Zürnen d'Enghien's Todesschrei:
> Der Dichter steht auf einer höhern Warte,
> Als auf den Zinnen der Partei.

[The salvo was fired: what more do you wish to know? | The salvo was fired: his eye did not blink! | "Load, fire!" Blasted and torn, | his noble face sank into the dust!— | Thus was his death! I call it a fine one! | It was a courageous, chivalrous fall, | and it deserves that verse should echo it, | sombrely, like the roll of muffled drums. | These verses you have heard—freely have I pronounced them! | Whether that pleases everyone: does a poet care about that? | Since the days of Priam he knows that there has been sin | in Troy and outside Troy! He bends his knee to the hero Bonaparte | and hears with fury d'Enghien's death-cry. | The poet stands above the ramparts of party.]

In his famous answer, which he explicitly addressed "To Ferdinand Freiligrath," Herwegh—in the same meter and rhyme scheme—took the diametrically opposite position. Although in German politics at that time there were no parties in the modern sense, the word "party" that Herwegh hurled at the reader with the effect of monotonous incantation, clearly took on the meaning of a passionate commitment to the concrete demands of current politics.

> *Partei! Partei!* Wer sollte sie nicht nehmen,
> Die noch die Mutter aller Siege war!
> Wie mag ein Dichter solch ein Wort verfemen,
> Ein Wort, das alles Herrliche gebar?
> Nur offen wie ein Mann: Für oder wider?
> Und die Parole: Sklave oder frei?
> Selbst Götter stiegen vom Olymp hernieder
> Und kämpften auf den Zinnen der *Partei!*
>
> Sieh hin, dein Volk will neue Bahnen wandeln,
> Nur des Signales harrt ein stattlich Heer;
> Die Fürsten träumen, lasst die Dichter handeln!
> Spielt Saul die Harfe, werfen *wir* den Speer!
> Den Panzer um—geöffnet sind die Schranken,
> Brecht immer euer Saitenspiel entzwei,
> Und führt ein Fähnlein ewiger Gedanken
> Zur starken, stolzen Fahne der *Partei!*
>
> Das Gestern ist wie eine welke Blume—
> Man legt sie wohl also Zeichen in ein Buch—
> Begräbt's mit seiner Schmach und seinem Ruhme
> Und webt nicht länger an dem Leichentuch!
> Dem Leben gilt's ein Lebehoch zu singen,
> Und nicht ein Lied im Dienst der Schmeichelei;
> Der Menschheit gilt's ein Opfer darzubringen,
> Der Menschheit auf dem Altar der *Partei!*
>
> O stellt sie ein, die ungerechte Klage,
> Wenn ihr die Angst so mancher Seele schaut;
> Es ist das Bangen vor dem Hochzeitstage,
> Das hoffnungsvolle Bangen einer Braut.
> Schon drängen aller Orten sich die Erben

Ans Krankenlager unsrer Zeit herbei;
Lasst, Dichter, lasst auch ihr den Kranken sterben,
Für eures Volkes Zukunft nehmt *Partei!*

Ihr müsst das Herz an eine Karte wagen,
Die Ruhe über Wolken ziemt euch nicht;
Ihr müsst euch mit in diesem Kampfe schlagen,
Ein Schwert in eurer Hand ist das Gedicht.
O wählt ein Banner, und ich bin zufrieden,
Ob's auch ein andres, denn das meine sei;
Ich hab' gewählt, *ich* habe mich entschieden,
Und *meinen* Lorbeer flechte die *Partei!*[54]

[*Party! Party!* Who would not take sides, | since party has
always been the mother of all victories! | How can a poet pro-
scribe such a word, | a word that gave birth to all things
magnificent? | Now openly like a man: for or against? | And
the password: slave or free? | Even gods came down from
Olympus | and fought on the ramparts of *party!* | Look!
Your people want to walk new paths; | a mighty army awaits
only the signal. | The princes are dreaming, let the poets act!
| If Saul plays the harp, *we* will hurl the javelin! | On with
your armor—the barricades are open, | break your lute in
two | and carry a pennant of eternal ideas | with the strong,
proud flag of *party!* Yesterday is like a faded flower— |
one may press it between the leaves of a book— | bury it with
its shame and fame | and stop weaving the shroud! | Now it
is time to sing a toast to life, | and not a song in the service
of flattery; | it is time to make a sacrifice for mankind, | for
mankind on the altar of *party!* Oh, stop the unjust lament |
when you see the fear of many a soul; | it is the anxiety be-
fore the wedding day, | the hopeful anxiety of a bride. |
From all over the heirs are already crowding | to the death-
bed of our time; | you, too, poet, let the patient die, | take
sides for your nation's future in a *party!* | You must risk
your heart on one card, | the calm up in the clouds does not
become you; | you must fight in this battle; | a poem is a
sword in your hand. | Oh, choose a banner, and I shall be
satisfied if it is another than mine; | *I* have chosen, *I* have
decided, | and *my* laurels will be plaited by my *party!*]

Neither Herwegh nor Freiligrath followed his own political pathos; developments ironically turned the personal destiny of each into the opposite direction. Freiligrath, who had defended the intellectual right of self-determination for writers, only a little later joined the Communist League and subordinated himself for years to Marx's dictates; Herwegh, on the other hand, who had protested against the "dismal indifference"[55] of the poets, was soon to become disaffected with communism because of its egalitarian indiscretions, its collectivism, its massive brutality. Political partisanship, within the limitations of social reality, was not without its own problems.

To be sure, it was some time before Herwegh became completely clear about the nature of contemporary communism. In 1842, while traveling through Germany in triumph and accepting the adulation of his readers, he met Marx personally for the first time: upon arriving in Cologne, he was formally greeted by a reception committee of the *Rheinische Zeitung,* of which Marx was in charge, and was given a banquet in his honor. In the course of further travels through France and French Switzerland, Herwegh made connections with groups of Communist workingmen, for whose concerns he felt an increasing sympathy. More than ever he was convinced that the modern writer had to try to reach the great mass of the as yet unawakened proletariat in order to carry out his political task. "He thinks," reported Carl Stahr on October 30, 1843, on his conversations with Herwegh, "there is nothing to be achieved with all our liberalism, with poems and dramas. One must reach the masses, one must awaken them who up to now have been sleeping the deepest sleep of death, by all possible means. Communism is this means. . . . Property relationships are . . . still those that will be listened to more readily than any others."[56] Herwegh's inclination to communism was of short duration; after he had observed the petty conflicts of the tailors and watchmakers of Geneva, he spoke contemptuously of the "mob" and conspicuously insisted that he had nothing in common with them because he hated "all banding together, [all] playing at conspiracy."[57] Like Ruge and Heine, Herwegh also came to the conclusion that a victory of communism would result in the "equality of all in slavery."[58]

For Marx, who had his own theoretical antipathies toward artisans' communism, Herwegh, standing at the height of his fame in the early forties, was a potential political confederate of no mean value. Marx did not give up hope of achieving closer collaboration. After Engels met Herwegh, whom he personally admired, at Ostend in the summer of 1843, Herwegh's poem "The Betrayal" ("Der Verrat")[59] appeared in the *Deutsch-Französische Jahrbücher* (1844). Ruge, the coeditor of the *Jahrbücher*, was, however, far less taken by Herwegh than Marx; differences of opinion between Ruge and Marx on the subject of Herwegh were the last straw that broke the long-withering friendship of the two editors of the *Jahrbücher*. In Paris, Herwegh had fallen prey to the fading charms of the Countess d'Agoult, who had just separated from Liszt; while Ruge looked askance at Herwegh's Paris affairs and regarded the liberal movement as a whole to be compromised, Marx felt himself obliged to defend the poet with a tolerance he had otherwise never exercised. In any case, as Ruge reported, "[Marx] defended Herwegh as a genius and expected him to have a great future."[60] Ruge, who had suffered for a long time under Marx's violent temper and irritability, saw his principles threatened and, making a sudden decision, moved out of the Paris pension in which Marx lived. Always in need of new allies, Marx hoped to replace Ruge immediately with Herwegh; he renewed friendly communications with the poet, a development that Ruge commented sourly upon from afar. Marx was living "more than before with Herwegh," reported Ruge to his mother on May 19, 1844, "not without youthful adventures, although each knows what divides him from the other, namely, that each considers himself the greatest genius. Marx mistreats . . . and despises him; he has . . . only attracted him, in order to make his party and people into vassals."[61]

By the spring of 1848 it was clear that Herwegh did not have the slightest inclination to follow Marx or the Communist League. In order to work successfully against the influence of the Paris

Workers' Society (a front organization of the League), Herwegh organized a German Democratic Association and began, in conspicuous opposition to the slogans of the League, to prepare an armed invasion of Germany. With the financial support of his wife (who in turn got her means from her father, a Berlin financier and silk merchant by appointment to the court), Herwegh succeeded in uniting a group of about six hundred German liberals and a few French radicals who were prepared to invade Germany and carry the revolution into the German heartland. The French government supported the undertaking with a meager subsidy—not so much in order to further the revolution as to get the tiresome troublemakers out of the country.

Herwegh's invasion troops were doomed to a quick and disastrous end as soon as they reached German soil. Regular Würtemberg army detachments took up the pursuit of the invaders and stopped Herwegh's six hundred in a short skirmish near Niederdossenbach (April 27, 1848); fifty revolutionaries were left dead on the field; the rest took flight. With his wife and friends, Herwegh succeeded in reaching the Swiss border; in the end, it appears, he even had to be careful of his own co-conspirators, of whom several wanted to earn the reward the government had offered for him. Continuing to live was a far more heroic achievement for Herwegh than death in battle with the Würtembergers would have been. Heine had once called him Germany's "iron lark"; now he had to waste away in the darkness of failure and ridicule, persecuted and mocked equally by the enemies of the revolution as by its all too theoretical friends from the ranks of the Communist League. Nevertheless, events like the one near Niederdossenbach are far too rare in modern German history. Even if the six hundred were predestined to defeat, the military failure alters none of the dignity of their political decision. They were lacking in ammunition, not in courage.

The defeat at Niederdossenbach also put an end to Marx's interest in Herwegh. Herwegh had played out his hand politically; neither Marx nor the League had any use for political bankrupts, however heroic their motives might be. To be sure, Herwegh for his part had no more interest in renewing contact with Marx. Not until the publication of his posthumous papers did it become clear to what insights Herwegh had come, having matured painfully through his experiences with his Communist friends. "I hate the absolute (communism or monarchy)," he wrote in his diary, "whether under a cap or under a hat."[62] And he added thoughtfully: "All triangles are equal to two right angles, and similarly all men—but the form of the triangles can be in reality larger or smaller, made of one material or another; similarly with individuals—this at the same time a criticism of communism."[63]

Ferdinand Freiligrath

Freiligrath (1810–76) had to earn his bread from an early age as a shopclerk and bookkeeper. His first literary impulses derived from French art, which, following French foreign policy, had turned to North African and Oriental themes. In opposition to the tame poetry of the German family magazines, Freiligrath wrote passionately of an imaginary realm of exotic harems and Moorish princes, surprising the German petty bourgeois with scenes at once gloomy and magnificent à la Delacroix. When he was twenty-seven, Freiligrath took a job with the merchant house of J. P. Eyneren in Barmen-Wuppertal and soon found himself surrounded by an admiring circle of young men; the schoolboy Friedrich Engels looked up to him from afar. In 1842, Freiligrath had a sudden stroke of luck: after he had achieved a surprising success with his first volume of collected poems (1838), Frederick William IV, upon the recommendation of Alexander von Humboldt, awarded him a royal pension; now his publications and political utterances were news. The liberals, of course, could not get over the fact that Freiligrath had raised his voice against a writer's political commitment and that he received his income from the private purse of the king; his wife complained in a confidential letter that one of her close friends in Bingen had met a certain Dr. Marx who had called Freiligrath an "enemy of Herwegh and of freedom."[64] But even Marx could not foresee Freiligrath's subsequent political development. In the Preface to his *Confession of Faith* (*Glaubensbekenntnis* [1844]), a collection of radical poems, Freiligrath declared that he too was stepping down from his Olympian perspective to the "ramparts of party" and that he was renouncing his royal pension on political grounds.[65] The next logical step was Freiligrath's voluntary exile, which took him first to Brussels.

In Brussels, Marx and Freiligrath met for the first time. Marx, who had just been expelled from Paris, did not lose a moment in gaining Freiligrath's affection. "After we had spent one night in Brussels," reported Heinrich Bürgers, Marx's traveling companion at that time, "just about the first thing Marx said to me in the morning was: 'Today we must go to Freiligrath, he is here, and I must make good what the *Rheinische Zeitung* did to him when he was not yet standing on the ramparts of party; his *Confession of Faith* has made up for everything.' "[66] It is difficult to decide whether Marx felt genuine regret or whether, as in other cases, he was once again concerned to lure a popular writer into political alliance for the future. In any case, definite publishing plans were considered as early as their first meeting. "Marx, too, has been here for a week," reported Freiligrath on February 10, 1845, to his friends in Germany, "an interesting, pleasant, unassuming chap. After a while he will probably found a newspaper here and then bring other people in."[67] Nevertheless, there was not enough time to develop the planned collaboration, for Freiligrath had decided to travel on to Switzerland. Not far from Zurich he wrote a series of six radical poems that he entitled *Ça ira* (1846);[68] the Jacobin title alone was proof enough that Freiligrath had come to a position to the left of the liberalism of prerevolutionary Germany.

Nowhere does Freiligrath's development from prerevolutionary liberal attitudes to proletarian postulates appear more clearly than in the centerpiece of this slender collection. In his ballad "From the Bottom Up" ("Von unten auf"),[69] Freiligrath drew a political image of the contemporary situation as it appeared to him on the occasion of a Rhine journey by Frederick William IV.

> Ein Dampfer kam von Bieberich: stoltz war die Furche, die er zog!
> Er qualmt' und räderte zu Tal, dass rechts und links die Brandung flog!
> Von Wimpeln und von Flaggen voll, schoss er hinab keck und erfreut:
> Den König, der in Preussen herrscht, nach seiner Rheinburg trug er heut!
>
> Die Sonne schien wie lauter Gold! Auftauchte schimmernd Stadt um Stadt!
> Der Rhein war wie ein Spiegel schier, und das Verdeck war blank und glatt!
> Die Dielen blitzten frisch gebohnt, und auf den schmalen her und hin
> Vergnügten Auges wandelten der König und die Königin.

[A steamer came from Bieberich: proud was the wake it left behind! | It steamed and wheeled downstream, so that the foam flew left and right! | Full of pennants and flags, it shot along pert and pleased: | today it carried the king who rules in Prussia to his castle on the Rhine! | The sun shone like pure gold! City after gleaming city appeared! | The Rhine was like a mirror, and the deck was shiny and smooth! | The planks glittered, freshly swabbed, and on those narrow planks | the king and queen walked back and forth with pleased eyes.]

Freiligrath is concerned here above all with the melodramatic contrast: not the king on the magnificent top deck of the Rhine steamer, but the half-naked stoker (a figure who survives in Hofmannsthal's poetry and Kafka's prose) appears as the actual master of the ship and the elements:

> Doch unter all der Nettigkeit und unter all der schwimmenden Pracht,
> Da frisst und flammt das Element, das sie von dannen schiessen macht,

Da schafft in Russ und Feuersglut, der dieses Glanzes Seele
    ist;
Da steht und schürt und ordnet er—der Proletariar-Maschi-
    nist!

Da draussen lacht und grünt die Welt, da draussen blitzt und
    rauscht der Rhein—
Er stiert den lieben langen Tag in seine Flammen nur hinein!
In wollnem Hemde, halbernackt, vor seiner Esse muss er
    steh'n.
Derweil ein König über ihm einschlürft der Berge freies
    Weh'n!

Jetzt ist der Ofen zugekeilt, und Alles geht und Alles passt;
So gönnt er auf Minuten denn sich eine kurze Sklavenrast.
Mit halbem Leibe taucht er auf aus seinem lodernden Ver-
    steck;
In seiner Falltür steht er da, und überschaut sich das Ver-
    deck.

[But under all the neatness and under all the floating mag-
nificence, | there devours and flames the element that makes
it all shoot along; | there labors in soot and fiery heat he
who is the soul of this lustre; | there he stands and stokes and
regulates—the proletarian machinist! | Outside the world is
green and laughs, outside the Rhine glitters and swirls— |
the whole live-long day he only stares into his flames! | In a
wool shirt, half-naked, he must stand before his furnace. |
Meanwhile the king above him breathes in the free breezes of
the mountains! Now the furnace is wedged shut, and every-
thing is working and everything fits, | so he allows himself
for a few minutes a short slave's rest. | With half his body he
emerges from his glowing lair; | he stands there in his hatch
and looks over the deck.]

In fact the rhetorical core of the poem is nothing but the traditional *topos* of human society as a ship, which is applied here in
the spirit of early communism—Freiligrath's proletarian machin-
ist has, to be sure, a classical education and knows his Horace:

Das glüh'nde Eisen in der Hand, Antlitz und Arme rot
    erhitzt,

Mit der gewölbten haar'gen Brust auf das Geländer breit
    gestützt—
So lässt er schweifen seinen Blick, so murrt er leis dem Für-
    sten zu:
"Wie mahnt dies Boot mich an den Staat! Licht auf den
    Höhen wandelst *Du!*

Tief unten aber, in der Nacht und in der Arbeit dunklem
    Schoss
Tief unten, von der Not gespornt, da schür' und schmied'
    ich mir mein Los!
Nicht meines nur, auch Deines, Herr! Wer hält die Räder
    Dir im Takt,
Wenn nicht mit schwielenharter Faust der Heizer seine
    Eisen packt?

Du bist viel weniger ein Zeus, als ich, o König, ein Titan!
Beherrsch' ich nicht, auf dem Du gehst, den allzeit kochen-
    den Vulkan?
Es liegt an mir:—Ein Ruck von mir, Ein Schlag von mir zu
    dieser Frist,
Und siehe, das Gebäude stürzt, von welchem Du die Spitze
    bist!

Der Boden birst, aufschlägt die Glut und sprengt Dich kra-
    chend in die Luft!
Wir aber steigen feuerfest aufwärts an's Licht aus unsrer
    Gruft!
Wir sind die Kraft! Wir hämmern jung das alte morsche
    Ding, den Staat,
Die wir von Gottes Zorne sind bis jetzt das Proletariat!"[70]

[The glowing iron in his hand, face and arms heated red, |
with his arched, hairy breast broadly spread upon the rail-
ing— | thus he lets his gaze rove, thus he growls quietly to
the prince: | "How this boat reminds me of the state! You
walk like light on the heights! | But deep below, in the night
and in the dark womb of labor, | deep below, spurred on by
want, there *I* stoke and forge my lot! | Not only mine, yours
as well, my lord! Who keeps the wheels in rhythm for you, |
if the stoker does not take hold of his irons with calloused

fist? | You are much less a Zeus than I, O king, a Titan! | Do I not rule the constantly boiling volcano on which you walk? | It is up to me—one jolt from me, one blow from me at this moment, | and behold! the structure collapses, of which you are the top! | The ground bursts, the fire leaps out and blows you up with a crash! | But we climb, fireproof, upward to the light from our crypt! | We are the power! We will hammer it young, the old, rotten thing, the state, | we who up to now by the fury of God are the proletariat!"]

Freiligrath paradoxically succeeds in intensifying the impact of this early example of Communist propaganda by freely handling the alexandrine as some contemporary French poets did. The long line, by its continuing hollow tone and the paired rhymes, gives the angry meditations of the stoker a powerful, striking force. Curiously enough, this poem—in which, thirteen years after Chamisso's still idyllic "Old Washerwoman" ("Alte Waschfrau" [1833]), the class-conscious proletarian makes his first appearance in German literature—found a very lukewarm reception in the Brussels headquarters of the Communist League. Marx passed over the literary event in icy silence, while Engels, in an unpublished review, poured his scorn upon Freiligrath's new radicalism. "One must admit," he wrote, "nowhere are revolutions made with greater cheerfulness and spontaneity than in the head of our Freiligrath."[71]

Hardly two years later, Freiligrath, Marx, and Engels began an extremely close collaboration. During the events of 1848 Freiligrath came to the forefront of the revolutionary writers; in his poem "The Dead to the Living" ("Die Toten an die Lebenden" [July, 1848]), he honored the dead of the March revolt in Berlin, demanding the continuation of the revolution in their name. The Prussian government imprisoned Freiligrath briefly for sedition, but was forced in a public hearing in Düsseldorf on October 3, 1848, to retract the accusation and release him, on which occasion his poem was read in the courtroom. The workers of Düsseldorf had already streamed to the building to celebrate the martyr of the revolution.

In nearby Cologne, Marx and the rest of the editorial staff of the *Neue Rheinische Zeitung* followed the Düsseldorf hearings with intense interest: Freiligrath's political importance had increased enormously as a result of the demonstrations by the Düsseldorf workers. Marx decided to make use of Freiligrath's popularity immediately for the *Neue Rheinische Zeitung*, which was completely in Communist hands, and at the same time for the Communist League. He hurried to Düsseldorf and offered Freiligrath an editorial position on the paper (October 3, 1848);[72] as it later appeared, Marx may also have urged Freiligrath on this occasion to become a member of the Rhenish Central Committee of the Communist League. Freiligrath seems to have accepted both offers. On October 12, his name appeared for the first time among the editors of the *Neue Rheinische Zeitung;* at the same time he may have taken part in the meetings of the Communist League. Freiligrath hoped at first to be permitted to write articles on foreign affairs, especially on the English situation, but at once it became clear that all important political articles were written by Marx, Engels, or their devotees, and that Freiligrath was expected to write useful propaganda ballads on political events in Paris, Frankfurt, and Vienna. Even in his poetic contributions he accommodated himself to the editorial policy of the *Neue Rheinische Zeitung:* although the editors were striving for a Communist state, for tactical reasons they were obliged to fight for the German liberal republic; only a democratic republic would be able to create the favorable conditions that would guarantee the subsequent success of the second, totally economic revolution. In Switzerland, Freiligrath had asked conspicuously for a "second, wild battle" against "the silver fleets of property";[73] in the *Neue Rheinische Zeitung* he contented himself with liberal postulates and a call for German republican unity. Only his last contribution deviated somewhat from this line. When the government succeeded in closing the paper, Marx replied with a farewell issue of sensational makeup, printed entirely in red. On the first page he put Freiligrath's "Farewell Words of the *Neue Rheinische Zeitung*," a touching picture of grieving proletarians bringing flowers to the grave of the "proud rebel's corpse."[74] In order to quiet any doubt about the strategic intentions of the *Neue Rheinische Zeitung,* Marx added a sharp declaration to the poem, to the effect that he and his friends, should they ever return, would not embroider their terrorism with apologetics. After this blow the editorial staff quickly dispersed: Engels took part in the struggles of the Baden insurgents; Marx fled to France; Freiligrath, who first attempted to find asylum in Holland, withdrew to a secluded life in a remote west German village. He did not abandon his political activity: when Marx sent an emissary from London with new instructions for the illegal work of the Rhenish Communists, Freiligrath was among the six delegates of the League who received the instructions and made copies of them.[75] Otherwise Freiligrath collected contributions for the wives of the imprisoned League members and for the exiled Marx; in a later document (November 19, 1852), Marx explicitly refers to Freiligrath as the treasurer of the Communist group.[76]

Not until 1851 did Freiligrath follow Marx into exile in London and was immediately and cordially welcomed by him as a personal companion and a "friend of the party." On English soil, however, Freiligrath noticeably hesitated to take any further part in the deliberations of the League. In one of his early communications to Freiligrath from London (December 27, 1851),[77] Marx stressed that the members of the League met in only one place, which was in Freiligrath's district; it was therefore expected that he would regularly take part in League meetings. Freiligrath continued to write political poems for Marx's various publications; Marx boasted to his colleagues that he knew how to get along with poets, particularly with Freiligrath, who could only be treated with kid gloves. "He is a real revolutionary and a thoroughly upright man," wrote Marx of Freiligrath on January 16, 1852, to the emissary of a German-American immigrant group; nevertheless it was necessary, he added, to pay some flattering attention to the poet: ". . . Poets are all, *plus ou moins,* even the best ones, *des courtisanes, et il faut les cajoler, pour les faire chanter.*"[78] Marx's attitude to Freiligrath in the first years together in exile in London remained most friendly. With some pride he reported to Engels that Freiligrath had declared upon his arrival in London that he belonged as before to the circle of the *Neue Rheinische Zeitung* and would only associate with Dr. Marx and his friends.[79] But Marx rejoiced too soon. As the years of the exile went by, it became ever clearer that Freiligrath, who at the beginning of his stay in London may have felt drawn to his former confederates, tried increasingly to avoid Marx and his circle, in order to attach himself finally to those liberal emigrants who gathered around Gottfried Kinkel (1815–82), who had once been condemned to life imprisonment and had been freed in a sensational raid.

A whole series of petty quarrels and conflicts were blown up into matters of principle in the stuffy atmosphere surrounding the German emigrants, and some of these helped to drive Marx and Freiligrath irreparably apart. The first opportunity of accusing Freiligrath of disloyalty arose when the unhappy wife of Gottfried Kinkel died a tragic death in November, 1858, and Freiligrath wrote a poem in which he made her death symbolic of the extinction of the German revolution. Marx, who in his vehemence was unable to distinguish personal from political motives, charged Freiligrath out-of-hand with political betrayal of the little group of Communist emigrants. "Freiligrath, who could not find a tone of pain in his lyre for the 'tragic' events, whether in his own party . . . , whether in the world *generally*,* complained Marx, ". . . suddenly [sings] of this miserable humbug."[80] Marx's anger increased considerably when he found out that Freiligrath had decided to join Kinkel in organizing the London celebration of Schiller's hundredth birthday in 1859. It was not only that Marx, like Hegel, personally had a rather low opinion of Schiller. Freiligrath's collaboration with Kinkel was clear proof that he had gone over to the liberals. From now on Freiligrath was referred to only as "the fat Philistine"[81] and his poems, which once had done such valuable service, as "pomp and circumstance."[82]

These troubled personal relations were finally severely worsened

---

* In English in Marx's original.—Translator.

by a third literary affair. Heinrich Bettziech (1813–76), a friend of Kinkel, published an essay in the German family magazine *Die Gartenlaube* (1859, No. 43), in which he reminded the German public of Freiligrath as one of its great poets. Bettziech's article closed with a sarcastic attack upon Marx, whom he accused of having nearly destroyed Freiligrath's muse by his dark influence. In vain did Marx protest on November 23, 1859, in a lengthy letter to Freiligrath: "If one wanted *wrongly* to ascribe to me any influence upon you, this could have been only in the brief period of the *N[eue] R[heinische] Z[eitung]*, when you wrote your very famous and certainly most popular poems."[83] Marx had to moderate his wrath for the present: Freiligrath meanwhile had become manager of the London branch of a Swiss bank. He repeatedly loaned Marx cash upon promissory notes for his American fees and saved Marx's family from many a precarious situation. Moreover, Marx knew very well that any public conflict with Freiligrath would be interpreted by the gossipy community of German emigrants in London as the final breach with the popular poet. But in his private correspondence he gave vent to his anger by calling Freiligrath simply "the cow"[84] or, no less sarcastically, "the fat rhyme-smith."[85]

But the break could not be avoided. In the years 1859–60 Marx was involved in a series of libel actions in London and Berlin that he considered "decisive for the historical vindication of the party and its subsequent position in Germany."[86] Forced by his opponents to lay before the court concrete evidence of the past activities of the Communist League, Marx turned to the former members of the group to assure their testimony, particularly to Freiligrath, from whom, as the only former member of the Rhenish Central Committee of the League[87] residing in London, he expected valuable help. But Freiligrath was not anxious to see his name dragged suddenly into public view on account of his radical past; and an excited scene took place between him and Marx in Freiligrath's office. Afterward Marx wrote to Engels that he could, if he wanted to, dip Freiligrath "into fire and brimstone up to the eyebrows";[88] at the same time he threatened Freiligrath that he would make public those "200 letters" containing sufficient material to substantiate Freiligrath's connections with the Party.[89]

In February, 1860, the moment of open reckoning between the former political allies arrived. Freiligrath answered Marx's pressing arguments (which were not lacking in a hint of blackmail) with a long, penetrating letter in which he reviewed his whole political development since 1848 and made it unmistakably clear to Marx why he could not agree to Marx's wishes in the matter of the League, from which he had kept at a distance for years. Going beyond the immediate occasion, Freiligrath's letter of February 28, 1860, raised questions that must have troubled him for a long time:

> Nevertheless, although I have always remained true to the banner of the *classe la plus laborieuse et la plus misérable* and always will, you know as well as I do that my relationship to the Party as it was and to the Party as it is are of a different nature. . . . I have kept myself at a distance from the Party throughout these seven years [1853–60], its meetings have not been attended by me, its decisions and acts have been unknown to me. Thus my relationship to the Party was *de facto* dissolved a long time ago, we never have deceived each other about it, it was a kind of tacit agreement between us. And I can only say that I have felt good about it. The Party, too, is a cage, and one can write poetry, even *for* the Party, better outside it than in. . . . I was a poet of the proletariat and the revolution long before I was a member of the League and an editor of the *Neue Rheinische Zeitung!* So I will continue to stand on my own two feet; I desire to obey only myself, and will manage my own affairs myself![90]

It was not only political subordination of the imagination that Freiligrath found unbearable. The more insight into politics and society he acquired in his long years in exile, the clearer it became to him that he had to avoid political affiliations for the sake of his personal purity; in the shadows of the League, his letter to Marx left no doubt, curious characters had emerged who were doing

their own questionable fishing in the troubled waters of conspiracy.

> Also another consideration has caused me never to regret my
> distance from the Party. When I think of all those ambig-
> uous and depraved elements that have already managed, de-
> spite all precautions, to push their way into the Party . . .
> then, just out of my sense of purity, I am more than glad that
> *de facto* I no longer belonged to an organization that could
> bring me into daily contact with such company.[91]

The importance of Freiligrath's letter of repudiation of Marx and
the Communist League as a paradigmatic document should not
be underestimated. To be sure, the personal and political elements
should be kept separate insofar as this is possible. The personal
opposition must not be oversimplified in melodramatic terms; each
was following his own star and could not avoid doing the other an
injustice.

The political relevance of Freiligrath's intimate confession ex-
tended far beyond the unfortunate occasion and the personal conflicts of the two friends, who continued to maintain a correspondence on a cool and occasional basis. Freiligrath was the first writer
who voluntarily subordinated himself to a modern Communist
organization, and accepted its dictates in artistic matters, only to
come, after a period of years, to the painful insight that the
"Party" that had written the slogan of freedom on its banner was
in reality a "cage," from which the instinct for self-preservation
of the imagination demanded an escape. More than two generations after Freiligrath, in a crisis similar to that of prerevolutionary Germany, it was the turn of a considerable number of European and American writers and intellectuals to find themselves
confronted with problems analogous to those with which Freiligrath and his friends had to contend. Silone, Malraux, Wright,
and Plievier are probably greater writers and more serious thinkers than their predecessors; nevertheless it was Freiligrath, the
poor schoolteacher's son from Detmold, who in his own way
anticipated and solved one of the central problems confronting
the modern intellectual.

Karl Marx's Commentary on Eugène Sue's
Les mystères de Paris

Unfortunately there is only a single extensive discussion of a novel to be found in Marx's writings. Although he confessed in his old age that Diderot was his "favorite in prose" and thought for a long time about writing a book on Balzac, he was so exclusively occupied with his political activity and later with his economic studies that he was never able to realize his literary plans. This is the only explanation for the fact that his single analysis of a novel deals with a contemporary best seller rather than with a work of enduring importance.

When Marx formulated his opinion about Eugène Sue's novel[92] in 1845, he could, to be sure, count on the lively interest of his readers. *Les mystères de Paris* (1842–43 in the *Journal de Débats*) caused an almost world-wide literary sensation; although Sue's book was by no means the first of the new novels published in instalments that were just then revolutionizing the press, it was certainly the most impressive of them. Sue's book is essentially a maudlin story of moral purification through the power of love and good will. The *deus ex machina* of the novel is Rudolf, the Grand Duke of Gerolstein, the ruler of a petty principality who goes out disguised as a painter and dandy in order to do good and prevent evil in the ballrooms and slums of Paris. During a stormy night he saves a young Paris grisette (who, of course, is unstained by vice in her innermost heart) from the hands of a burly assailant and brings the victim back to the straight and narrow path of virtue. Fleur de Marie, the young girl, is sent to a model farm managed by Rudolf's friends; her former assailant is sent to the French provinces where he is given an opportunity to sublimate his murderous instinct in a butcher shop. But Fleur de Marie is oppressed by inexplicable secrets and fates: among others, the Maître d'École, a brutal criminal, and his companion La Chouette, stick to her heels, at the same time mysteriously negotiating with a Scotswoman, Lady Sarah MacGregor, who seems to know a good deal about Fleur de Marie's background. In an immensely involved series of thrilling adventures the plot finally leads to a moving operatic finale, in which even a blessing from on high does not seem to be lacking. It turns out that Fleur de Marie, who had been forced into the oldest profession, is none other than the love-child of the Grand Duke and Lady Sarah; when the latter dies, Rudolf brings his noble daughter with him to his German duchy, where she enters a nunnery to lament her past. On account of her piety and seriousness the former street girl is elected abbess of the nunnery but dies transfigured on the day of her enthronement. Fortunately her father does not remain without consolation in the days of his grief; Rudolf marries the charming Countess d'Harville, a woman of means in the best years of her life, and can continue to take the beleaguered poor and endangered virtue under his grand-ducal protection.

The clever mixture of elements combined in this trash assured Sue unusual success. The actual basis of the book is the literary convention of the Gothic novel that Sue learned from the works of Mrs. Ann Radcliffe (1764–1823), whom he much admired. Like Mrs. Radcliffe, Sue engaged upon a literary search for the terrifying; like her, he turned out to be a master of the labyrinthine plot at the end of which persecuted innocence, pressed by criminals and monsters, emerges as the dearly beloved child of a father whose name stands prominently in the *Almanach de Gotha*. But Sue significantly changed the nature of the Gothic monsters. He promised his readers to reveal scenes out of the life of a new class of monsters *dehors de la civilisation,* and he kept his word by extending the boundaries of his light novel far into the sphere of criminal life, the proletariat, and the dregs of the big city. In principle, the modern social novel as well as the detective story owe much to him: instead of leading his readers into the Radcliffean haunted castles and terrifying death palaces, Sue opened their eyes to those frightening "caves and dens in which children and adults, legitimate offspring and bastards, lie with no order whatsoever on common mattresses, the most pernicious examples of drunkenness, of violence, of licentiousness, of murder, constantly before their eyes."[93] Indeed it was Sue's particular achievement that he combined the heritage of the Gothic novel with early naturalistic motifs; for example, in his portrait of the impoverished stonecutter Morel and his daughter, wasting away from tuberculosis in a garret, Sue created a naturalist *locus classicus* more than a generation before Zola and his colleagues. Like the later naturalists, Sue also pursued his scientific and philological inclinations; he, too, had his poor people speak argot for the sake of naturalistic verisimilitude; he, too, described his criminal types in the terminology of the then fashionable science of phrenology. In the case of the criminal family Martial, which appears in the second part of *Les mystères de Paris,* Sue even called upon heredity and environment in order to explain the degeneration of whole groups of people.

To these elements of the traditional Gothic novel and anticipated naturalism Sue added, with a feeling for contemporary fashion, the salt of socialist ideas. It was just this seasoning à la Saint-Simon and Fourier with which a critic of the stature of Sainte-Beuve reproached him. Sue, Sainte-Beuve claimed, had renounced his native literary instincts in order to smuggle "les systèmes du jour"[94] into the plot of his novel, with an eye to the political education of his readers. Other readers were far less averse to Sue: Balzac devoured the book; George Sand sent compliments to its author; in Germany Gutzkow chose him as model for his own lengthy novels;[95] in Russia even the skeptical Belinsky was moved to admit at least symptomatic importance for the book.[96] Only writers such as Gautier who adhered to stricter poetic standards did not spare their sarcastic remarks: "Tout le monde a dévoré *Les mystères de Paris,* même les gens qui ne savent pas lire."[97]

Marx's tiresome and often confusing review of the book was intended less to expose the weaknesses of the French author than to take one of his Young Hegelian commentators to task. The necessity of reviewing Sue arose when Marx, along with Engels, was occupied with deriding his former Young Hegelian friends for their ignorance of the economic motivating forces of the world and for "absorbing" (*aufzuheben*) their ideas philosophically. The first target of these attacks, which were all out of proportion to the insignificance of their victims, was the short-lived *Allgemeine Literatur Zeitung*,[98] edited in Berlin-Charlottenburg by the three Young Hegelian brothers Bruno, Edgar, and Egbert Bauer. Marx and Engels called their critical pamphlet against this philosophical brotherhood *The Holy Family* (*Die Heilige Familie* [1845]); in it they set themselves the sterile task of thoroughly picking apart the essays in the *Allgemeine Literatur Zeitung* one after the other and carrying them *ad absurdum*. Thus it happened that Marx busied himself with a more confused than difficult philosophical interpretation of *Les mystères de Paris* that a young Prussian officer named Franz Zychlin von Zychlinski (1816–1900)[99] had contributed to the Bauer brothers in June, 1844. Marx squandered his intellectual energy upon a literary dilettante; only a little later did it appear that von Zychlinski, who was accustomed to hide his essays modestly behind the pseudonym Szeliga, was more inclined to textbooks of tactics and the Prussian manual of arms than to Hegel. Zychlinski survived Marx by many years and died as a general in the Prussian infantry reserve.

It was not too difficult to mock Zychlinski's critical interpretations. The young infantry officer had taken it into his head to declare Sue's novel, in the true Young Hegelian manner, a philosophical essay; all that needed to be proven, he reasoned, was that an essential idea of the present situation of the world (Zychlinski called this idea "the secret," that is, *mystère*) was developed in this novel through actual situations and characters. By attempting to pursue in detail the unfolding of the "secret," which he obviously too hastily equated with Hegel's *Weltgeist*, he found himself chiefly fascinated by Sue's frequent changes of scene; for, he declared, epic change of scene was nothing other than the essential movement, the various stages of the presentation of the "secret." Zychlinski concerned himself especially with Sue's ball scene in the embassy of————; in it Sue was clearly attempting to confront the world of the poor with the sphere of glittering wealth. In Zychlinski's opinion, this scene was important because

in his description of the ball Sue touched upon the phenomenon
of the dance, which in turn was identical with "sensuality as a
'secret.' "[100] Marx condemned this strained philosophical construction, which had nothing to do with the text of the novel, most
angrily: the critic, wrote Marx, talked "about the category of the
dance that isn't danced anywhere but inside his critical skull."[101]
In contrast to a philosophical construction that ignored the text,
Marx pointed with justifiable emphasis to the decisive importance
of the literary convention. Sue's ball scene, which corresponded
to similar scenes in current French novels of society, had the same
function to fulfil as the frequent descriptions of hunting parties in
the fashionable novels of the English: namely, to concentrate the
most important persons of the plot for a while in a manageable
epic space. "Eugène Sue does not describe the dance with a single
word," remarked Marx, who showed that he was more familiar
with the text than his idealistic opponent. "[Sue] does not mix
with the dancing throng. He uses the ball only as an opportunity
to bring the principal group of aristocrats together."[102]

Zychlinski departed further from the text of the novel when he
declared Sue's fictional characters to be allegorical manifestations of the unfolding "secret"; even the relatively unimportant
secondary figure of the concierge Pipelet he interpreted as " 'secret' as ridicule."[103] Marx condemned "this philosophical construction of the concierge"[104] most sharply. Peculiarly enough,
however, he immediately fell into the trap of his own methodological prejudices: while he condemned the philosophical interpretation, he fell victim to the principle of sociological counterconstruc-
tion and for his part declared Sue's characters to be concentrated
embodiments of sociologically comprehensible realities. This appears when Marx in his own discussion of the figure of Pipelet
refers to the incontestable facts of French social history: in order
to refute Zychlinski's interpretation, Marx defended the verisimilitude of Sue's fiction by giving a brief historical summary of the
activities and duties of the Parisian concierge from the days of
the Revolution until the Restoration and, adding a few whimsical
anecdotes, measured the fictional character according to the criteria of sociological reality. From the frying pan of philosophical

interpretation, Marx leaped into the fire of unrestrained sociologism.

This confusion of modes of being appears even more clearly in Marx's criticism of the figure of the fictional Grand Duke Rudolf. Marx judges Sue's hero with an abstract earnestness and moral outrage as though he had been a petty prince of German history. " 'Good' Rudolf," sneered Marx; "only lucky accidents, money, and rank save the 'good man' from prison."[105] With astonishing naïveté, Marx concerns himself with Rudolf's past, at which the novel for the sake of a mysterious effect only barely hints, and even refers to the budget of his little state. "It is impossible for [Rudolf] to lead this kind of life," asserted Marx, "without sucking the last drop of blood out of his little German land like a vampire. According to Sue's own report he would belong to the mediatized German princes, had not the protection of a French marquis . . . saved him. The size of his principality may be estimated on the basis of this statement."[106] By calling Sue's novelistic hints "reports" and "statements," Marx clearly betrays how closely bound his critical assumptions were to the "positive" criteria of the nineteenth century as they appear most starkly in Russia in the essays of Pissarev and Dobrolyubov and from thence flow into the literary criticism of Soviet Russia. Marx's criticism of Sue's Grand Duke Rudolf anticipates Dobrolyubov's famous condemnation of Goncharov's Oblomov[107] as a repulsive good-for-nothing as well as those judgments of Stalinist literary criticism that, after the war, forced Konstantin Fadeyev to rewrite his best seller, *The Young Guard*,[108] because his fictional hero did not meet the political requirements of Soviet society. Political moralism replaces the literary interests of the critic.

Marx's and Engels' Criticism of Ferdinand Lassalle's Franz von Sickingen

It is both fruitful and difficult to examine Marx's and Engels' occasional utterances upon tragedy. Lassalle's *Franz von Sickingen* (1859), as well as Marx's and Engels' commentaries upon it, moves in a world bounded by Hegelian horizons that generates much resistance to literary examination.[109] There are also other difficulties to overcome: in this case the author and his critics agree in certain ideological assumptions that permit them to push political questions into the foreground of their correspondence; furthermore, it is of some importance that Marx and Engels were examining the literary experiment of a potential political ally and therefore had reason to moderate their usual rude tone considerably. But if allowances are made for terminological difficulties and the particular personal circumstances, the study of the literary argument between Lassalle and Marx/Engels is a fruitful one.

Lassalle (1825–64) probably knew that he was not a gifted playwright. His philosophical work on *Heraclitus* (1858) won the admiration of Alexander von Humboldt; with his tragedy *Franz von Sickingen* he was far less fortunate. The Hoftheater in Berlin declared itself uninterested; the Weimar theater, too, showed little eagerness to examine the manuscript. Even Lassalle's political friends, whose views differed considerably from those of theater directors, felt serious doubts as to whether it had been a happy inspiration to transform Franz von Sickingen into a tragic hero.

Even before Lassalle, several German liberals, in despair at their present ineffectiveness, had enthusiastically studied the Reformation and its powerful German characters. Literature and historiography found the issues of the Reformation and the Peasants' War a most welcome substitute for revolution. In Lassalle's *Franz von Sickingen*[110] the historical figure (1481–1523), who possessed some of the characteristics of an adventurous *condottiere*, is given the qualities of a national revolutionary of 1848. Lassalle's Sickingen appeals to the emperor, Charles V, to follow Luther and the German knights in the fight against Rome; but Charles has no other choice than to refuse Sickingen's demand. Thereupon Sickingen unites the German knightly opposition in order to launch a decisive battle in the local feud against the Elector of Trier; not until Trier has fallen does he try openly for the German imperial crown. But the siege of Trier drags out too long: Charles threatens Sickingen's allies with imperial proscription and Sickingen finds himself in his last stronghold at the mercy of the imperial troops. A friend devises a desperate plan of resistance. Sickingen is to renounce his knightly rank and join the peasants who are preparing their revolt. But it is too late; the last sally fails, and Sickingen is brought back to his castle badly wounded. Once more he sees his friend Hutten, who has slipped to his bed disguised as a priest—both know that their cause is lost. Over Sickingen's corpse Hutten speaks the final monologue, which predicts the defeat of the peasants and recommends Sickingen's struggle to future revolutionary centuries.

Zusammenbricht mit diesem *einen* Mann
Das deutsche *Vaterland*—in Scherben liegen
Die Hoffnungen, für welche wir gelebt.
Machtlos mit seinem Tod, weicht bang zurück
Der Adel, wirft ans Fürstentum sich hin,
Das um sich greifend unser Reich zerreisst;
Zu seinen Schranzen sinkt er schnell herab!
Des Halts beraubt, sich selbts misstrauend, spinnt
In seines Weichbilds Sondervorteil sich
Der Städter ein und stirbt dem Ganzen ab.
—Der *Bauer* bleibt nur treu dem grossen Zweck,
Er greift zum Schwert—doch auf sich selbst beschränkt,
Schleppt er zur Metzgerbank nur seinen Leib
Zur blutigen, bedeckt mit seinem grässlicht
Gevierteilten Gebein die weite, deutsche Erde,—
Die schaudernde!
. . . *Du* stirbst und nimmst in deine Grube mit,
Was dieses Leben lebenswert gemacht.
Mich trägt mein flücht'ger Fuss jetzt ins Exil,
Doch nicht auf lange; wen'ge Wochen, und—
Es *eint* sich meine Asche deinem Staub.
Künft'gen Jahrhunderten vermach' ich unsre *Rache!*[111]

[With this *one* man the German | fatherland *collapses*—in shreds lie | the hopes for which we lived. | Powerless with his death, the nobility fearfully draws back, | throws itself upon the princes who, | grasping all around them, tear our empire to pieces; | they quickly become toadies! | Robbed of their

support, mistrusting himself, | the townsman envelops him-
self in the special privileges of his town | and his interest in
the larger issue dies. | Only the *peasant* remains loyal to the
great purpose, | *he* reaches for the sword—but limited to his
own resources, | he only drags his body to the slaughter-
house, | that murderous place; the broad German earth is
covered with his horrible quartered bones, | the shuddering
earth! . . . *You* die and take with you to the grave | what
made this life worth living. | My fleeing foot will carry me
now into exile, | but not for long; a few weeks, and— | my
ashes will be *united* with your dust. | To *future* centuries I
bequeathe our *revenge!*]

Lassalle completed his tragedy, which was conceived as an
elegy upon the revolution of 1848, in the early spring of 1859 and
sent copies of the long text to Marx and Engels, along with a short
theoretical essay[112] on tragedy, asking for their critical comments
(March 6, 1859).[113] But the author had to wait a considerable
time for an answer from his two friends; neither of them seemed
willing to spend time on Lassalle's literary experiment. But since
Marx wanted to find a German publisher for his *Critique of Political Economy* through the good offices of Lassalle, there was finally an end to the wait: Marx answered Lassalle on April 19,
1859;[114] Engels wrote four weeks later on May 18.[115]

Engels opened his critical comments with the somewhat ambiguous remark that doubtless none of the "current official poets of
Germany would be even remotely capable" of writing such a
tragedy.[116] Marx admitted that "the composition and the action"
of the play left him not unimpressed.[117] But the praise was immediately tempered: Marx complained about the rough iambic
lines, although he still admired them more than the "formal
smoothness" of the "current pack of epigones."[118] Engels added,
with some insight into the exigencies of the stage, that the over-
long monologues and dialogues might well prevent a performance
of the tragedy in an established theater. Both Marx and Engels
justly pointed out in addition that Lassalle's characters were very
thinly drawn and lacked sensual richness. Marx recommended to
Lassalle that he should "Shakespearize more" than he had done

instead of "Schillerizing [*Schillern*]."[119] Engels went into this decisive question more patiently and formulated his own idea of a successfully conceived dramatic character: the true dramatic figure, he observed, combined in himself individual as well as typical elements. Dramatically successful characters were not only symbols of impersonal forces, but also possessed their own, native, personal richness. Lassalle should try to present the moving forces of the world not only in mere dialogues, but in specific action; if he could succeed in this, his characters would immediately come into the foreground "alive, active, so to speak rooted in nature."[120] Clearly Engels' recommendations were here determined by the concept of the concrete universal as defined by German classical philosophy; Lassalle, in neglecting the concrete, had stressed the general principle too exclusively. Like Marx, Engels also recommended that Lassalle should bring himself closer to Shakespeare in his art; Shakespeare, he wrote, had been of essential importance in the development of the drama. In this recommendation, too, Hegelian ideas emerge: Hegel himself had criticized the abstract and merely formal method of characterization of the French and Italian theater, pointing to the English, above all Shakespeare, who had known how to combine the immediacy of living existence with the ideal greatness of a dramatic character.[121] The disparagement of Schiller, in which Marx and Engels were oddly in agreement, had also clearly appeared in Hegel's *Lectures on Aesthetics*. Schiller, Hegel had declared, had given way to a stormy violence that expanded outward without a real core (". . . ist in eine Gewaltsamkeit verfallen, für deren hinausstürmenden Expansion es an dem eigentlichen Kern fehlt").[122]

Thus far Marx and Engels had developed their criticism of Lassalle's *Franz von Sickingen* in the spirit of Hegel. The curious turn that indeed separated their criticism from Hegel's appeared as soon as Engels, after calling the "formal aspect" of the play a "secondary matter,"[123] made the explicit demand that the play should be subjected to a more thoroughgoing political and historical examination. From a political point of view Lassalle's experiment was most embarrassingly disappointing. Marx de-

clared categorically that the basic mistake lay in the choice of a
hero: Franz von Sickingen had not, after all, been a real revolutionary, but merely an odd character who had rebelled in his
imagination; it was fatal that he and Hutten, "just like the educated Polish aristocracy of 1830, made themselves into organs
of modern ideas, on the one hand, but, on the other hand, represented a reactionary class interest."[124] Sickingen had to fall,
added Marx, "because he as *knight* and *representative of a disappearing class* rebelled against the existing order."[125] Obviously
it was impossible to base a tragedy upon such a figure; by overestimating the Protestant knightly opposition, Lassalle had neglected the plebeian opposition that had found its leaders in figures
like Thomas Münzer. Engels stressed the same problem in his
own letter, though he formulated his objections somewhat more
tolerantly by connecting them with the dramaturgical exigencies
of the theater. In Engels' opinion Lassalle had criminally neglected "the non-official plebeian and peasant elements with their
concomitant theoretical representation."[126] This was to be regretted for purely technical and dramaturgical reasons: actual
representation of the peasant and beggar would have given the
play that Shakespearean roundness and richness it so noticeably
lacked; the popular element would have functioned as a truly
"Falstaffian background"[127] that in such a play "would have to
have [been] more effective than in Shakespeare"![128]

Lassalle answered Marx and Engels on May 27, 1859, in a long
letter in which he tried to refute their objections.[129] To be sure,
Lassalle knew that Marx's and Engels' criticism of his maladroit
blank verse and his thin characterization was just. His answer
was aimed at their more important objections to the *content* of
the tragedy; he stressed that he, too, was definitely interested,
for "party reasons," in the historical and political questions his
tragedy raised.[130]

Lassalle's sharp intelligence unfailingly grasped the actual core
of his critics' arguments. "Your objections," he wrote to Marx
and Engels, "reduce, in the last analysis, to the fact that I wrote
a *Franz von Sickingen* at all and not a *Thomas Münzer* or some

other tragedy of the Peasants' War."[131] Lassalle was determined to defend his choice of a hero. Opposing an equally frank reply to a thinly veiled "wholesale"[132] condemnation, he declared that Marx's view of the Peasants' War rested upon a dogmatic and therefore mistaken estimate of the historical facts. Marx and Engels thought of the Peasants' War as a necessarily progressive action of the lower class; they were not willing to admit that the rebelling German peasants (as Lassalle stressed) fought for political ideas that had long since belonged to the past. "The Peasant Wars," declared Lassalle, "[are] . . . *not* of the nature you appear to give to them. They are, rather, (*a*) not revolutionary (*b*) and even in the highest degree—*ultimately reactionary, quite as reactionary* as . . . the *historical* aristocratic party itself."[133] Even Thomas Münzer hardly appeared to him as a tragic hero; it was quite impossible for him, declared the rationalist Lassalle, to take a positive attitude toward religious fanaticism.[134] In Lassalle's opinion it was just the religious and mystical element that had condemned Münzer's revolts to hopeless failure.

In his reply to Marx and Engels, Lassalle showed clearer insights into German history than the dogmatic founders of historical materialism. Lassalle, who kept the ability of being convinced by the raw materials of history, did not close his eyes to the fact that, as he said, the brutal rebels were "reactionary through and through,"[135] just as reactionary as the knights they slaughtered in the burning castles. The founder of the first German workers' party did not hesitate to point out vigorously to Marx and Engels that historically the lower classes were certainly not always the vanguard of progressive periods of history.

As a writer, Lassalle felt that such historical and political arguments were only temporary prologues to a more significant answer to Marx's and Engels' criticism of his aesthetic efforts. In contrast to his friends, Lassalle insisted in principle upon the difference between Sickingen as an actual historical person, whose deeds one might, if one chose, subject to a political value judgment, and Sickingen as the fictional figure of a knight, who, he pointed out, was subordinate only to aesthetic illusion. How could a figure existing only as artistically ordered language come to false decisions in the concrete realm of history? Were not Marx and Engels confusing the two distinct worlds of historical reality and of aesthetic illusion? Were they not equating the work of art with a political document? ". . . Though you may be completely right with respect to the *historical* Sickingen," Lassalle wrote to Marx, "you are not right in respect to *my* Sickingen. And does the author not have the right to idealize his hero, to give him a *higher* consciousness? Is Schiller's Wallenstein historical? Homer's Achilles the real one?"[136] It was the privilege of the author, added Lassalle, to concentrate the best ideas of the age in his hero "as in a single focal point."[137] In the historical figure of Sickingen one might very well sense "a conflict of diverging forces that indeed remains undecided"; in its task of organizing the historical raw material in a fictional character the "creative imagination is free."[138]

Despite the successful defense of aesthetic illusion against the illegitimate claims of political commitment that were raised by Marx and Engels, Lassalle's reply lacked logic. His inconsistency results from his vacillation between a Hegelian (or better, monistic) and a dualistic position. This vacillation, which robs many of his counterarguments of their force, appears first of all in the fact that Lassalle's tragedy—as Ludwig Marcuse has remarked[139] —by no means corresponds to Hegelian postulates as a whole. According to Hegel, protagonists and antagonists of a tragedy are both equally justified in their necessarily hostile positions, which are absorbed (*aufgehoben*) into the restored majesty of the ethical substance without regard for the suffering individual. Lassalle bases his powerful scene between Sickingen and Charles V upon this Hegelian concept of tragedy. In many other instances, Lassalle's tragedy shows a dualistic spirit that insists upon an irreconcilable opposition of forces. In his theoretical essay on the tragic idea (March, 1859), Lassalle speaks not of a Hegelian resolution of antitheses, but, in the Heraclidan sense, "of the deep dialectical contradiction inherent in the nature of all action, especially revolutionary action."[140] Lassalle's tragedy (like Georg

Büchner's) moves away from Hegel in the direction of providing shattering insights into the eternally implacable chaos of existence without ending in the questionable consolation of a reconciled ethical substance at the cost of the individual.

Lassalle's reply, finally, is seriously weakened by the dual na · ture of his hero, which corresponds to the vacillating philosophical position of his author. On the one hand, Lassalle's Sickingen moves in the Hegelian world of the pure idea; his tragic failure is in not believing ardently enough in the power of the absolute spirit. According to Lassalle's own interpretation, Sickingen is tragic because of his "lack of confidence in the ethical idea and its infinite power in and of itself."[141] On the other hand, Lassalle's conception of the tragic hero is clearly infected by the postulates of economic materialism: for in order to motivate Sickingen's lack of confidence dramatically, Lassalle, in a fateful twist, turns to economic and social causes; the tragic hero, his face turned to the sun of the absolute idea, has a personality determined by the early quality of his class situation.[142]

Even if Lassalle was unable to find a consistent path between the Hegelian tradition and economic determinism, nevertheless as a playwright he was clear-sighted enough to feel the essential failure of Marxist theory in its relation to tragedy. Lassalle defended the principle of aesthetic illusion against the alien standards of partisan politics and arrived at the insight that the Hegelian view (and with it, Marxism) threatened the existence of the hero in literature *and* reality. "This critical, philosophical view of history, in which iron necessity is tied to iron necessity," he remarked in his manuscript on tragedy, "is . . . no soil either for *practical revolutionary action* or for *imagined dramatic action*. For both elements, rather, the indispensable basis is the assumption of the reforming and decisive effectiveness of *individual* decisions and actions, without which neither a *dramatic*, igniting interest nor a bold deed is possible."[143] This fundamental insight of Lassalle's—which neither Marx nor Engels was inclined to discuss—has lost none of its validity in the course of time.

5

The Later Engels as a Critic of Marxist Literary Doctrine

A Different Taste

Official apologists of Communist literary theory and also more scholarly observers often fall victim to rash conclusions that as a rule derive from the mistaken premise that Marx and Engels present a monolithic intellectual unity. Onetime defenders of Stalinist literary doctrine like Georg Lukács,[1] as well as sober and informed interpreters of recent Russian literary criticism,[2] speak of the literary taste of Marx and Engels as though it were thoroughly uniform and proceeded from similar sources. This assumption of monolithic unity does not fit the facts: Marx and Engels are not identical twins either in their social theories or in their literary judgments but rather distinct personalities of a unique stamp; their literary tastes exhibit nuances just as important as those of their theoretical formulations. The more precisely these nuances of taste and the chronology of their literary judgments, are examined the more undeniably differences appear; not infrequently even those theoretical deliberations that aim at universal validity are colored by their strongly differentiated tastes.

Engels remained, at heart, the talented young man of good family: tall, with brown hair and alert blue eyes, he could be seen even in his old age, when he was suffering from cancer of the larynx, striding energetically through the rainy streets of

London. He had always loved the fresh air: he fenced, danced, hiked, and swam with enthusiasm; his military service he regarded as a pleasure; and he described the four skirmishes in which he took part in the company of west German revolutionaries with the understatement of the gentleman to the manner born. He was excellent company; he composed, sang, and conversed with wit and sparkling good humor. His occasional dilettantism was mitigated by his genuine pleasure in differing surroundings, people, and ideas; of extraordinary personal courage, he maintained an infinitely touching loyalty to anyone whom he had once taken into his perpetually youthful heart. Although he was a respected member of the Manchester stock exchange and several gentlemen's clubs, and often seems to have taken part, cheerfully pink-jacketed, in the foxhunts of the well-born, he spent his evenings and nights with Mary Burns, a plain Irish working girl for whom he built a little house on the edge of Manchester, and, after her death, with her sister, to whom he transferred all his affections. His exemplary friendship with Marx shows a similar constancy; he bore Marx's domineering whims without contradiction, yielded to his demands, wrote articles in his friend's name, sacrificed his working time, supported him for decades by sending him money, took up the pen where his friend had laid it down, fought against his enemies, defended his errors, forgave him time and time again his tyrannical egotism, his coldness, and his insensitivity. Engels remained attuned to the surface of the world, preferring to deal with individual phenomena; to be sure he lacked his friend's penetrating intellectualism, but he was able to defend Marx's ideas with native conciliatory ease.

Young Marx plunged into his literary and philosophical studies with a fury that made his father speak of a dangerous obsession; later observers were more inclined to talk of unrestrained ambition, unbearable moodiness, and wicked arrogance. With the exception of Engels, who knew how to subordinate himself, his former friends turned into bitter enemies: from Ruge to Lassalle, from Freiligrath to Bakunin, the number and annoyance of those whom Marx alienated with his mistrustful, undisciplined polem-

ics and explosions of hatred increased steadily. His world was
one dominated by the word: his senses were impervious to natural,
visual, or musical beauty; the reading room of the British Museum
was his real home, where he poured his thoughts into endless
notebooks; and as soon as he found himself without theoretical
reading matter, he stilled his hunger for the printed word with
trashy multivolume novels. Unwilling to be enslaved by the cheap
journalism of his time, he muddled along as head of a household
of seven in a musty two-room flat in Soho, not infrequently pawn-
ing his bed linen in order to pay for his children's daily bread.
This truly obsessed thinker was the gentlest of husbands and a
most touching father. The institution of marriage was sacred to
him in the old religious sense, and he always regarded his wife
Jenny as the tenderly won beloved of his youth; she, who had
followed him into unbearable misery from the noble house of the
Westphalens, remained devoted to him in unshakable affection
as he did to her. Marx, said Engels, really died on the day when
Jenny passed away.

The essential differences of background, education, and temperament could not fail to have important consequences for
Marx's and Engels' estimate of works of art. Marx's father knew
his Goethe, Schiller, and Lessing, and was more than willing to
see in his son's literary talents a particular qualification for his
future career as a Prussian civil servant. From his earliest childhood Karl Marx had grown up in an atmosphere very friendly
to classical literature; Ludwig von Westphalen, his paternal friend,
expanded his knowledge of the classics to include Homer and
Shakespeare and induced the young student to take courses at
Bonn and Berlin on the mythology and literature of the Greeks
and Romans. In Berlin, Marx was highly impressed by a performance of the first part of *Faust* with Carl Seydelmann in the role
of Mephisto; Marx recognized in Mephisto elements of his own
personality, and Seydelmann's performance remained a persistent
memory. Even in his old age Marx remained loyal to those writers
whom he had admired in his student years. When his daughters
asked him to write down the names of the three writers he most

dearly loved, Marx named Aeschylus, Shakespeare, and Goethe without hesitation.[3]

Engels' literary *education du cœur* took a completely different direction. His family belonged to the most famous of the Pietistic communities of the Rhineland, led by Pastor Krummacher (1774–1837); in such circles people were opposed to belles-lettres in principle. Without receiving the slightest encouragement from family or older friends, Engels had to find his own way to literature; since he had received no systematic training, he turned almost unavoidably to that which was popular and fashionable. He was convinced that the political literature of the forties was the fulfilment of the German literary tradition. In contrast to Marx, Engels enthusiastically tried to follow the spokesmen of German chauvinism: what occupied him was not the Greek past but the heritage of the Germanic tribes that affected the German present. Nowhere, Engels believed, did the poetic element express itself more purely than in his mother tongue. In a patriotic poem, "The German Language" ("Die deutsche Sprache" [1839]), he compared German with English, French, Greek, and Portuguese, and praised its unique power, paradoxically enough in the epic meter of the Greeks:

Aber die Sprache Germaniens—sie tönt, wie die donnernde
    Brandung
An den gezackten Korallen—die tragen ein liebliches Eiland,
Dorthin schallet das Rauschen der langen Wellen Homeros,
Dort erdonnern die riesigen Blöcke aus Äschylos' Händen,
Dort auch siehst du der Feldhernnhand cyklopisches Bau-
    werk . . .
Syrinx tönet im Schilf, und die Bächlein runden den Sand-
    stein,
Dort auch steht manch' Hünengebäu, umsaust von den
    Winden,
Das ist Germaniens Zunge, die ewige, wunderumrankte.[4]

[But the language of Germania—it roars like the thundering surf | on the serrated corals—they support a lovely island, | thither resounds the roar of the long waves of Homer, | there thunder the giant blocks from Aeschylus' hands, | there, too, you see the Cyclopian structures by the hands of generals ... | the Panpipe sounds in the reeds, and brooks round off the sandstone, | there stands also many a giant's building, the winds howling about them, | that is Germania's tongue, eternal, overgrown with wonders.]

Engels' early reviews are permeated by references to the Germanic myths; he counted old Danish heroic lays like *Lord Oluf He Rides So Far* (*Herr Oluf han rider saa vide*)[5] or folk songs like "Herr Tidmann"[6] among the incomparable treasures of folk poetry; later he angrily defended the original, pure atmosphere of the *Nibelungenlied* against Richard Wagner's "total falsification of the primitive world."[7] Instead of occasionally quoting Dante, as Marx did,[8] Engels liked to refer to "our Wolfram von Eschenbach,"[9] of whose works, to be sure, he by far preferred the "three wondrously beautiful albas"[10] to *Parzival*. To such a view, Martin Luther also appeared as one of the most important poets in the German language. "Luther not only swept out the Augean stables of the Church, but also those of the German language";[11] Engels praised the chorale "A Mighty Fortress Is Our God ("Ein feste Burg ist unser Gott") as "the Marseillaise of the sixteenth century."[12]

In his youthful preference for the Germanic myths, the *Nibelungenlied*, Middle High German courtly poetry, and the German chapbooks, Engels followed, although at the significant distance of almost a generation, the sympathies of the younger German Romantics. Walking in the footsteps of Jakob and Wilhelm Grimm (even where they led astray), Engels tried to deepen his knowledge of the Germanic and ancient Germanic world through occasional study of comparative philology. In later years he willingly turned back to the interests of his youth, wrote a well-intentioned essay on the "Franconian Dialects,"[13] said that he had read Hafiz in Old Persian,[14] and in the fifties pursued a somewhat superficial study of Slavic literatures.

As a good classicist Marx was not in the least interested in the Germanic past. Instead of occupying himself with Middle High

German as Engels did, Marx was curious to know what artistic achievements might have preceded those of the ancients. In *Capital* he explained the great mass of Asiatic and Egyptian art by reference to economic conditions, administrative co-operation, and the immense concentration of material and human resources in the hands of despotic rulers and administrative systems. "Their command over the hands and arms of almost the whole non-agricultural population and the exclusive disposition of the monarchs and priesthood over that surplus value supplied them with the means for the erection of those mighty monuments with which they filled the land. . . . In the movement of colossal statues and enormous masses, whose transport arouses astonishment, human labor was extravagantly and almost exclusively applied."[15] This explanation, though it sounds so characteristically Marxist, in fact comes from the *Textbook of Lectures* of the English economist Richard Jones (1779–1855), where Marx had found it (pp. 77–78).

Further characteristic differences in literary taste appear in Marx's and Engels' respective studies in Greek art. Marx, in his own way, remained true to the traditional German Grecophilia in the spirit of Winckelmann, Goethe, and Hegel. In his fragmentary manuscript of August 23, 1859, Marx tries in vain to apply his economic theory to the stubborn subject of Greek art; in order to bridge the gap between the imperatives of his classical taste and the relativism of his economic theory, he has no choice but to seize upon the ideas of organic development contained in the tradition of Vico and Herder to give at least the impression of a resolution. Greek art continued to disturb Marx as an astonishingly timeless example of aesthetic achievement.

Engels' commentaries upon Greek art appear, in comparison with Marx's self-tormenting studies, far more insignificant. Engels read Homer's epics as social and economic documents illustrating certain early political and technological developments in Greece. Thus the *Iliad* appears not only as a textbook of Greek economic history; it also indicates, declared Engels, the increase of "population . . . with the expansion of herds and agriculture, the begin-

nings of artisanship," and, connected with this, the intensification
of the "differences in wealth of the aristocratic element within
the old, indigenous democracy."[16] Similarly, the Homeric poems
illustrate the development of early Greek instruments of production and the accomplishments of a higher stage of civilization;
they refer to "developed iron tools: the bellows, the hand mill,
the potter's wheel; . . . a developed skill of metalworking in the
process of becoming artisanship; the chariot and the war chariot;
shipbuilding with beams and planks; the beginnings of architecture as an art. . . ."[17] This dry catalogue offered by Engels certainly has nothing in common with Marx's enthusiasm for the
timelessness of Greek art.

Marx's inclination to the classical appears also in his distinct
predilection for the French authors of the seventeenth and eighteenth centuries, whom he most explicitly recommended to Engels.
Marx's extraordinary respect for the French mind became apparent above all in his late years: in the early summer of 1869 Marx
reread De la Rochefoucauld's *Réflexions*[18] earnestly and approv-
ingly, and sent his friend Engels one of his two copies of Diderot's
Le neveu de Rameau with the strongest recommendations.[19] Marx
himself admitted why he was so devoted to this piece of penetrating irony: referring to Hegel, he declared himself in agreement with the philosophical interpretation appearing in the *Phenomenology of the Mind (Phänomenologie des Geistes)*.[20] Along
with Hegel, Marx, too, is fascinated by the "self-conscious and
self-expressing pessimism (*Zerrissenheit*) of the consciousness,"
"by the scornful laughter at existence,"[21] by that imperious spirit
that destroys the emptiness of existence through its own self-
affirmation. By identifying himself so explicitly with Hegel's
view, Marx turns decisively against the sociological interpretation
formulated by the French critic Jules Janin in his book, *Le fin
d'un monde et du neveu de Rameau* (1861). With angry sarcasm
Marx calls the critical development from Diderot's complexity to
Janin's simplicity a "regressive metamorphosis"[22] and ridicules
the attempt to explain "that Rameau's whole perversity comes
from his chagrin at not being a 'born *gentilhomme*.' "[23] Here,

at least, Marx, who in his high opinion of the *Neveu de Rameau* was in essential agreement with Goethe and the most brilliant minds of the twentieth century, prefers the metaphysical interpretation to the dull sociologizing of his own age.

As an admirer of De la Rochefoucauld and of Diderot, Marx could not develop the least liking for the French Romantics. In his letter of November 30, 1873, he admits to Engels that he completely agreed with the deadly verdict of Sainte-Beuve upon Chateaubriand, who was "always odious to him"; Sainte-Beuve's remarks on Chateaubriand merely confirmed him in his own dislike of the latter, whose "false depth, byzantine exaggeration, flirtation with feelings, motley iridescence, *word painting**" were intolerable to him.[24]

Although clear differences appear in Marx's and Engels' personal inclinations for the literary phenomena of western Europe, their concern with the traditions of Slavic culture exhibit common characteristics—above all the common failure to penetrate Slavic cultural questions. In their concern with Slavic matters three often overlapping phases can be distinguished: first, their dislike of the world of reactionary Slavs in the revolutionary days of 1848; about eight years later, their purely philological interest in certain examples of Slavic folk literature; and finally, after 1870, a growing political interest in the possibilities of a social revolution in Slavic eastern Europe. Certainly Marx and Engels as Hegelians could only look down upon the Slavic sphere with some distrust: in Hegel's later Prussian concept of historical development the Slavs were given a very modest and uncertain place. Hegel relegated them to the periphery of world history, where their task was to maintain contact with Asia;[25] the Slavs had appeared too late on the stage of world history. Despite the enthusiastic asseverations of Herder in his *Ideas toward a Philosophy of the History of Mankind* (*Ideen zur Philosophie der Geschichte der Menschheit* [1784–91]), their national individuality did not appear distinct enough to Hegel; he thought the Slavic national groups faded into each other.[26] In the revolution-

* In English in Marx's original.—TRANSLATOR.

ary days of 1848, this Hegelian concept of the peripheral, vague Slavic world nourished Engels' bitter indictment of the Slavs in the *Neue Rheinische Zeitung*. As a German radical, Engels had additional reasons to bear the Slavs a grudge: in the Frankfurt Diet the Czech historian František Palacký (1798–1876) had declared in the name of his people, at that time still clinging to the Austrian monarchy, that the Czechs wanted to have no part of a pan-German empire, and only a little later the Russian army invaded Hungary and slaughtered Kossuth's revolutionary soldiers (1849). No wonder that Engels was only able to see in the fashionable pan-Slavism a thoroughly sentimental mysticism or an ideological camouflage of the Russian knout.[27]

This revolutionary anger did not ease until the middle of the fifties, when Engels turned to Slavic culture for purely philological reasons and asked Marx to look up Slavic anthologies and reference books in the rich library of the British Museum. In this indirect way Marx, too, was moved to get an insight into Slavic traditions. On March 5, 1856, Marx reported to his friend in Manchester that he had paged through F. G. Eichhoff's *Histoire de la langue et de la littérature de Slaves* (1839);[28] although he could not claim to be an expert in Slavic matters, he was still astonished at the questionable way in which Eichhoff (1799–1875) declared the Lithuanians and the Latvians to be Slavic tribes. In Eichhoff's book Marx saw for the first time excerpts of an epic poem that in his letter to Engels he called *Igor's Expedition*. This is the only proof that he was at least superficially acquainted with the *Song of Igor*, the oldest document of Russian literature. The *Song of Igor* appeared to him to be "Christian-heroic, although the pagan elements still show up strongly."[29] Marx also leafed through a German anthology of Old Czech heroic epics, published by the philologists Václav Hanka (1791–1861) and Václav Svoboda (1781–1849); he was amazed to find in these old poems a definite anti-German and anti-Christian mood of a very modern kind. Marx could not suspect, of course, that the fragments, which belonged to the so-called Královodvorský Manuscript, would be proved by T. G. Masaryk to be romantic forgeries by Hanka *ad maiorem nationis gloriam*. Among other collections of Slavic folk poetry that Marx found in the library of the British Museum, he mentioned Goetze's German version of the Russian heroic poem *Prince Vladimir and His Round Table* (1819), *Voices of the Russian People* (1828), Siegfried Kapper's *Slavic Melodies* (1844), *Songs of the Serbs* (1852), and a German translation of the *Wedding Songs* of the Serbian philologist Vuk Stefanović Karadžić (1787–1864). Engels had his own opinion on these works. Eichhoff, he declared, was a "philological swindler";[30] Siegfried Kapper "a Prague Jew" whose translations were not trustworthy;[31] Hanka and Svoboda "complete asses."[32] Thus the extent of Marx's and Engels' studies in Slavic literature was modest to say the least. In an article by Engels in the *New York Daily Tribune* there is a quotation from Derzhavin;[33] Marx refers once to Pushkin's *Eugene Onegin*.[34] But in the age of Gogol, Goncharov, and Dostoevsky, this hardly suggests a penetrating or comprehensive knowledge of Slavic literature.

However, added to this occasional philological interest there appears a more lively concern with the social problems of Russia. In 1870, Marx met German Aleksandrovich Lopatin (1845–1918), an exiled member of the *Narodnaya Volya* ("Popular Will"); by him he was introduced to the angry debates of the Russian emigrants. The terrorist Lopatin, who had unsuccessfully tried to blow up the tsar's special train, could hardly have been a source of impartial information. However, the important thing was that Lopatin, as an enthusiastic reader of Chernishevsky, may have called Marx's attention to the radical tradition of Russian cultural criticism that appeared also in the works of Belinsky (1811–48), Dobrolyubov (1836–61), and Pissarev (1840–68). In any case, on December 12, 1872, Marx asked the Russian economist Danielson for further details about Chernishevsky; he wanted, said Marx, to awaken "interest in the West" for this excellent writer who had to endure so much in his Siberian exile.[35] Marx's interest in Chernishevsky was shared by Engels, who praised him and Pissarev in the *Volksstaat,* at that time the central organ of the growing democratic socialism, as "two Socialist Lessings."[36] But neither Marx nor Engels appear to have known of the specific efforts of Chernishevsky or Pissarev in the theory of literature. Although overestimating the political aspects, they never realized that Russian radical literary criticism, which had been influenced by the German idealist tradition and the Young Hegelians, had developed ideas that were frequently close to their own. The more clearly the possibility of a Russian revolution appeared on the horizon, the more frequently Marx and Engels, often against their will, found themselves drawn into the conflicts of the Russian emigrants in London and Geneva. After they became acquainted with the co-operative agrarian program of the *Narodniki* ("Populists") and the terroristic principles of the *Narodnaya Volya*, they came into contact with those emigrants who had established themselves as the "Liberation of Labor" and who had been the first to accept a consistently Marxist program. No doubt Marx's and Engels' attitude to the Slavs underwent a thorough change: when Engels on March 6, 1884, directed a friendly letter to Vera Zassulich (1853–1919), one of the founding members of the "Liberation of Labor," he declared to her that the beautiful Russian language has "tous les avantages de l'allemand sans son horrible grossièreté."[37] Marx was clear in his own mind about the metamorphosis that had taken place; when he heard from St. Petersburg that a Russian publisher intended to bring out the first translation of *Capital,* he wrote to his friend Dr. Kugelmann that it was astonishing how the Russian people, against whom he had fought for twenty-five years of his life, were now the first to seize upon and further his ideas.[38]

Marx's and Engels' particular agreement on Slavic questions should not obscure the essential differences in their literary inclinations. Without doubt Marx remained within the boundaries of the classicistic canon of the late eighteenth century: he liked the ancients, Shakespeare, Goethe, and the authors of the *ancien régime.* Engels' literary sympathies, on the other hand, which were nourished by the Romantic impulses of the early nineteenth century, turned to nationalistic German poetry and the basically

Romantic questions of comparative philology. Engels was prepared to submit his personal taste and judgment to the dictates of the times and to enjoy such literature as political theory required; Marx, however, remained true to his favorite authors and to Greek art against his own theory. In matters of literary taste Marx was by no means a Marxist.

A Theory of Socialist Realism?

Ever since the decrees of the CPSU (1932) and the First Soviet Writers' Conference (1934), Marxist literary doctrine in the sphere governed by Stalinist functionaries has been presented as a theory of socialist realism. It is the task of the writer, it is claimed, to provide "a truthful, historico-concrete portrayal of reality in *its revolutionary development*";[39] but yet "the truthfulness and the historical concretization of the artistic portrayal must take into account the problem of *ideological transformation* and *the education* of the workers in the spirit of Socialism."[40] In order to justify these political postulates, the official commentators and apologists, among whom even such intelligent minds as Georg Lukács were occasionally found, refer as a rule to Marx, Engels, Lenin, Belinsky, and the lesser lights of Communist aesthetics; and the argument is regularly concluded with the demonstration that social revolution has always been in the most intimate alliance with realistic literature, which concentrates its messages into a literary type. The massive argumentation of the official critics necessarily directs attention away from an inner paradox: how realism, as an accurate portrait of historically shaped reality, is to be linked to the yet-to-be-realized postulates of socialism. There arises a confusion of ideas that can only be resolved by appeal to the elusive idea of the dialectic.

In Marx's works one seeks in vain for sustained remarks about realism in literature or in the visual arts. One may well doubt whether a serious and thoroughly conservative connoisseur who named Aeschylus, Shakespeare, and Goethe as his favorite authors would have been able to feel much appreciation for the realism of the late nineteenth century; even if Marx thought highly of Balzac, about whose realism critics disagree, it is difficult to speak of Marx *and* Engels in one breath as the ancestors of a theory of socialist realism. Marx had nothing in common with a "socialist" or any other kind of realism; he did not even use the word.

It is Engels alone whom the official apologists can burden with the responsibility of having inspired a discussion of literary realism in intimate connection with the question of social tendencies in the work of art. But even here his responsibility does not go beyond mere occasional suggestions. Engels never even remotely suggested that he regarded realism as the only fruitful method of art; even less did it occur to the onetime admirer of Börne and Gutzkow to proclaim realism as the only permissible mode of proletarian literature. One seeks in vain in Engels' important theoretical writings for a systematic exposition of these problems; it seems that he occupied himself with the question of realism and the problem of tendentious art not out of theoretical interest, but out of pure politeness. More than once it happened that Engels, in his function as the grand old man of the radical movement after Marx's death in 1883, was obliged to occupy himself with new books and pamphlets that writers of his acquaintance and ambitious friends sent to him. This was so in the case of the two radical writers Minna Kautsky (1837–1912) and Margret Harkness, whose new novels Engels provided with well-meant criticism. Engels would have been impolite not to thank the ladies, with whom he was on friendly terms, for sending him their books or not to add a few words of personal criticism; Mrs. Kautsky was the mother of Karl Kautsky, who studied in London and worked as Engels' private secretary; Miss Harkness, who lived in the same house as Engels, could lay claim to the privileges of a neighbor.

After Minna Kautsky had visited her son Karl and his young wife in London and had taken the occasion to meet Engels as well, she sent him, in the fall of 1885, her recent book *The Old and the New* (*Die Alten und die Neuen*). She knew that Engels was not unacquainted with her earlier novel *Stefan von Grillenhof* (1881), in which she had attacked the Austrian clergy and praised Darwinism as a social panacea. The novel, *The Old and the New,* in which Mrs. Kautsky endeavored to draw attention to the class conflicts of modern Austria, was quite appropriate to the political program of the Social Democrats. But her idiom took the edge off her socialist outrage; it seemed to be derived exclusively from the hardly proletarian style of the popular middle-class magazine *Die Gartenlaube* ("suite of chambers," "virginal form," "tasteful traveling habit"). But it could not have escaped Engels that this book, an awkward mixture of kitsch and pamphlet, drew the first literary portrait of his deceased friend Marx. At the beginning of her plot (which she concluded, clumsily enough, with a sudden mountain slide), Mrs. Kautsky introduced the imposing figure of the economist Marr, who, on his return to Europe from England, devoted himself completely to his studies and "the ancient classics."[41] Marr's "mighty head with the silver-white mane flowing about it"[42] clearly proved whom Mrs. Kautsky had in mind.

Though Engels did not touch at all upon questions of literary realism in his letter of thanks to Mrs. Kautsky, his remarks upon the problem of tendentiousness in art are of symptomatic importance. Engels sternly asserted that a writer is wrong to side openly with a partisan cause. The late Engels was distinctly averse to explicit partisan bias: although he characterized Aeschylus, Aristophanes, Dante, Cervantes, Schiller, and "the modern Russians and Norwegians" (thinking, no doubt, of Tolstoy and Ibsen) as "tendentious writers,"[43] he distinguished—as in his interpretation of Balzac—in principle between an overt and a latent political attitude with a clear preference for the latter. Political postulates, declared Engels, must not be the superficial concern of the work of art; they must rather "arise out of the situation and action itself, without express reference being made to them";[44] the writer must not feel moved by his political enthusiasm "to hand his reader the future historical solution to the social conflicts he describes."[45] Engels explained his sympathy for political partisanship that was hidden only in the depths of the work of art by reference to the necessities of the class conflict. Since the modern novel found its public above all in bourgeois circles, an open confession of belief on the part of the radical writer would only frighten away the potential readers of the book. It was therefore necessary to conceal the political message in order to attract the bourgeois reader to the book and then, with a single blow, destroy "the . . . prevailing conventional illusions" and shake "the optimism of the bourgeois world."[46] The political time bomb hidden in the depths of the aesthetic structure should not explode until the work of art had found access to the bourgeois sphere; not until then could it fulfil its destructive task.

The aesthetic success of such a novel, in Engels' view, is determined by the art with which the writer delineates his characters and the social contrasts they represent. Although Engels had much to criticize in the character of Arthur, the all too virtuous hero of *The Old and the New,* he praises Minna Kautsky's "familiar sharp individualization of the characters."[47] Engels' courtesy here triumphs over his critical judgment: "each one," he says of Minna Kautsky's figures, "is a type, but at the same time a definite individual person, a *'Dieser,'* as old Hegel expressed it."[48]

The reference to Hegel proves once again how often Engels' aesthetic conceptions were determined by the concept of the "concrete universal," or derived from Hegel's spiritual principle crystallizing itself in sensory semblance. In this Hegelian concept of the successful literary character Engels agrees closely with Hippolyte Taine, another late disciple of Hegel. In his study *L'idéal dans l'art* (1865), Taine demands of the writer that he create representative figures (*caractères*) who unfold their spiritual essence to the reader in sensory form.[49] In his recommendations to Mrs. Kautsky Engels does not, in any case, go beyond those Hegelian postulates he had professed almost thirty years earlier in his letter to Lassalle (1859).

Engels sketched his conception of realism, not to Mrs. Kautsky, but in the draft of a letter with which he thanked Margret Harkness for sending him her new novel, *A City Girl* (1887).[50] It was hardly very tactful to measure the modest effort of the

Englishwoman against the mighty achievement of Balzac, as Engels did; the tone of the letter also indicated that Engels was in much less agreement with the assumptions of her story than with Mrs. Kautsky's Social Democratic principles. In her little book, Miss Harkness tells the story of the poor, blond seamstress Nelly Ambrose, who toils to support herself and her rowdy brother with piecework. To be sure, she longs to marry her shy admirer George, a former soldier, as soon as he succeeds in getting a better job; meanwhile he must earn his weary bread as janitor and lamplighter in one of the gloomy London tenements. During a Sunday walk, Nelly and George meet their friend Jack Strange, who in turn introduces them to Arthur Grant, a self-satisfied intellectual who speaks in the radical workers' clubs. Although the wily Grant is married and the father of two children, he pursues charming Nelly, hoping for an affair. He easily succeeds in beguiling her; he takes her to the theater, where the poor innocent is overwhelmed by the unaccustomed magnificence, and charms her with a courtesy that conceals his dark purposes. On a weekend excursion to Kew the inevitable occurs: Nelly yields to Arthur, who revels arrogantly in his new role as seducer. Poor Nelly finds herself with child, but as she is about to confront the cause of her ruin in his own house, she glimpses through the rain-spattered windows a touching picture of Arthur's family happiness, which she, in noble self-sacrifice, cannot destroy. Hungry and unemployed, abandoned by family and friends, the pregnant Nelly finds help from Captain Lobe, an energetic officer of the Salvation Army, who finds her shelter and work with which she can support herself and her child in honor. Just as everything seems to be showing a turn for the better, Nelly's child falls ill. When Nelly appears at the hospital to see her child, she is shown the empty bed; Nelly breaks down, recognizing the secretary of the hospital who is bending over her as none other than her seducer Arthur Grant. After this last trial comes a happier dawn for Nelly: her admirer George reappears, forgives her magnanimously, and the couple lives happily ever after. Once again love and the generosity of the English Salvation Army have won the victory over a world of baseness, humiliation, and want.

Miss Harkness insisted on calling her tale, in which she gives the traditional epic *topos* of seduced innocence a proletarian twist, "A Realistic Story." Following contemporary usage, she claimed that her book would throw light upon the life of the poorer classes with exact faithfulness of detail and portray those sad and outrageous things that the strict conventions of the Victorian novel of manners had kept from the reader's view. But it was just this subtitle that Engels took as the starting point of his criticism. Engels declared that Miss Harkness' story was "not quite realistic enough."[51] "Realism, to my mind, implies," he said, "besides truth of detail, the truthful reproduction of typical characters under typical circumstances."[52] Engels did not object to the representation of the individual characters; with a polite compliment, he even called the figure of the complacent intellectual, Arthur Grant, "a masterpiece."[53] But he did not at all agree with the representation of the typical circumstances of the London proletariat: "the circumstances which surround them [the characters] and make them act are not perhaps equally [typical]."[54] Engels had political doubts about the image of the London proletariat as Miss Harkness had drawn it. The helpless, inactive mass of individuals misled by ministers or in need of the Salvation Army's help did not seem to him at all like those pugnacious descendants of the Chartists whose political rise he believed he had followed since the first fiery proclamations of Thomas Carlyle. In Miss Harkness' story, Engels pointed out,

> the working class figures as a passive mass, unable to help itself and not even making any attempt at striving to help itself. All attempts to drag it out of its torpid misery come from without, from above. Now if this was a correct description about 1800 or 1810, in the days of Saint-Simon and Robert Owen, it cannot appear so in 1887 to a man who for nearly fifty years has had the honour of sharing in most of the fights of the militant proletariat. The rebellious reaction of the working class against the oppressive medium which surrounds them . . . at recovering their status as human beings, belong to history and must therefore lay claim to a place in the domain of realism.

One might well ask in passing whether Engels' theoretical arguments were not a good deal over Miss Harkness' head. There seems to be little common ground between Engels' typological concept and the conventional, sentimental, and melodramatic realism that characterized the novels of Miss Harkness and of some of her contemporaries. But the difference in usage of the term "realism" is of considerable importance for more recent Communist literary doctrine; the question must be approached, first of all, by way of a brief survey of the development of those ideas that contributed to the definition of the typical in literature as the later nineteenth century understood it. It can only be examined and judged from the perspective of the history of ideas.

Every concept of type[55] derives primarily from an originally theological tradition, which, presuming a divine order of the universe, interprets particular figures and events of the Old Testament as prefigurations of future realities of salvation (Rom. 5:14; I Pet. 2:21). Thus the faithful Abraham appears as a prefiguration of the Christian (Gal. 3:9); Melchizedek, of the priestly office of Christ (Heb. 7:15); the serpent in the wilderness, of the Son of Man on the Cross (John 3:14). As Erich Auerbach points out in his Dante studies,[56] the typological method of interpretation goes back to pre-Christian rabbinical traditions of Messianic expectation, unfolds powerfully in primitive Christianity, and permeates the whole Middle Ages in theological doctrine, liturgical symbolism, iconographic representation, and literary associations. Even in the age of the Enlightenment, Johann David Michaelis made a final attempt to defend the method in his *Draft of a Typological Theology* (*Entwurf einer typischen Gottesgelehrtheit* [1752]), whereas Christoph Semler in his *Essay toward a Freer Mode of Theological Instruction* (*Versuch einer freieren theologischen Lehrart* [1777]) tried to exclude typology from the area of true religion. Basically, however, the secularization of typology had progressed irresistibly since the Renaissance: the theologian Herder, in a theoretical essay on the fable (1801), characterizes its figures as "living, continuing, eternal types who stand before us and teach us" (XXIII, 253 [B. Suphan ed.]).

Similarly, the concept of type appears in the work of Schelling and Friedrich Schlegel as an aesthetic idea of purely human possibilities; from Schlegel's work it was transferred into the literary theory of France by Charles Nodier (1780–1844) and turns up, in the age of Taine, in Victor Hugo's *Shakespeare* (1864). "A type," declared Hugo, "is a lesson which is man, a myth with a human face so plastic that it looks at you . . . an idea which is nerve, muscle or flesh."[57] Although the concept of the type has here been removed from the area of theology to that of aesthetics, it has lost none of its ancient prophetic and inspirational character.

A second tradition flowing into the more recent literary concept of the type can be followed back to Theophrastus' *Characters.* Casaubon's Lyons edition (1592) raised the "character" to a fashionable European prose genre. La Bruyère (1645–96) and Vauvenargues (1715–47) developed it in France; and Hall (1574–1656), Overbury (1581–1613), and Butler (1612–80) in England, where it survived long afterward in the portraits of the *Tatler* (1709–11) and the *Spectator* (1711–12), which were directly dependent upon La Bruyère and which, in turn, had a strong influence upon Gottsched (1700–1766) and the beginnings of German journalism. In the dramaturgical theory of the new bourgeois play, Diderot defined his own, theatrical version of Theophrastus' "character" by demanding that the modern playwright must compass concrete situations of life in representative figures (*conditions*) and stress appropriately their dependence on the social and even on the economic element. Lessing concerned himself with this problem in the ninety-fifth section of his *Hamburger Dramaturgie* (1768).

For the formation of the literary concept of the type in the later nineteenth century, however, a third tradition—the scientific—is of decisive importance. In the absence of more detailed studies, I can only put forward the hypothesis that important aspects of the modern literary concept of type correspond to those principles of classification elaborated by the advancing science of the late eighteenth and early nineteenth centuries. To the mind of the early nineteenth century, the basic classifications of the scientifically ordered world were brilliantly exemplified in Georges-Louis Leclerc Buffon's *Histoire naturelle, générale et particulière* (1749–89) and in Georges Cuvier's *La règne animal distribué d'après son organisation* (1817), to which an *Atlas représentant les types de tous les genres* was added. But Buffon and Cuvier stand only at the beginning of an extraordinarily complex development: Goethe in his osteological studies occupied himself, in his own particular way, with the type that he saw in his mind's eye;[58] Schiller spoke of the type in a botanical, Humboldt in a geographical, and Oken in a mineralogical, sense.[59] The more seriously the age concerned itself with the question of objective classification of natural reality, the more clearly the concept of the typical emerges as a topic of literary discussion; the writer who intends to comprehend the whole of society necessarily reaches for a category, the usefulness of which in creating order had been brilliantly proven by the example of natural science. The most famous attempt to use scientific categories for literary control over social reality appears in Balzac's Foreword (1842) to his *Comédie humaine*.[60] Balzac confessed that his great undertaking arose from his plan to compare the realm of men and of animals ("une comparaison entre l'humanité et l'animalité");[61] he points out that there are differences between particular groups of men, such as between soldiers and workers, which are just as great as those between lions and foxes. Buffon, Balzac says, fortunately succeeded in representing the totality of the natural realm in a single work; why should the writer hesitate for his part to comprehend the whole of human society in a single overwhelming labor? Although Balzac does not overlook the difficulties that necessarily arise from the application of a zoölogical concept to literary material, he insists upon creating human types that combine various distinguishing qualities of several homogeneous characters ("en composant des types par la réunion des traits de plusieurs caractères homogènes").[62] In the age of Balzac, the literary idea of the type dominated criticism of the novel; in the sixties of the last century it became a literary cliché. It appears simultaneously (to name only a few) in Dickens

and in the prose of Annette von Droste-Hülshoff, in the correspondence of Dostoevsky and Goncharov, in the works of Hippolyte Taine and Gottfried Keller, and in the novels of Theodor
Fontane and Henry James.[63]

The popularity that the literary concept of the type enjoyed in
the epoch of realism should not, however, be allowed to obscure
the fact that in this ubiquitous word theological, literary, and
scientific traditions often fuse in a peculiar way; the result is a
labile balance of the elements. Where the theological model pre-
ponderates, the type will imply a prophetic and normative element; a more scientific temperament will aim at the sober description of experienced reality. The two concepts of type are differentiated by the criterion of time: the type in the theological
sense points from a still imperfect present to the perfection of
future fulfilments, or, in the language of Aristotle's poetics, to
"things as they ought to be";[64] the scientifically colored concept
of the type is satisfied with the representative example of what
is already existent, of "things as they are."[65] Out of this dual concept of the type, a dual concept of realism results: on the one
hand, a scientific view, which endeavors to express observations of
a world existing independently of consciousness; on the other
hand, an ultimately theological conception of "realism," which in
an age of secular values turns into ideology, or an a priori vision
of what the future world order ought to be. A scientifically oriented realism will always appeal to the actual world of experience,
whereas the ideologically defined "realism" looks to the potential
as its true realm.

The conflict between the theological and the scientific implications of the modern literary concept of the type appears clearly in
the novels of George Sand (1804–76) and in the critical objections Vissarion Belinsky (1811–48) brought to bear against the
attempts to justify the novels theoretically. As early as 1832 George
Sand spoke of her Indiana as the type of a woman in whose heart
all the passions suppressed by society flowed together.[66] But Indiana was not the only exaggerated character offered by George
Sand to her European public. The idealization of her representa-

tive heroes raised much critical protest; in 1851 she found herself forced to defend explicitly her conception of the literary character she called a type. Her apology concentrated upon her novel *Le compagnon du tour de France* (1840) and its hero, Pierre Huguenin, an extraordinarily virtuous and educated craftsman, whom George Sand presented as her chief witness, as it were, for the validity of her theory of the novel. Although she had not intended to flatter the working masses, she declared, still her Pierre Huguenin was "un type d'ouvrier."[67] The novel as a genre was by no means "la peinture de ce qui est."[68] Following her own concept of realism, she defined her idealized figures as embodiments of man as he should be ("tel que je crois qu'il doit être"),[69] or as she wished he were ("tel que je souhaite qu'il soit").[70] It was not surprising that George Sand angered her skeptical critics. Especially in Russia she found little appreciation for her theory of type; in a country in which every literary critic was painfully aware of unsolved social problems, the idealistic exaggeration of representative characters, who so obviously transcended social reality, necessarily met resistance. No less a critic than Vissarion Belinsky declared in his "Survey of Russian Literature for the Year 1847" that his concept of the type deviated from that of George Sand. Despite his enthusiasm for the social pathos of the French authoress, he criticized her work as being "a mixture of novel and fairy tale"; she created "fantastic characters" and combined literature with ideological rhetoric.[71] In other words, Belinsky (on this occasion) clung to the concept of the type as a model representation of experience, whereas George Sand, more devoted to her visions than to the facts, used the type to indicate an ideal image of man. Belinsky demanded a realism that describes conditions; George Sand defended the reality of her utopian norm.

Belinsky's criticism of George Sand (1847) anticipated Engels' objections to Miss Harkness (1887). Curiously enough, the theoretical positions are diametrically opposite: contrary to all expectations, the Victorian bluestocking is of one mind with the radical Belinsky; Engels, on the other hand, proceeds from the theoretical presuppositions of George Sand. Obviously Engels, like the French authoress forty years before him, was aiming at a dogmatic conception that would compress the raw material of reality into a form of the typical predetermined by partisan considerations. Only for this reason could Engels claim that Miss Harkness' "realistic story" was not "realistic enough"; he meant to say that the *realia* represented by her did not conform to the realities postulated by his ideology. Without realizing it, Engels returned to the most ancient traditions and revived the theological concept of type in his own way; he, too, demanded from the writer the image of the desirable man—*tel qu'il doit être;* and thus his conservative followers, in a central concept of their official aesthetics, return to exactly that point where Messianic expectation, centuries before Christ, began to unfold its typology of future truth.

Engels as a Revisionist?

"Yesterday at noon," Engels reported to his friend F. A. Sorge on March 15, 1883, "I came to [Marx's] house. . . . Everybody was in tears, the end seemed to be coming. I inquired, tried to find out, to give consolation. A small hemorrhage, a sudden collapse had set in. Our good old Lenchen, who took care of him like a mother for her child, went up, and came down again; he was half-asleep, I could come along. When we entered, he lay there sleeping never again to wake. Pulse and breathing were gone. In those two minutes he had passed away quietly and painlessly."[72] A few days later Karl Marx, who had survived his beloved Jenny by only fifteen months, was buried in Highgate Cemetery in London.

Marx had passed the last years of his life in scholarly seclusion. After the failure of the First International (1864–72), Marx returned to his economic studies; he did not give up hope of being able to finish further sections of *Capital.* But his advancing illness frustrated his plans. Engels, who had worked with him since the summer of 1844, rather suspected what would happen after the death of his friend. "The local experts and the little talents, if not the swindlers," he wrote one day after Marx's death to Sorge, "will get a free hand. Well—we've got to scrape through, what else are we here for?"[73]

After Marx's death, it became the task of Engels to pursue questions of Marxist theory that still required clarification and to explain the ideas of his friend in personal commentaries to a growing number of interested disciples. From this period come Engels' numerous popularizations of Marxist theory and his spirited polemical writings against the second generation of opponents. But at that time, in the period of the rapid growth of the Social Democratic parties, literary questions were not in the center of interest; and Engels treated them mainly, as he had already done in the cases of Minna Kautsky and Miss Harkness, in his lively correspondence. Five of these communications are of decisive importance for the interpretation of Marxist literary doctrine; they are the comments to Conrad Schmidt (August 5, 1890), the warnings to the young writer Paul Ernst (June 5, 1890), two further letters to Joseph Bloch and Conrad Schmidt (September 21 and October 27, 1890), and finally the communication to young Hans Starkenburg (January 25, 1894), in which Engels appears as a judicious critic of early Marxist theory. Even the chronology of these communications is of some importance here: the sequence of the letters itself indicates that as time went by Engels moved farther and farther away from the strict principles of economic determinism; and it seems that he was on the way to a philosophical position that would provide a new place for the independent intellect when his death ended the development for good and all.

Although Engels' letter to Conrad Schmidt (August 5, 1890) does not suggest any new concepts of literary theory, it does provide important methodological suggestions. Engels warns the younger generation not to confuse the ideas of his deceased friend, to whom he ascribes in retrospect a rather tolerant sensibility, with the rigid dogmatism of Hegelian philosophy. Marx's theories, Engels stresses, are to be used merely as a "guide to study,"[74] by no means as a crude "lever"[75] for ideological constructions out of touch with historical and social realities. The younger generation must begin anew to study devotedly individual phenomena in their characteristic elements: "All history must be studied anew," wrote Engels; "the conditions of existence in the various forms of society must be investigated individually before one attempts to derive from them the political, legal, aesthetic, philosophical, religious, and so on, ways of viewing things that correspond to them."[76] The concept of the correspondence between intellect and the material basis intimated here shows how closely Engels was still bound to Marx's ideas as expressed in the Preface to the *Critique of Political Economy* (1859). The principles remain untouched; only the strictness of application becomes progressively relaxed.

How much the younger generation of Marxists needed advice and instructive hints appears from Engels' trenchant warnings to Paul Ernst (1866–1933), the later defender of a classical theater and the conservative German empire. Ernst wrote to Engels in connection with a series of articles on Scandinavian questions in the *Freie Bühne für das moderne Leben,* which were of paradigmatic importance for the young Naturalists of that time. On March 12, 1890, the journal published a first article, signed by L. Marholm, on "The Woman in Scandinavian Literature," in which the author expressed the astonishing opinion that the emancipation movement in the north had long since come to an end, for August Strindberg, "the thinking mind among the best in the coming generation,"[77] had demonstrated in his bitter plays and inexorable novels that the elementary nature of women instinctively denies the ideas of emancipation. In his youthful radicalism, Ernst felt himself obliged to give L. Marholm the appropriate Marxist answer; in his reply of May 14, 1890,[78] entitled "The Question of Women and the Social Question," he defended the view that the " 'elemental' in woman"[79] was not essential for an understanding of the shipwreck of emancipation; the problem could be explained "very simply . . . out of the social aspect of the petty-bourgeois class situation."[80] According to Paul Ernst's view, the emancipation movement was only "a phase in the last-ditch battle of a disappearing class";[81] the movement's problems were to be solved by the progress of industrial production, which would destroy the psychological differences between the sexes, quickly, "without ink and paper."[82]

Ernst's economic determinism aroused the Viennese critic Hermann Bahr to a sharp and intelligent rejoinder. Hermann Bahr's condemnation of Ernst on May 28, 1890, was not relieved by any politeness; even the title of his contribution, "The Epigones of Marxism,"[83] indicated what he thought of Ernst's intellectual accomplishment. The young radical reaped unmitigated scorn; Bahr called him one of those "wise would-be Marxes" (*weise Gerne-Märxe*)[84] who presume to apply economic theories in a completely mechanical manner to the most difficult questions and transform Marxism "from a critical method for ordering experience" into a "dogmatic axiom as a substitute for experience."[85] In a merciless metaphor, which has lost little of its validity, Bahr compared the young Marxists to a tin vending machine: "As soon as one deposits the shabbiest ten-penny question in the top, unfailingly a long chapter of Marxist wisdom comes out the bottom; a first-rate, reliable mechanism that never fails."[86]

When Ernst found himself so sharply attacked in the most important organ of the young German avant-garde, he appealed to Engels for a public statement that he could use in his argument with Bahr. The young writer was doubtless not a little surprised when Engels, though very politely, took Bahr's side and added some serious warnings to the latter's scorn. "So far as your attempt to treat the matter materialistically is concerned," wrote Engels with almost fatherly calm, "I must say above all that the materialistic method turns into its opposite when it is not used as a guide to historical study but rather as a prefabricated pattern according to which one adjusts the historical facts. . . ."[87] Engels flatly refused to assist Ernst with a declaration against Bahr; not only did he want to avoid a quarrel with the influential Viennese critic, but it appeared to him much too questionable to defend a young radical who had degraded the ideas of his late friend into a rigid dogma. "If Herr Bahr thinks he has caught you on this wrong track," Engels added in his letter of June 5, 1890, "he seems to me to have a little shadow of right on his side."[88]

Engels was not content to urge the younger generation merely to study the Marxist canon. The more penetrating the questions he had to answer, and the more concrete the problems raised by the younger people, the more inclined he felt to combine the old theories with new observations, whose judicious flexibility contrast with the polemic rigidity of earlier years. He was aware of the difficulties he invited by doing this; from time to time he even admitted that he and Marx had not been without fault in the dogmatism and one-sidedness of their earlier formulations. In the heat of controversy they had had to defend above all else the "denied main principle" and had not always had an opportunity "to do justice to the remaining . . . elements."[89] But Engels underestimated the gulf that separated his later interpretations from the formulations of the forties and fifties: he thought he was talking about only a more sensitive application of the immutable principles of dialectical materialism, whereas the implications of his interpretations were clearly beginning to erode the absolute primacy of economics in human affairs. This is to be seen for the first time in his letter to Joseph Bloch (September 21, 1890); unquestionably Engels introduced concepts into this discussion that contradict in many ways the theories Marx put forward in the Preface to his *Critique of Political Economy.*

> According to the materialistic view of history, production and reproduction are *ultimately* the determining element in history in real life. . . . But now if someone twists that around to mean that the economic element is the *only* determining one, then he transforms that proposition into a meaningless, abstract, absurd phrase. The economic situation is the basis, but the various elements of the superstructure—political forms of the class struggle and its results, constitutions established by the victorious class after the battle has been won, and so on—legal forms—and even the reflexes of all these real struggles in the minds of those taking part in them, political, legal, philosophical theories, religious ideas and their further development into systems of dogma—also have their effect upon the course of the historical struggles and in many cases predominantly determine their *form*. It is a mutual interaction of all these elements, in which, finally, through all

the infinite number of accidents (that is, of things and events whose inner connection to each other is so distant or so indemonstrable that we can disregard it as not present) the economic movement wins through by necessity.[90]

This explanation immediately raises a series of questions. First of all, it is surprising that Engels noticeably reduces the importance of the economic elements. Although they may be "ultimately" of importance, they seem robbed of their absolute hegemony. Any other assertion, Engels stresses, would be "meaningless, abstract, absurd. . . ." Meanwhile Engels ignores the fact that the *Deutsche Ideologie* (1845) as well as the *Critique of Political Economy* (1859) took a most rigorously economic position; here, in his late commentary, Engels wants the younger generation to believe that the dogmas of earlier years were only excusable hyperboles that had arisen out of the tensions of the philosophical situation at that time.

In his letter of September 21, 1890, Engels in all seriousness tries to propose a new ordering of the relationship between the economic basis and the intellectual superstructure. This proposal can hardly be brought into harmony with the earlier rigid conception. Marx was interested above all in the components of the economic basis, for example, in "the particular stage of development of the material productive forces" and the "necessary relationships of production"; a generation later Engels neglects this outline of the economic basis and turns his whole attention to the intellectual superstructure. There he distinguishes four clearly defined levels: (1) primary political forms, such as the class struggle; (2) secondary elements, such as legal forms; (3) "the reflexes" of the conflict "in the minds of those taking part in it"; and finally, (4) the "further development" of these reflexes to "complete systems of dogma." In contrast to Marx, Engels thus unfolds in the intellectual superstructure a finely organized system of differentiated spheres; and he attempts to replace the compact chaos of the superstructure as it appears in earlier explanations with a surprisingly structured order that in each of its fields possesses a certain undeniable autonomy.

A third important divergence from earlier formulations appears in Engels' clear effort to define the relationship of economics and intellect through a new concept of mutual interaction. Where Marx was satisfied with the plain linear dependence of the superstructure upon the economic foundation, the late Engels limits the effect of the economic forces and postulates at the same time the possible effectiveness of the intellectual epiphenomenon. There is little philosophical continuity between Marx's formulations in the *Critique of Political Economy* and Engels' explanations in his late correspondence; two diverging ontological sketches of reality stand opposed to one another in sharp distinction.

Engels expands his concept of a relative mutual interaction between matter and intellect in what is certainly a decisive step, by admitting that a whole series of elements that escape a strictly scientific determination of causal connection have a part in this process. Even Marx in his fragmentary Introduction (1857) was disturbed by similar questions; he too was obliged to note that the questions of the "justification of accident" and of "freedom and other things as well" needed to be more thoroughly examined. Thirty-three years later Engels found himself forced to declare that in its analysis of reality dialectical materialism must take into consideration an "infinite number of accidents." Once again there is a hesitant glance in the direction of a world of nuance, of indeterminability, of freedom.

In similar passages in his correspondence Engels breaks down the theory of economic determinism in a series of concrete examples that prove the determining force of the state, of the legal administration, of the intellectual tradition—in short, of the superstructure. Among other things, Engels examines the economic development of prehistoric society and indicates that it was partly determined by the false conceptions of nature held by man at that time.[91] Even if such arguments might be doubted from the standpoint of modern anthropology, they demonstrate clearly that the linear theory of exclusive economic causation of culture was in the process of disintegration. Even the terms "superstructure" and "foundation" begin to lose their specific meanings.

The progressive collapse of the rigid theory becomes still clearer in another letter to Conrad Schmidt (October 27, 1890). Although Engels here too clings to economic forces as the ultimate factor, their effect appears suddenly limited, reduced, and transformed by the specific laws inhering in the individual levels of the organized superstructure. A new "level theory" of the intellectual superstructure, to which Engels begins to incline more and more, is here clearly sketched.

> . . . In France as well as in Germany, philosophy, like the general flourishing of literature in that time was also [!] a result of the economic upsurge. The ultimate supremacy of the economic development over even these areas I am convinced of, but it takes place within the conditions prescribed by the individual area itself: in philosophy, for example, through the effect of economic influences (which usually have an effect only in their political, and so on, disguise) upon the existing philosophical material provided by previous philosophers. The economy does not create anything here *a novo*, but it determines the kind of change and continuation of the existing ideas, and that too for the most part indirectly, insofar as it is the political, legal, and moral reflexes that exercise the greatest direct effect upon philosophy.[92]

This interpretation is based upon two basic assumptions that limit the theoretical validity of economic determinism. Engels admits that in every moment of human history there exists a level of intellectual traditions removed from the area of economic forces. Even if Marx expressed similar doubts in his Introduction of 1857, he could never bring himself to allow any artistic phenomenon other than the Greek a quality of timelessness. Engels here goes a step further: for him not only the Greek tradition of art is removed from the *direct* confines of formative economic forces but every intellectual tradition whatsoever. The economic impulses are incapable of creating *new* intellectual phenomena; they are merely able to determine *changes* and *continuations* of intellectual traditions. This reduction of the economic aspect is supported by Engels' new conception of reality as a richly complex cosmos of differentiated spheres of an intellectual and economic kind, in which complexity triumphs once more over the linear differentiation of matter and intellect. In this newly conceived hierarchy of being, there is a direct contact, a possibility of effectiveness, only between those levels immediately bounding on one another, for example, economics and politics. Only between these directly adjacent areas can a process of undisturbed, one-sided determination arise; between two spheres of reality that are farther apart an unmediated, linear effect is not possible. These levels that are farther from one another are separated by a whole series of intermediate spheres, which do indeed permit the formative impulses to pass through them, but subject these impulses, following their own law of being, to significant transformations. It follows, therefore, that the sphere of literature remains basically inaccessible to the concentrated forces of economics. Before the economic impulses can have a formative effect upon the sphere of literature, they must make their way through intermediate levels that do not leave them unchanged; their effect "takes place within the conditions prescribed by the individual area itself." No further proof is required that here strict economic determinism is replaced by a complicated conception of a hierarchically structured world that seems to suggest, even though quite remotely, an Aristotelian image of the universe.

Engels' letter to the young writer Hans Starkenburg applies the new results arising from the radical devaluation of economic determination to literary questions. Unfortunately Starkenburg's original letter to Engels seems to have been lost; since neither Franz Mehring nor the Russian editor of the *Gesamtausgabe* quotes its contents, the direction in which Starkenburg's questions must have moved can only be deduced approximately from Engels' answer. It may be assumed that these questions were aimed at Hippolyte Taine's literary theory; it is in any case surprising how many of Taine's key concepts turn up in Engels' declaration and are there given their importance for Marxist doctrine. On January 25, 1894, in one of his very last letters, Engels defines the bases of Marxist cultural doctrine in the following way:

By the economic relationships that we view as the determining basis for the history of society, we understand the
manner by which men of a particular society produce their
sustenance and exchange their products among one another.
. . . Included further among the economic relationships are
the geographical base upon which they occur and the actually inherited remains of earlier economic stages of development that have survived, often only through tradition or
vis inertiae, naturally also the milieu surrounding this form
of society on the outside. We see the economic determinants
as the factors ultimately determining the historical development. But race itself is an economic factor. . . .

The political, legal, philosophical, religious, literary, and
so on, development is based upon the economic. But they all
react upon one another and upon the economic basis. It is
not so that the economic situation is *cause, active by itself
alone,* and all the rest only passive effect. Rather it is mutual
interaction based upon economic necessity that always real-
izes itself ultimately. . . . The further the area we are investigating is removed from the economic sphere and approaches
that of purely abstract ideology, the more we will find that
it shows accidentals in its development, and the more its
curve will run in a zigzag. But if you draw the mean axis of
the curve, you will find that the longer the period in question and the larger the area under consideration, the more
closely this axis will approach *the curve* of the economic
development.[93]

In this communication Engels concerns himself with three of
Taine's central concepts ("geographical base," "surrounding
milieu," "race"). It seems probable that Starkenburg's questions
forced Engels to confront his own doctrine with that of Taine;
here, for a fleeting moment, that rare point is reached where the
literary doctrine of Marxism meets that other, more ambitious
doctrine of determination of literature produced by the later nineteenth century.

In his many studies, Hippolyte Taine proceeded from the axiom
that a serious scientific investigation would reveal those forces
from which art arises and by means of which can be exhaustively

explained. Like Herder a century and a half before, Taine was fascinated by the biological metaphor of organic growth: the work of art grew—in the north like a poor moss, in the south like a magnificent oleander—out of a certain earth, a certain climate, a certain moment. Literary history was nothing other than "a kind of botany" applied to works of art. Taine avoided the dangers of the botanical analogy by the theoretical inconsistency with which he tried to describe the various causes of art in ever new ways: essentially he stressed that the origins and development of art were determined by an "aggregate" compounded of the *Zeitgeist* and the surrounding elements. Popular representations of his theories, which usually consider only his famous preface to his *Histoire de la littérature anglaise* (1863), restrict themselves to proclaiming the concepts *moment, milieu,* and *race* as the exclusive causes of creative achievement; in fact Taine began most of his studies with a look at the geographical region, the climate, and popular traditions. Nevertheless, his work is rich in complex attempts at interpretation going far beyond a naïve materialism to include political, philosophical, and religious motivations.

Engels' interest in Taine's concepts clearly avoids the element of time (*moment*). Seen from his own standpoint, Engels was perfectly right in ignoring this concept: in his stress upon the element of time he was of one opinion with Taine. It was no accidental philosophical agreement: the onetime Young Hegelian Engels postulated the importance of the specific moment for the emergence of a work of art just as axiomatically as Taine, who had probably taken his expression *moment* from his own translation of Hegel's *Philosophy of History*.[94] It seemed superfluous to the Hegelian Engels to go into this concept of Taine's any further. Engels' conception of race as a culturally determining factor, however, deviates significantly from Taine's. Taine uses *race* in an extremely indefinite way; he applies the same concept, without being aware of the contradictions, equally to linguistic, political, and national groups. For him—as for his less educated disciples in Nazi Germany—*race* was basically a mystical idea. Taine not infrequently postulates a community of blood and spirit; elsewhere he speaks, a little recklessly, of Germanic, French, or Gallic "races." Engels' concept of race, on the other hand, is thoroughly determined by economic elements; according to Engels' view, races are products of historical economic developments; that is, racial groups are formed by a united economic pressure. This concept of Engels' is older than might appear at first glance; even in his youthful work, *The Situation of the Working Classes in England (Die Lage der arbeitenden Klassen in England* [1845]), similar ideas turn up. Describing the rich and the poor of Lancashire, Engels speaks of the "two entirely different peoples,"[95] of which the Continental observer customarily sees only the more prosperous. In a later edition (1892) of the same work Engels added a footnote confirming this passage, in which he says he is in agreement with Disraeli (1804–81), who brought out the same fact in his novel *Sibyl, or the Two Nations* (1845). It would be irrelevant to raise the question which of the two—Engels or Disraeli—was the first to use this concept of economically formed groups of men; probably both of them took up a popular idea of that age, which appears also, for example, in W. C. Taylor's contemporary work, *Notes of a Tour in the Manufacturing Districts of Lancashire* (1842). Taylor points out that the "isolation of classes in England has gone so far [as] to divide us into nations as distinct as the Normans and the Saxons."[96]

In the development of Marxist theory Engels was not the only one who concerned himself with the concept of race as a culturally creative element. Marx, too, was plagued by occasional doubts as to whether race and other biological factors did not have a share in the formation of economic relations. In his Introduction of 1857, he notes briefly that a treatment of this question would have to take its "starting point" from the elements of "natural determinacy" (such as race and tribe);[97] in a somewhat isolated remark in *Capital* he adds that the productivity of human labor is bound up with natural determinants that in turn are "traceable" to the races of men and their natural surroundings.[98] Engels follows Marx's fragmentary discussion of the contemporary problem of race but distinctly rejects the supra-economic elements that Taine ascribed to this concept. But Engels was beginning to approach an ideological compromise with Taine in other respects. The late Engels is prepared to investigate the importance of the "geographical base" and the "surrounding milieu" and to stress their formative force. Once again factors are brought to bear that weaken the concept of economic determinism; the "economic" basis no longer consists of homogeneous economic elements but also includes geographical and organic aspects. Engels' thinking in his later period, as he suggests in his letter to Starkenburg, moved on a peculiar middle ground between the rigid dogma of the *Critique of Political Economy* (1859) and Taine's *Philosophie de l'art* (1865). Engels stands on materialist ground when he insists upon the decisive, if not exclusive, importance of economic determinants; however, he approaches Taine where he expressly expands the economic basis to include geographical and biological factors. To be sure, Engels maintains his distance from Taine by means of a last, decisive nuance in his thinking: Engels stubbornly continues to believe in the ultimate self-realization of the economic impulses, whereas Taine considers the economic element to be one of many elements in the "aggregate" that determines the development of the arts. This intermediate position, however, permits Engels to achieve important insights into the complexity of the intellectual sphere; in this regard he is significantly superior to both Marx and Taine. Marx concentrated his attention upon the economic bases of existence; Taine was no less determined to disregard the question of intellectual complexity and, strictly in the spirit of Hegel, to comprehend science, religion, and literature as manifestations of an originally identical creative impulse. In evident contrast to Marx and Taine, the late Engels stressed the variegated structure of the intellectual levels; the specific laws of the intellectual forms are of such independent force that they are even able to transform economic impulses.

As soon as we once again look over the whole of Engels' late correspondence as a contribution to Marxist literary doctrine, we inevitably become aware of the gulf that separates it from the rigid formulations of earlier years. In the *Deutsche Ideologie*

(1845), *The Communist Manifesto* (1848), and the Preface to the *Critique of Political Economy* (1859), an inflexible dogma of the linear dependence of the intellect upon economics appears; not until a generation later is the polemical but barren rigidity replaced by a more relaxed and tolerant constellation of ideas, which Engels, modestly enough, presents as a concrete interpretation of the inherited canon (1890–94). To be sure, it would be a simplification to ignore Marx's Introduction (1857), in which he himself emerges as the first critic of his inflexibility. But since he repudiated this fragment, which was not put before a wider public until Kautsky published it in 1902–3, it cannot be given a prominent place in the totality of nineteenth-century literary doctrine.

Engels' letters of his late years sketch a hierarchically ordered conception of economics and creative intellect. The economic basis seems to be expanded through the influence of Taine's concepts; the superstructure unfolds into a surprising complexity of intellectual fields. The relationship between foundation and superstructure is now characterized by the possibility of mutual interaction; moreover, this interaction is subject to the scientifically indeterminate effects of "a whole series of accidents." There is no longer a direct contact between more distant spheres; economics may exert its influence upon the neighboring area of politics, but it can no longer force the more distant sphere of literature directly under its tyranny. The more abstract fields of the superstructure are only lightly touched by economic impulses, which, in turn, are subjected to serious metamorphoses on their way through the intermediate levels. Undoubtedly the creative intellect acquires a new dignity: the higher its achievement rises above the economic basis, the more freely the laws of its own being will operate once more.

6

Three Interpretations: Shakespeare, Goethe, Balzac

Shakespeare

Marxist literary criticism of the thirties, in the West and in the East, complacently identifies itself with Shakespeare's supposed position on the side of the progressive demands of the fighting Renaissance bourgeoisie. "Shakespeare sided with . . . the commercial class," writes the American Donald Morrow in his pamphlet *Where Shakespeare Stood* (1935); "any play he wrote was a blow against feudal aspirations."[1] A. A. Smirnov's Russian essay on Shakespeare, which is available to the Western public in an English translation (1936), tries to avoid such a meaningless simplification by an apparently more realistic understanding of the complexity of artistic development. Smirnov stresses that even Shakespeare vacillated in his loyalty to the cause of the bourgeois class; even his allegiance was not free of flaws and suffered at times from the countercurrents of the age. The Soviet critic differentiates three periods in Shakespeare's career, each of which corresponds to a different social and economic element of the historical moment. In the first period (1590–1600), Shakespeare's work, in Smirnov's opinion, is permeated by a joyful optimism and a happy affirmation of life that still proclaims the organic harmony of all social groups; in his second period (1601–9), Shakespeare reflects the slow disintegration of Elizabethan society in somber tragedies; in the third period (1609–11), he finally feels himself forced by the anti-aristocratic tendencies of bourgeois Puritanism to make his peace with the aristocracy that supported the theater and thus he falls victim to the reactionary and royalist taste of his lords and patrons.[2]

Neither Morrow's coarse simplification nor Smirnov's all too neat division into periods can, however, be based upon source texts of Marxist literary criticism. In Marx's and Engels' written remarks upon Shakespeare one will look in vain for the slightest trace of economic determinism; there is not the faintest hint of how future Marxist critics are supposed to treat Shakespeare. That does not mean, of course, that Marx and Engels did not have their opinions about Shakespeare; all their lives they spoke of him with the same unchanging, ardent, completely non-political admiration. Basically they both were rooted so deeply in the German Shakespearean tradition that it never occurred to them for a moment to motivate their personal enthusiasm, shared with whole generations of German writers, with political or economic arguments.

The German admiration for Shakespeare reaches far back into eighteenth-century classicism. In his seventeenth *Literaturbrief* (1759), Lessing declared Shakespeare to be the true fulfilment of Aristotle: French tragedy had followed Aristotle only in its mechanical arrangement, whereas Shakespeare alone had understood Aristotle in his essence. The young men of the period of "storm and stress" chose Shakespeare (as their present descendants have selected Brecht) as a private symbol of their revolt against narrowness and the restriction of rules; and Gerstenberg's extreme enthusiasm for Shakespeare was a symptomatic predecessor of the attitude of Herder and the young Goethe. To the Romantics, Shakespeare appeared as the great "hieroglyphic" of literature: like Goethe, the author of *Wilhelm Meister*, Shakespeare, too, was the real prototype of all literary, indeed of all intuitive, possibilities of creative man. Hegel codified the preceding Shakespearean tradition in a strict system. In his *Lectures on Aesthetics* he followed the Romantic generation by judging Schiller skeptically and playing off Goethe and Shakespeare, both of whom had created works of genuine life and richness, against the literary Kantian. So powerful was the fascination Shakespeare exercised upon generations of German writers and critics that the very history of this spell—Gundolf's *Shakespeare and the German Spirit* (*Shakespeare und der deutsche Geist* [1911])—itself turned into a work of almost Shakespearean grandeur and breadth.

Marx and Engels moved completely within this traditional admiration for Shakespeare. Marx was fortunate enough to have enjoyed an early literary education by his paternal friend Ludwig von Westphalen, who had inherited his enthusiasm for the Briton from his Scottish mother and faithfully passed it on to his young friend. In later years Marx continued in Westphalen's footsteps. At times he occupied himself with Dr. Johnson's commentaries to the Shakespeare edition of 1765, prided himself on his ability to quote from memory, and passed on his delight in Shakespeare's works to his three studious daughters. Marx's son-in-law, Paul Lafargue (1842–1911), reports in his *Memoirs* that in Marx's household there was a real Shakespeare cult.[3] In this respect Engels could not be compared with his friend. In his writings important references to Shakespeare's tragedies are lacking; even *Timon of Athens*, which young Marx admired above all, was not mentioned by Engels with the same enthusiastic appreciation. Engels occasionally preferred lighter fare and very much enjoyed *The Merry Wives of Windsor*.

Shakespeare's name appears three times in the writings of Marx and Engels: first in Marx's *Economic-Philosophical Manuscripts* (*Ökonomisch-Philosophische Manuskripte* [1844]); a second time in the correspondence of both with Lassalle on the subject of *Franz von Sickingen* (1859); and a third and last time (1873) in the personal correspondence between Manchester and London. In his *Economic-Philosophical Manuscripts*, Marx refers to *Timon of Athens* in order to explicate his ideas about the characteristics and the social function of money. *Timon* is not a bad choice; in the scene Marx quotes, Timon wanders through the forests by the sea, hoping in his despair for restoration and consolation from the sun and nourishment from the virgin earth. His hopes are cruelly shattered: the earth provides him not with nourishment but with gold. Marx quotes the following lines from Timon's monologue:

> Gold? yellow, glittering, precious gold? No, gods,
> I am no idle votarist: roots, you clear heavens!
> Thus much of this will make black white, foul fair,
> Wrong right, base noble, old young, coward valiant.
> Ha, you gods! why this? what this, you gods? Why, this
> Will lug your priests and servants from your sides,
> Pluck stout men's pillows from below their heads:
> This yellow slave
> Will knit and break religions; bless the accurs'd;
> Make the hoar leprosy ador'd; place thieves,
> And give them title, knee, and approbation,
> With senators on the bench: this is it
> That makes the wappen'd widow wed again;
> She, whom the spital-house and ulcerous sores
> Would cast the gorge at, this embalms and spices
> To the April day again. Come, damned earth,
> Thou common whore of mankind, that putt'st odds
> Among the rout of nations, I will make thee
> Do thy right nature.
>
> (Act IV, scene 3, lines 26–44.)

In order to stress his theoretical standpoint more exactly, Marx also adds the following lines from the same scene and underscores certain key words that seem to him to be of particular importance.

> O thou sweet king-killer, and dear divorce
> 'Twixt natural son and sire! Thou bright defiler
> Of Hymen's purest bed! thou valiant Mars!
> Thou ever young, fresh, lov'd, and delicate wooer,
> Whose blush doth thaw the consecrated snow
> That lies on Dian's lap! thou *visible god*
> That *solder'st* close *impossibilities,*
> And mak'st them kiss! that speak'st with every tongue,
> To every purpose! O thou touch of hearts!

> Think thy slave, man, rebels; and by thy virtue
> *Set* them into confounding *odds*, that beasts
> May have the world in empire!
>
> (Act IV, scene 3, lines 384–95.)

"Shakespeare," Marx asserts, "particularly stresses two characteristics of money:

> 1. It is the visible god, the transformation of all human and natural qualities into their opposites, the general confusion and perversion of all things; it solders impossibilities.
>
> 2. It is the common whore of mankind, the common procurer of men and nations.[4]

In this short paraphrase of the quotation from Shakespeare, Marx actually continues his rudimentary discussion of economic alienation that he first initiated (possibly under the impact of Moses Hess) in the concluding passages of his deliberations *On the Jewish Question*. Early in 1844[5] he defined the cult of money as "Judaism"; and his use of the religious image of money as a powerful God and his stress on its power to transform clearly anticipated the central ideas of the *Economic-Philosophical Manuscripts*. "Money," Marx wrote in his remarks *On the Jewish Question*, "is the jealous one God of Israel beside which no other god may stand. Money dethrones all the gods of man and turns them into a commodity. Money is the universal, independently constituted value of all things. Money is the alienated essence of man's work and his being. This alien being rules over him and he worships it."[6]

Shakespeare's *Timon* provides Marx with a wealth of paradoxes which he used to define his idea of monetary perversion more exactly; and in unfolding his bitter vision of the mythic power of money, Marx combines the core of his earlier "Judaic" theory with a series of violent contrasts that derive from Shakespeare's text (IV, 3, 28–29). "Then [money] appears," he writes in his *Economic-Philosophical Manuscripts*, "as this *perverting* power against the individual and against social bonds, and so on, which claim to be of essence in themselves. It turns loyalty into treason, love into hate, hate into love, virtue into vice, vice into virtue, vassal into lord, lord into vassal, nonsense into reason, and reason into nonsense."[7]

Of course it can be argued that Marx falsely identifies the dramatic hero with his author and, adding to the confusion of speakers, blends his own early idea of money (*Geld*) with Shakespeare's *gold*—this "common earth"—relying, perhaps, too strongly on the fact that these words are genuine cognates in German. Yet these legitimate philological objections would ignore much of the dramatic quality of the timing of Marx's development. Groping toward one of his central ideas, he resolutely if not brutally seizes upon Shakespeare's conceits in order to continue his own articulation, and it is as if Shakespeare, at a crucial point of Marx's developing thought, has loosened his tongue.

Fifteen years after the *Economic-Philosophical Manuscripts*, Marx, with Engels, turned once more to a discussion of Shakespeare. As their criticism of Lassalle's *Franz von Sickingen* proves, Marx and Engels regarded Shakespeare as the most important playwright of world literature: Lassalle neglected the Shakespearean example and therefore drew his idealized figures too thinly. But for the modern dramatic writer, according to Marx and Engels, there is no other way than Shakespeare's; it is necessary to turn away from Schiller's lifeless idealizations and find help and inspiration in Shakespeare's truly living characterization. Hegel makes the same point in the third volume of his *Lectures on Aesthetics*.

In 1873 it was Engels who began a final dialogue on Shakespeare: he had come across Roderich Benedix' book against what he called *Shakespearomanie* and, full of righteous anger, reported the details of the deplorable undertaking to Marx. Roderich Benedix (1811–73) had begun his career as a touring player in provincial Germany, later achieving astonishing success with his own plays. As a belated and indifferently talented successor of Iffland, he knew how to praise petty-bourgeois comfort and the sweet reward of virtue in skilfully constructed plays that

were applauded all over Continental Europe. Many of his plays—
such as *Dr. Wespe* (1843)—were even performed in London and
New York, a success that has come to few German playwrights. It
is another question whether such successes entitled the former
touring player to pillory the German tradition of admiration for
Shakespeare as "accursed xenomania (*verfluchte Ausländerei*)."[8]
For lack of more artistic arguments, Benedix based his three-hun-
dred-page lampoon, which masquaraded as a Platonic dialogue,
upon the lowest kind of chauvinism that had suddenly burgeoned
after the military victories in France. The veneration of Shakespeare, declares Benedix, "poisons the healthy sense of our
people, it poisons the self-assurance of our people by disparaging
and belittling German authors and trying to rob us of our enjoyment of them."[9] Benedix supplements his chauvinistic arguments
with the invectives of a literary Philistine who attacks Shakespeare
with heavy self-righteousness. In Shakespeare's *Tempest*, writes
Benedix, the very first scene is against all reason: in the uproar of
the hurricane and in the crashing tackle of the shipwreck it would
be impossible to understand the words of the actors. Prospero,
who richly deserved his fate, was nothing more than a "Sunday
preacher";[10] Stephano's profligacy was simply insulting. "A really
drunken man belongs in bed," argued Benedix for the decorum of
the Wilhelminian age, "but not on stage."[11]

As though fate itself wanted to pass judgment on Benedix' nonsense, he died shortly before the publication of the manuscript.
"That lout Roderich Benedix," declared Engels on December 10,
1873, with dry humor, "has left behind an evil stench in the form
of a thick volume against Shakespearomania."[12] To be sure, there
was no need of an extensive defense of Shakespeare against
Philistine envy. "In the first act of the *Merry Wives* alone,"
asserted Engels with a side glance at Benedix' comedies, "there is
more life and reality than in all German literature, and Launce
alone with his dog Crab is worth more than all the German
comedies put together."[13] Marx's answer was terse. "Rod[erich]
Benedix does not surprise me. If he and his like understood
Shakespeare, where would they get the courage to produce their
own handiwork before the public?"[14]

Shakespeare's radiance is far too magnificent to be tarnished by the venom of the jealous: after Lessing, Herder, Goethe, after the Romantics and Hegel, any further defense of Shakespeare would have been only immodest folly. Marx and Engels remained imperturbable in their admiration. The anxiety of their successors to categorize Shakespeare as a "progressive bourgeois" would have appeared to them as an absurd inanity.

Goethe

Twelve months after the bicentennial conferences of 1949 were held in London and Aspen, the Soviet Academy of Arts and Sciences hastened to pay homage to Goethe.[15] Rather belatedly, it published a volume by one of the leading Soviet scholars in the field of German studies, the Armenian writer Marietta Shaginian (b. 1888). In 1950 Miss Shaginian had just received the Stalin Prize for her Armenian travel impressions;[16] it is probably because of this commendation that students in the Western world as well as the satellite countries had a chance to study Miss Shaginian's book on Goethe in Czech, Hungarian, German,[17] and other widely advertised translations.

Miss Shaginian undeniably presented an official Soviet view of Goethe. Her fluently written book contained few surprises: only the trimmings, the bons mots aimed at Mr. Barker Fairley and the Marshall Plan, are of more recent origin. Basically, the volume elaborated on the traditional arguments of Marxist criticism that have outlived all the purges in astonishingly good health. "Goethe," Miss Shaginian asserted, "entered into literature as a courageous, almost revolutionary son of the third estate, whose attack against old values and traditions announced the dawn of a decisive revolution. Goethe stepped into literature as a fighter against the gods, against the enslavement of man by religion. He postulated freedom for man."[18] Yet, according to this view, Goethe was not only Prometheus, but a Prometheus chained to the feudal rocks of Weimar. "If Goethe's knowledge of social matters," writes Miss Shaginian, "was relatively inadequate, it was because of the misery prevalent in his times and because of his position in society."[19]

But Miss Shaginian freely admitted an important error to which Soviet scholarship had been victim for a long time. The fundamental passage in the Marxist canon from which all other later Goethe interpretations were derived had been ascribed to the wrong source. The culprit, according to Miss Shaginian, was Franz Mehring, who had ascribed the key passage—a review of Karl Grün's Goethe book of 1846—to Karl Marx instead of correctly to Friedrich Engels.[20] Having discovered this mistake,[21] Soviet scholarship should now, Miss Shaginian stated, "commence new studies of Goethe the basis of which would be exclusively Friedrich Engels' classical interpretation."[22]

From an official Soviet point of view, then, Engels provides the exclusive foundation for a prescribed Goethe interpretation. Only Heinrich Heine is mentioned in passing; this irresponsible poet, of course, could not penetrate into Goethe's problems as deeply as could Engels. "Engels' evaluation fundamentally differs from that of Heine," Miss Shaginian remarked, ". . . because it is deeper, more serious, and more important for scholarship. Engels condemned Goethe's servility . . . but he also pointed toward the positive elements that he discovered, analyzing the negative according to the law of dialectics."[23]

It is exactly at this point that a more detailed study of the early sources and instances of developing Marxist literary theory yields some unexpected results. Did Friedrich Engels really work out an elaborate Goethe interpretation of his own? Or did he again rely on his usual sources, the publications of the Young Germans or the Young Hegelians, from which he had derived most of his early ideas about literature?[24]

Friedrich Engels arrived rather late on the battlefield upon which friend and foe struggled for the true image of Goethe. As is well known, Wolfgang Menzel was among the first to launch a bitter attack against Goethe. Menzel combined moral with political criticism: to the *Turner* Goethe appeared as an effeminate dandy of a decadent age, to the *Burschenschaftler* as an aesthetic sybarite, indifferent to the important problems of the nation.[25] In his political attacks, Menzel soon found a powerful ally in Ludwig Börne, who started publishing his ideological criticism in Menzel's journal. Unlike Menzel, Börne was fully aware of Goethe's poetic achievement, and yet he continually attacked the courtier (*Fürstendiener*) who had avoided political action in support of liberalism. Comparing Goethe with Dante, Alfieri, Montesquieu, Voltaire, Swift, Byron, and Thomas Moore, Börne accused Goethe of not speaking up for the German people: "God has given you a tongue of fire, but did you ever once defend the people's rights?"[26]

Not until Heinrich Heine did critical interpretation of Goethe's legacy become firmly based on a sensitive and intimate knowledge of his life and work. Both Menzel and Börne had merely projected all the ideas they hated into the figure of Goethe. Menzel had made him the playboy of the age; Börne saw in him only the submissive friend of Duke Karl August of Weimar. Heine's ambiguous relationship to Goethe was characterized by subtle enchantments and subtler disillusionment. Heine spoke as a lover of Goethe's works who had first found himself vehemently attracted, then bitterly repelled, by the complexity of Goethe's personality and achievement. For Heine, Goethe was not an ideological scapegoat as he had been for Menzel and Börne; rather, he found it much easier to trace both the virtues and the faults of Goethe to his religious view of God and the universe. At the core of Goethe's idea of the universe, according to Heine, lies pagan pantheism. Yet this pantheism, though revolutionary when contrasted with orthodoxy, makes Goethe consider all phenomena as of equal value, and thus leads him on toward complete indifference and ideological neutrality. Heine criticized Goethe's political inactivity from a Saint-Simonian point of view. According to Heine, modern pantheism had left Goethe's ideas far behind; it no longer believed in the *Dieu Esprit* of political indifference whom Goethe continued to worship, but had embraced the belief in the *Dieu Progrès* of historical action. "God is not merely a substance as

Wolfgang Goethe thought," Heine declared, "but motion and action, manifesting itself in time."[27] The belief in the *Dieu Esprit* had inspired the achievements of the old Goethe and thus had condemned them to a realm without life or blood.

In a famous paragraph, Heine compared the lifeless perfection of Goethe's later works to the Egyptian statues in the Louvre that seemed to feel "that they cannot suffer and cheer with us, that they are not men but unfortunately half-castes of gods and stones."[28] For the ensuing interpretation of Goethe, especially that by Young Germany, these paragraphs pointing out the aloof perfection of Goethe's *Kunstperiode* remained of utmost importance.

Scarcely a year after Heine's essay *On the History of Modern Literature in Germany* (*Zur Geschichte der neueren schönen Literatur in Deutschland* [1833]) appeared, Ludolf Wienbarg (1802–72), a young scholar at the University of Kiel, offered a series of twenty-four lectures on contemporary aesthetic problems. Regarded by German youth as a statement of the liberal viewpoint, these lectures were immediately published by Hoffmann and Campe under the title *Aesthetic Campaigns* (*Ästhetische Feldzüge*). In his twentieth and twenty-first lectures, Wienbarg concentrated on Goethe and, proceeding from the theories of Jean Paul and Schelling, offered an interpretation that tried to combine Menzel's, Börne's, and Heine's points of view into a single new image.

Certainly it was more Wienbarg's enthusiasm than the depth of his ideas that attracted his young audience. Yet he was by no means as superficial as some other members of the Young German movement. Wienbarg had carefully studied German literature from the Middle High German period to the days of Goethe, and had gone about his extensive reading with both sensitivity and an impressive vigor. His *Aesthetic Campaigns,* or rather, rhapsodies, were to a great extent based on Menzel's criticism as well as on Börne's liberal aggressiveness. However, Wienbarg had been fortunate enough to enjoy Heine's company and conversations, and had become suspicious of too extreme an ideological evaluation of literature.[29] Wienbarg synthesized and summed up the preceding Goethe criticism by combining aesthetic praise with political reproach. Taking the middle of the road, Wienbarg fully recognized the aesthetic achievement of the poet (which Menzel refused to acknowledge), and yet did not hesitate to criticize Goethe, following Börne's political ideas. In order to bring the highly conflicting views of his forerunners into harmony, Wienbarg elaborated a point already hinted at by Heine in his *History of Modern Literature in Germany*. Wienbarg distinguishes between the revolutionary splendor of Goethe's youth and the politically indifferent aestheticism of his old age. In the fundamental dualism of Goethe's life and work, the first part of *Faust* marks the turning point separating the young Prometheus from the elder Philistine.

Ludolf Wienbarg's writings, which inspired a whole generation of young German liberals, also had their impact upon Friedrich Engels. Gutzkow, of course, seemed of greater importance during the early days of Engels' literary career; yet Wienbarg's name usually followed very closely whenever young Engels spoke of the excellence of contemporary literature.

In almost every one of his early letters to his friend Gräber, Engels referred to Wienbarg as one of the leaders of Young Germany. He also mentions Wienbarg's exemplary review of the Swabian writer, Gustav Pfizer,[30] and recommends Wienbarg's most recent work, *The Playwrights of Today* (*Die Dramatiker der Jetztzeit* [1839]).[31] Wienbarg appeared to Engels as "the master of the modern style"[32] who wrote "warmly and radiatingly."[33] Even after Engels had discarded his fervent enthusiasm for Young Germany, Wienbarg continued to occupy a permanent place in his affections. Wienbarg, Engels wrote as late as 1842, was, among the writers of Young Germany, "the most noble, a real strong man, a statue of ore, a monolithic figure on which there is no stain."[34] Among the few sentences in which Engels refers to Goethe in the period between 1839 and 1847, there is a hint that he already had definite knowledge of Wienbarg's *Aesthetic Campaigns*. Writing about Karl Leberecht Immermann, Engels expressed his belief that this writer from the Rhineland aimed "at the elevated perspective of Goethe's calm sculptures."[35] These words are analogous to the famous passages in Wienbarg's *Aesthetic Campaigns* in which the Young German scholar discussed the aloofness of the later Goethe.[36] It was not until 1847 when Engels tried to give a Goethe interpretation of his own that Wienbarg's ideas reappeared more distinctly in his writings. But already an abyss had opened between master and pupil. Wienbarg had been the enthusiastic spokesman of the rising German liberalism; Engels now simplified Wienbarg's ideas in order to justify the tactics of a small group of radicals that by then, under Marx's dictatorial guidance, was vehemently attacking early German liberalism. Among the Goethe critics of the 1830's and 1840's, Friedrich Engels was perhaps the one least interested in aesthetic discussion. In 1846, Marx and Engels were involved in one of their lively controversies with a radical group which did not agree with the developing Marxist program of action. The main target at that time was one of the German pupils of Proudhon, Karl Grün, who had sketched in his *The Social Movement in France and Belgium* (*Die soziale Bewegung in Frankreich und Belgien* [1843]) a rather glowing portrait of Proudhon and his followers in western Europe. Marx and Engels decided to finish off Grün, each in his own particular field of interest. Marx condemned Grün's political pamphlet in the *Westphälisches Dampfboot* as "philanthropic";[37] Engels took over the task of ridiculing another of Grün's books.

Grün had attempted in his *Goethe from the Human Standpoint* (*Göthe vom menschlichen Standpunkt* [1846]) the formidable task of revealing the links between feudal Weimar and the people of Paris, between Goethe and Proudhon. "Goethe as the poet of pure humanity," Grün had declared with genuine enthusiasm, "has given us a codex for the radical transformation of mankind."[38] Stressing *Prometheus* and *Werther*, Grün vehemently disagreed with the liberal interpretation of Goethe as a courtier (*Fürstendiener*) and pointed out Goethe's humane activity in the service of the underprivileged.

Friedrich Engels' review of Grün's *Goethe from the Human Standpoint* appeared in six instalments between November 2 and December 9, 1847, in the *Deutsche Brüsseler Zeitung*.[39] The review is hardly important as a refutation of Grün's arguments. Engels had to condemn the book regardless of its virtues because the author belonged to an opposing group of the German radical movement for the mastery of which Marx had already begun to fight. However, a few paragraphs in the sixth article were to prove of importance for the later Marxist approach to literature. In this article dated November 8, 1847, Engels tried to refute Grün's ideas by sketching a portrait of his own. But this portrait distinctly shows Engels' dependence on preceding liberal criticism of literature; beyond any doubt Engels is here deeply indebted to the Goethe clichés of Young Germany.

In fact, the Goethe image of Friedrich Engels is hardly more than a somewhat dramatized restatement of the Young German idea of Goethe as expressed in 1834 by Wienbarg in his *Aesthetic Campaigns*. From Wienbarg Engels has derived all the key words about the revolutionary and the Philistine, the dilemma of the creative spirit at the Weimar court, the difference between the old and the young poet, as well as the paradoxes that were supposed to give an adequate definition of Goethe's elusive personality.

The trouble with orthodox Soviet interpretation of Goethe is that it relies upon the judgment of a young critic who possessed a relatively restricted knowledge of Goethe; here, too, Engels could hardly be compared with his friend Marx. Of course, young Engels knew of the Pietist opposition to Goethe,[40] but his early letters mention Goethe's poems and *Faust* in a most superficial way.[41] Only Goethe's remarks "For Young Writers" ("Für junge Dichter" [1832]), which Gutzkow had particularly recommended, caught Engels' attention.[42] Not until 1840 did he acquire an edition of Goethe's works; even then he did it, as he pointed out, because everyone was constantly chattering about Goethe.[43] It is not hard to make out who stood between young Engels and Goethe. A young liberal who had trained himself by Börne's example would hardly feel very inclined to read, to admire, or to love the writer whom Börne had accused of betraying the German people. Marx, who had read and revered Goethe from his youth, was never plagued by similar ideological doubts. Faust, or rather, Mephisto, he had always regarded as a brother under the skin, and in the *Economic-Philosophical Manuscripts* (1844) he quoted the infernal dialectician in order to support poetically his own vision of the transforming and alienating power of money.

> Was Henker! Freilich Händ' und Füsse
> Und Kopf und Hintre, die sind dein!
> Doch alles, was ich frisch geniesse,
> Ist das drum weniger mein?
> Wenn ich sechs Hengste zahlen kann
> Sind ihre Kräfte nicht die meine?
> Ich renne zu und bin ein rechter Mann,
> Als hätt' ich vierundzwanzig Beine. (*Faust*, I, 1820–27.)

> [Why, Zounds! Both hands and feet are, truly—
> And head and virile forces—thine:
> Yet all that I indulge in newly,
> Is't thence less wholly mine?
> If I've six stallions in my stall,
> Are not their forces also lent me?
> I speed along, completest man of all,
> As though my legs were four-and-twenty.—BAYARD TAYLOR.]

The question, Marx observes in his fragmentary commentary, is what man and his individuality actually are; money drives being and individuality apart. "I—my individuality—am lame, but money provides me with twenty-four feet," runs Marx's variation on Mephisto; "I am a bad, dishonorable, unscrupulous, crass person, but money is honored, and thus also its possessor. . . . I, who through money can do anything that a human heart desires—do I not possess all human ability?"[44] These personal thoughts upon Mephisto's questions do not stoop to inherited criticism; in his violent treatment of the passage isolated from its dramatic scene Marx does not have the least intention of subordinating himself to an outside authority and even less to a second-hand literary tradition. He is being completely himself as he violates the poet's text.

Friedrich Engels, in distinct contrast to Marx, owes the central impetus of his Goethe interpretation to the German liberal tradition. Looking at the man and poet through the eyes of others, he sketches his portrait in the *Deutsche Brüsseler Zeitung* by playing upon Wienbarg's idea of Goethe's ambivalent relationship to his time and his environment. A comparison of Wienbarg's and Engels' sentences discloses interesting resemblances, not to say striking analogies.

Wienbarg (1834)	*Engels (1847)*
Thus two large parts and sections . . . may be distinguished . . . Goethe's youth and Goethe's old age. . . . In his youth he wrote those immortal plays . . . the chivalrous *Götz, Egmont, Faust.* . . .[45] All this was of a revolutionary nature, took a position in contrast to the political and moral order. . . .[46] Goethe was not to maintain this sharp, lyrical character in politics. Perhaps it lay in his nature . . . perhaps . . . in the political condition of Germany, that Goethe . . . honestly reconciled himself to the political and social situation and until the day of his death declared himself thoroughly unsympathetic . . . to all thoughts of revolution.[47]	Goethe's relation to German society of his time in his works is of two kinds. At one time he is hostile to it . . . he rebels against it as Götz, Prometheus, Faust. . . . At another time he is friendly to it, "accommodates" to it . . . indeed, defends it against the pressing historical movement . . . particularly in all those writings when he speaks of the French Revolution.[48]

Moreover, Engels followed Wienbarg's point of view very closely when he wrote of the old man who was all too willing to sacrifice his Promethean youth to the pleasures of the court and the contentment of the German Philistines. Again Wienbarg's sentences sound much more authentic than Engels' pamphleteering restatements.

So far as the greatest and last series of Goethe's productions is concerned, these novels and dramas that the Philistines . . . find not only bearable and comfortable, but also poetic, they suit the German who has become a husband and has acquired office, honor, and title . . . and, upon going to bed, crosses out the day in his calendar he has lived through as an honest husband and citizen.[49]	We reproach Goethe . . . that at times he could also be a Philistine, that he . . . could pursue the tiniest affairs and *menus plaisirs* of one of the tiniest German courts with solemn earnestness.[50]

Engels, following in Wienbarg's footsteps, sees Goethe's life as a dilemma of creativeness and servility stemming from the contrast between personality and environment. It is interesting to note that Wienbarg had defined this dilemma in more powerful words; undoubtedly because he still believed much more in the importance of the personality than in the relevance of the environment.

It is true that Goethe was an aristocrat in politics, an admirer of the system of courts and princes, a eulogist of hereditary power. . . . The same political aristocrat, this man who regarded the great historical element of the nations from such a small, courtly standpoint, surveyed religious, moral, and scientific life with the gaze of an eagle.[51]	There is still a continuing struggle in him between the poet of genius who was disgusted by the wretchedness of his surroundings and the . . . privy councillor of Weimar. . . . Goethe found himself in this dilemma continually, and the older he got, the more the mighty poet, *de guerre lasse,* retreated behind the Weimarian minister.[52]

In their final judgment, both Wienbarg and Engels used a series of paradoxes that were to define more closely Goethe's ambiguous personality. Again Engels used a pattern and a vocabulary that were not unlike Wienbarg's in his *Aesthetic Campaigns* thirteen years earlier.

I shall speak my last word upon him by trying to explain his dual character as servile and liberal, as great and small, as a genius and a man of the world. . . .[53]

Thus Goethe is at one time colossal, at another petty; sometimes a defiant, scornful genius full of contempt for the world, other times a cautious, contented, narrow Philistine.[54]

Friedrich Engels' dependence upon a preceding Goethe interpretation, to which both his knowledge of Young German writings and his enthusiasm for Wienbarg point, becomes even clearer against the background of his earlier literary career. Young Engels had begun to write his literary articles under the impact of Gutzkow and his Young German friends. Young Germany had initiated Engels into the current problems of literature and set him farther on his way toward pure political radicalism. Engels' enthusiasm for Wienbarg was part of his infatuation with Young Germany. Yet, in contrast to his declining interest in Gutzkow, some of Wienbarg's ideas proved to be of more lasting attraction for him. As the hard core of Young German thinking about Goethe, they were to survive critical scrutiny by the later Engels who had abandoned the liberal basis of his ideas. From Engels' essays they were taken over by Soviet criticism and finally embalmed as the official Stalinist interpretation of Goethe. Ludolf Wienbarg, who died half-forgotten, would have been indeed surprised at the strange migration of his ideas.

Balzac

The *Great Soviet Encyclopedia* (1950 ed.) honors Honoré de Balzac's social insights and his unrelenting fight against the bourgeoisie in seven columns of small print.[55] Because of his revolutionary virtue, declares the official Soviet reference work, Balzac is numbered among the most important writers of all nations in the world. Many other Marxist treatments of Balzac, in the West as well as in the East, hardly deviate from the principles of the *Soviet Encyclopedia:* even if Vladimir Grib's slender pamphlet (1937) or Georg Lukács' study *Balzac and French Realism* (1952) present individual ideas more thoroughly, they tend to draw conclusions of monumental uniformity. Balzac's greatness, asserts Lukács, lies in his unified conception of capitalist development, in his tendency to derive ideological developments from the economic basis.[56] Vladimir Grib praises Balzac as a clairvoyant psychologist who reveals the predatory instincts of capitalist society, and also points with particular stress, as does the *Soviet Encyclopedia*, to Marx's and Engels' judgments on Balzac. "It is well known," writes Grib, "that Marx and Engels admired Balzac's sharp and pitiless insights extraordinarily. . . . If the *Comédie humaine* had not been written, the first chapter of the *Communist Manifesto* would perhaps not have sounded so clear and sanguine."[57] Certainly Grib's comment must be read with the accent upon the "perhaps": the *Communist Manifesto* was written in 1847–48, and to the present time there is not the slightest evidence that either Marx or Engels concerned himself with Balzac before 1852.

Marx and Engels were not the first to discover Balzac as an anatomist of bourgeois society. In Germany, the elderly Goethe welcomed Balzac's early work; Börne and Heine reported on his new books from Paris. The Young Germans were well aware of the social questions Balzac raised. Balzac, wrote Karl Gutzkow in his *Observations on Recent Literature* (*Beiträge zur neuesten Literatur* [1836]), "anatomizes this great cult to which Paris sacrifices and about which one hardly knows whether it is merely the cult of fashion or the cult of money. . . . Balzac is the writer of money, of the new machinery that has its miracles just as the old epic did."[58] Twenty years later this idea was a commonplace of Balzac criticism. Even Taine's famous study on Balzac (1858), with its stress upon the economic element, remained thoroughly dependent upon a whole generation of preceding interpreters.

Without any doubt, Marx's and Engels' judgments on Balzac are also part of a general European tradition to which Gutzkow, Villemain, Taine, and Chernishevsky had contributed for a long time. When Marx stressed Balzac's economic interests, he was only repeating a cliché of Balzac criticism. Thus in *Capital* he referred to Gobseck, in whose character the author "studies all the nuances of avarice so thoroughly";[59] elsewhere in the same work Marx praised Balzac's *Les Paysans* for its "deep grasp of the real situation."[60] In a letter to Engels of December 14, 1868, Marx quoted a passage from *Le Curé de village* treating the economic basis of commerce and asked Engels, the Manchester businessman, whether he agreed with Balzac.[61]

So far as one can determine from the concrete evidence, for theoretical reasons Marx seems to have been primarily interested in Balzac's *Gobseck* (1830), *Le Curé de village* (1839), *Les Paysans* (1844), and *Cousine Bette* (1846). But, being a bookworm with an insatiable hunger for reading, he also knew other works of Balzac that he personally rated much more highly. Paradoxically enough, it is two of Balzac's shorter stories, namely, *Melmoth réconcilié* (1835) and *Le Chef d'œuvre inconnu* (1831), which Marx numbered among his favorite works.

It would probably be difficult to explain to Marx's dogmatic followers why he preferred these shorter stories, which completely disregard political and economic questions, to the great social novels. In view of the fact, however, that he often sat for whole nights poring over the works of Paul de Kock (1794–1871) and other long subliterary novels of his time, it is hardly surprising that he read *Melmoth réconcilié*, a Gothic story in the tradition of E. T. A. Hoffmann and Maturin, with such interest. Marx probably recognized that in this story Balzac had used a variation of the Faust-Mephistopheles motif that had so fascinated Marx in his own "Oulanem"; the mysterious bond holding the counterfeiter Castanier to his tempter John Melmoth recalls all too clearly Faust's shifting relationship to Mephisto. In Balzac's story, too, Faust-Castanier is tempted by the promise of limitless power, of the fulfilment of all sensual desires, of absolute knowledge; he, too, wants to be, in his way, *sicut Deus*. Balzac sharpens the con-

trast between victim and tempter with his reference to the anti-
thetical ideas of "omnipotence"[62] and "nothingness (*le néant*)";[63]
he insists upon contrasting the great abundance of life with its
absolute negation. For a reader like Marx, who liked to see the
moving principle of the dialectic even in its incarnation in literary
characters, Balzac's *Melmoth réconcilié* offered attractions of a
particular kind.

This does not explain why Marx chose another of Balzac's fantastic stories, *Le Chef d'œuvre inconnu*, as one of his favorite
works and recommended it to Engels, whimsically enough, as a
"*chef d'œuvre* full of delightful irony" (February 25, 1867.)[64]
One may well doubt whether Engels reacted to this story with the
same approval as his friend. The hero of the tale, Master Frenhofer, strives with Faustian violence to exceed the final limits of
his art: in his paintings he attempts to achieve "the roundness and
relief"[65] of nature and to surpass "the method of the sun";[66] "the
air playing around the objects"[67] is also supposed to appear on
the canvas. In order to prove his new ideas, he asks the young
Nicholas Poussin to bring his beloved Catherine into the studio.
The direct comparison of her living, breathing beauty with the
charm of the female figure on Frenhofer's new painting is to convince Poussin of the new theory. But Frenhofer has exceeded the
intrinsic laws of his art: Poussin stares at the canvas, on which
only the trace of a woman's foot appears in the midst of "confused
masses of colors (*de couleurs confusément amassées*) and a multitude of bizarre lines."[68] Frenhofer recognizes that he has failed
and dies that same night.

Paul Lafargue suggests that his father-in-law liked *Le Chef
d'œuvre inconnu* so much because he felt himself at one with
Frenhofer's Faustian urge.[69] This is a friendly, if quite vague, con-
jecture—Lafargue forgets that as early as "Oulanem" Marx was
attracted to Mephisto rather than to Faust. If it is necessary at all
to find a reason for Marx's attraction to one of Balzac's excitingly
written stories, the answer is probably to be found in another
direction. Balzac shows in his story the collapse of the classicist
theory of art, the dissolution of genres and of intentional mimesis

—did Marx also feel that an art was coming which, like Master Frenhofer's, was striving to imitate "the method of the sun" in order to create in its revolutionary pictures "confused masses of colors and a multitude of bizarre lines"? Did Marx suspect that in his *Chef d'œuvre inconnu* Balzac had anticipated a still unknown, impressionistic art with light irony?

Unfortunately, Marxist interpretation of Balzac does not proceed from Marx's personal sympathies for the work of art but rather—as in the case of Goethe—from the statements of Engels, who was far inferior to his friend in his knowledge of the writer and friendly insight into his work. Engels' thoughts on Balzac lack the warmth of personal confrontation; Balzac is praised because the materialistic theory requires it. His interpretation of Balzac is contained in the draft letter to Miss Harkness in which he expounded his ideas on realism. The specific problem of Engels' Balzac interpretation appears immediately in the opening paragraphs, which hardly go beyond the commonplaces of contemporary Balzac criticism. Like Gutzkow in 1836, fifty years later Engels also reads Balzac's novels as a textbook of the development of French society.

> Balzac, whom I consider a far greater master of realism than all the Zolas *passés, présents et à venir*, in *La Comédie humaine* gives us a most wonderfully realistic history of French "Society," describing, chronicle-fashion, almost year by year from 1816–1848, the progressive inroads of the rising bourgeoisie upon the society of nobles, that reconstituted itself after 1815 and that set up again, as far as it could, the standard of *la vieille politesse française*. It describes how the last remnants of this, to him, model society gradually succumbed before the intrusion of the vulgar moneyed upstart or were corrupted by him; how the *grande dame* whose conjugal infidelities were but a mode of asserting herself in perfect accordance with the way she had been disposed of in marriage, gave way to the bourgeoisie who corned her husband for cash and cashmere; and around the central picture he groups a complete history of French Society from which, even in the economic details (for instance the re-arrange-

ment of real and personal property after the Revolution) I have learned more than from all the professed historians, economists and statisticians of the period together.[70]

Inevitably, Engels finds himself forced to explain more carefully why he, the close collaborator of Marx, extravagantly praises a passionate royalist who all his life defended church and throne as the pillars of human existence. Engels here touches upon a question of some theoretical importance:

> Well, Balzac was politically a legitimist; his great work is a constant elegy on the irretrievable decay of good society; his sympathies are all with the class doomed to extinction. But for all that, his satyre [*sic*] is never keener, his irony never bitterer, than when he sets in motion the very men and women with whom he sympathizes most deeply—the nobles. And the only men of whom he always speaks with undisguised admiration, are his bitterest political antagonists, the republican heroes of the Cloître Saint Méry, the men who at this time (1830–1836) were indeed the representatives of the popular masses. That Balzac was compelled to go against his own class sympathies and political prejudices, that he *saw* the necessity of the downfall of his favorite nobles, and described them as people deserving no better fate; and that he saw the real men of the future where, for the time being, they alone were to be found—that I consider . . . one of the grandest features of old Balzac.[71]

Engels' Balzac interpretation proceeds (like Lenin's commentary on the works of Tolstoy) from a potentially valuable differentiation between the overt and the latent message of a work of art. In his letter to Minna Kautsky, Engels had touched upon similar questions. On the surface, Engels tries to explain, the legitimist Balzac stresses his loyalty to king, church, and dynasty; in the secret depths of the work, however, he betrays "undisguised admiration" for his "bitterest political antagonists, the republican heroes of the Cloître Saint Méry."

It is remarkable that Émile Zola, in his collection of essays *Les romanciers naturalistes* (1881), developed similar thoughts, without, to be sure, seeking for examples from among the fighters on the barricades of 1832. Balzac, remarked Zola, "was of aristocratic opinions. How strange . . . this supporter of absolute power, whose talent is essentially democratic and who has written the most revolutionary *œuvre* one can read."[72] One should analyze, Zola added, the forceful blows Balzac struck against the old society, perhaps while believing that he was solidly supporting it; "there would be a curious question to study, which I would pose thus: how the genius of a man can go against the convictions of that man."[73] It is difficult to decide whether Engels, the busy reader, had missed Zola's essay collection or not, but were not English admirers of Zola near at hand? Engels' neighbor Miss Harkness, whose works conjured up the names of Balzac and Zola, published with the firm of Henry Vizetelly (1820–94), whom Zola himself referred to in a letter as *l'ami Vz.*[74] Was Engels closer to a London circle of Zola admirers than his published correspondence suggests?

Engels' theoretical distinction between an "open" and a "hidden" message may be highly valuable for a structural examination of the novel, but its relevance seems endangered by the ideological prejudice which predetermines the results before the analysis begins. Engels' conclusions suffer from a grave weakness: they are not corroborated by Balzac's works. The claim that Balzac secretly admires *only* the republican heroes proves to be completely misleading as soon as the text itself is examined.

A critical examination of Engels' argument (which is of some importance because of its continuing survival in Soviet literary criticism) must first separate the concrete historical events from Balzac's fictional presentation. As a historical event, the battles in the Rue du Cloître-Saint-Merri[75] are part of a long series of republican attempts at revolt against the government of Louis-Philippe. On June 5, 1832, the republicans and legitimists decided to turn the funeral of General Lamarque into an armed test of strength. The funeral was followed by bitter street battles, which the government soon suppressed; only in the immediate neighborhood of the old cloister church of Saint-Merri did a determined little group of republicans maintain their barricade until June 6. Finally the government was forced to supplement the National Guard with regular troops and artillery in order to wipe out the nest of revolt that was being celebrated in Paris as a symbol of the republican will to resist. "Thus in the middle of this city of more than a million inhabitants, in the most populous quarter of Paris, in broad daylight, one saw sixty citizens defy a government, hold an army in check, negotiate, deliver battle" (Louis Blanc).[76] Heine, incidentally, who had arrived in Paris the year before, was fascinated by the event and reported on it graphically and at considerable length to the German public.[77]

Balzac formulated his thoughts on the events of Saint-Merri in his novels *Un grand homme de province à Paris* (1839) and *Les Secrets de la Princesse de Cadignan* (1839). Balzac's attitude is far more complicated than Engels admits. In any case it is peculiar that of the more important figures of Balzac's world, only one—Michel Chrestien—turns up as a participant in the battles around the cloister. Although Michel Chrestien fights on the side of the republicans, Balzac is rather obviously concerned with separating him from the mob of republican partisans and surrounding him with an aura of his own. "Michel Chrestien fell," explains Balzac, "fighting for ideas that were not his own (*périt pour d'autres doctrines que les siennes*); his ideas were more rational and less undisciplined than the violent notions of those young fools (*les jeunes insensés*) who regarded themselves as the heirs of the Convention."[78] In evident contradiction to Engels' claim, Balzac admires neither the republican youths of Saint-Merri nor abstract republicanism: his admiration is reserved for the individual Michel Chrestien, whose energy and purity he praises as exemplary.

It is just this purity and energy that Balzac stresses as the highest possession of individual and social existence. Good and evil in this world are not distributed according to a political pattern; in his joy in pure and strong characters Balzac overlooks the political dividing lines. It is not accidental that Michel Chrestien belongs to a circle of friends that binds liberals and royalists, re-

publicans and legitimists in the *Cénacle* of the Rue de Quatre
Vents into intimate discipline. After the death of Chrestien, a
young nobleman from Picardy named Daniel d'Arthèz emerges as
leader of the circle. This vehement royalist possibly represents
what Balzac himself wanted to achieve: a simple life and an
existence uncorrupted by sudden riches. D'Arthèz' house, declares
Balzac, is like a cloister; d'Arthèz lives and works like a Benedic-
tine monk; even after he becomes a deputy in the Chamber and
takes his place "on the benches of the right (*au coté droit*),"[79] he
remains a pure human being in a corrupt society. The royalist is
not alone: like him, his friends Fulgence Ridal and Joseph Bri-
deau remain unspoiled; even former radical skeptics like Léon
Giraud, whom d'Arthèz converts to the cause of the king, loyally
fulfil their new tasks. If Engels had read Balzac's novels more
attentively and without prejudice, it could hardly have escaped him
that Balzac's sympathies belong to all those who, regardless of
where their political sympathies lie, raise themselves above the
level of the imperfect many by means of strength, purity, and the
intense passion of their character.

7

The First Disciples

A Survey of Developments

A rigid system of literary criticism, equally binding for readers, writers, and scholars, appears in the history of modern communism about a hundred years after the first literary essays of Marx and Engels. It is the result of a late development that indicates intellectual sterility, if not the destruction of intellectual inquiry by the managers of the political administration. In the period of the first Communist League (1847–52), other questions came first. Marx and Engels were just on the point of developing their earliest and most extreme theories on the all-encompassing force of economics; literary and aesthetic principles were either implied in their general theory of culture or derived from personal preferences resulting from their youthful literary activities and the German tradition. Nor did the First International (1864–72) contribute much to change this situation. It would have been extremely difficult to force a systematic theory of art (even if it had existed) upon the battling members, whose inner disunity disrupted the organization before it had a chance to define a consistent attitude.

But with the need of the growing mass parties in Austria, Germany, and Russia to articulate a coherent relationship to the intellectual tradition of their own nations and to contemporary literature appeared the urgent necessity to develop a compact theory of the arts. Politically, the first decades of the Second International (founded in 1899) were characterized by revisionism, which far preferred the sober analysis of contemporary political problems to Hegelian philosophy. In England, the young people in the Fabian Society, among them George Bernard Shaw, protested against the damage that German metaphysics had done to the cause of socialism; in France, Jean Jaurès drafted his *Organisation Socialiste* (1895–96); in Germany, Eduard Bernstein— hardly a year after Engels' death—published his strategic essays in the *Neue Zeit* (1895), the central organ of the Social Democratic party, and summarized his ideas in his *Hypotheses of Socialism* (*Voraussetzungen des Sozialismus* [1899]). Sober political efforts and the daily practice of parliamentary activity were the fundamental concerns.

Franz Mehring and G. V. Plekhanov formulated the cultural postulates of socialism at the time of the Second International. These two men still combined political strategy and literary criticism; specialization was to be left to the next generation. In fighting against the same currents of the *Zeitgeist*, both were concerned with contemporary science and especially with Darwinism; similarly, both were willing to come to terms with Kant's aesthetics and ultimately followed the Königsberg philosopher in his stress on self-sustained laws of art and the disinterested enjoyment of the beautiful. Personal inclinations also had some relevance: Mehring (following Lassalle and German liberalism) recommended Friedrich Schiller to a liberal-minded working class; Plekhanov turned to the study of ethnography and sketched the foundations of an anthropological theory of artistic development, in which the young English Marxist Christopher Caudwell was to support him a generation later. The age of Mehring and Plekhanov required the free exchange of opinions and ideas as a matter of conscience; the critic developed his ideas without being persecuted by his political confederates at every step.

The period of the Third International (founded 1919) and the later organizations of similar purpose subordinated the requirements of Communist literary criticism as well as the taste of the reader to the interests of the Soviet state. In the first fifteen years, writers and independently thinking critics retained a relative possibility of continuing their work. In the shadow of the terror, a prolonged moment of suspense developed in which even basically anti-Marxist literary theories—for example, Russian formalism—were frankly discussed. Only with the consolidation of Stalin's power position in the early thirties did this peculiar period of suspense, which was unusually productive of intellectual achievements, come to an end; a single theoretical prescription, the application of which was ultimately determined by the political police, became binding for the public, the critics, and the universities alike. The most interesting figure of this frosty period is undoubtedly Georg Lukács, who, as long as Stalin ruled, was able to subordinate his private theory of nineteenth-century realism to the demands of the administration; his dialectical opposition was often indistinguishable from service to official interests. The specialist began to function: whereas Mehring and Plekhanov had been able freely to defend their ideas about politics and literature against their own allies, critics in many nations now found themselves demoted to assiduous commentators upon official decrees of cultural policy.

In the period after Stalin's death (1953) and the subsequent uprisings in Poznań and Budapest, the political and cultural centralization gave way to a polycentrism of interests that allows critics and writers renewed scope and at least limited possibilities of development. The aging functionaries of the Stalinist period still hold fast to power and the sterile concepts of socialist realism; occupying key positions in the administrative apparatus, they are exposed to constantly recurring attacks from the "reformers." The resistance comes above all from two groups: from the older generation that still remembers the time before Stalin's consolidation of power, and the youngest intellectuals who did not experience personally the terror of Stalinism and justly reject the demand for realistic art as an anachronism in the age of electronically programmed industrial production; they talk about Kafka, but they mean renewed possibilities for seeking uninhibited access to world literature. While the aging Lukács

(Budapest) tries in the first volumes of his thoughtful *Aesthetik* to define an intermediate, almost Aristotelian, position, methods and practices of a criticism derived from Hegel and Marx are being refined in the industrial societies of the West: Ernst Bloch and Hans Mayer, once the stars of the University of Leipzig, have emigrated to universities in West Germany; Theodor W. Adorno, who during his exile worked in Oxford, New York, Princeton, and Los Angeles, is now teaching again in Frankfurt, where he was born; and Lucien Goldmann, who took his doctoral degree in Zurich, continues to develop ideas of the early Lukács' within the sphere of the French philosophical and literary tradition. Fundamentally, with these thinkers and critics, a new age of the sociological theory of literature has begun.

Franz Mehring (1846–1919)

Franz Mehring was the first to try to apply Marxist principles systematically to German and European literature. Yet his varied efforts, which still await a complete critical analysis, were not exhausted by literary criticism; as an important political essayist, Mehring contributed his part to the definition of theory and tactics for German Social Democracy, and for almost a generation he put his stamp on the political and literary sympathies of the Central European workingman.

Mehring began his career neither as a Marxist nor as a Social Democrat.[1] He was born in 1846 into a prosperous Pomeranian family, studied at the universities of Berlin and Jena, and, after a brief period of enthusiasm for the far left, published his first writings in the liberal journal *Zukunft* ("Future"). Marx, upon reading these articles, called them "very boring and shallowly written."[2] The beginnings of Mehring's intellectual development were determined by the liberal editors Johann Jacoby and Guido Weiss, men who continued to burn with disappointment at the incomplete revolution of 1848; from them Mehring inherited his hatred of the Hohenzollerns, Bismarck, and the Prussian bourgeoisie. In the early eighties, the young man began his study of Marxism, and his radical turn from liberalism took place in the following decade. After he had angrily attacked Paul Lindau (1839–1919), the most influential drama critic of his time, and had published a pamphlet with the title *Kapital und Presse* (1891), Mehring joined the Social Democratic party and was soon directing the editorial policies of its official central organ. But Mehring's loyalty was to the Prussian patriot Lassalle rather than to the cosmopolitan Marx; he could never bring himself to accept Marxist theory in its entirety, especially the economic aspects which he hardly understood. In his old age he made another personal and political decision of importance: at nearly seventy years of age he left the Social Democratic party, which, in his opinion, had collaborated far too successfully with the Prussian bourgeoisie. He associated himself with Karl Liebknecht and Rosa Luxemburg and died as one of the spiritual fathers of the German Communist party.

To be sure, Franz Mehring was by profession neither a philosopher nor a philologist. He excelled in stubborn polemics, tactical arguments, and incisive commentaries on specific situations. He had quite superficial notions of philosophy and its history; accepting the assumptions of a rather naïve materialism, he called speculative philosophy *simply* a chimera.[3] Neither did the philosophical system of dialectical materialism, in Mehring's view, require any very complex demonstration; daily experience and Feuerbach were quite sufficient. The theories of Marxism are valid simply because "men must first eat, drink, and have a place to live and clothes to wear before they can think or write poetry"; man's consciousness "is determined by his social being, not conversely his social being by his consciousness."[4] Mehring defined his conception of Marxism in his essay "On Historical Materialism" ("Über den historischen Materialismus" [1893]). There he essentially agreed with Marx's rigorous arguments in the *Critique of Political Economy* (1859); for Mehring, too, economics was the primary basis out of which the intellectual superstructure grew. Yet, in the nineties, he had to cope with a new wave of opponents who forced him to make significant modifications. He had to defend Marx's concepts against the new followers of Darwin as well as against the virulent Neo-Kantianism of the universities, and, half accepting some of the fashionable ideas of his enemies, he finally arrived at an ideological conglomerate that contained Marxist, Darwinian, and Kantian motifs in almost equal measure.

As inveterate Hegelians, neither Marx nor Engels concerned themselves much with the most recent achievements of the natural sciences. Engels read Darwin's *Origin of Species* (1859) shortly after it was published; in his letter of *ca.* December 12, 1859, he referred Marx to this "quite splendid" Darwin who was trying to demonstrate "historical development in Nature as well."[5] Marx, in a letter to Engels on December 19, 1860, confirmed that Darwin's work contained "the basis in natural history"[6] for their own views. The two friends were content to examine Darwin's work from the point of view of their own ideas; the rest was of little significance. For the Hegelian Marx, the exhaustive study of the concrete phenomena of nature lay, after all, outside the range of serious intellectual effort; although in *Capital* he made at least metaphorical use of Darwin's terminology,[7] he considered P. Trémaux's *Origine et Transformations de l'Homme et des autres Êtres* (1865) more significant than Darwin's work.[8] It remained for Engels to defend his friend's ideas in an age in which intellectuals from London to Odessa were professing the theories of Darwin. Although in his *Anti-Dühring* (1878) as well as in his fragment on *Dialektik und Natur* Engels made a sincere attempt to come to terms with Darwin, he tends to acknowledge only those ideas of Darwin that easily harmonized with his own Hegelian postulates, that is, primarily, the idea of continuous development. Engels' ultimate judgment on Darwin can be found in a letter to the Russian Socialist Pyotr Lavrov (1823–1900). "Of Darwin's teachings I subscribe to the doctrine of development . . . ," declared Engels on November 12, 1875, "but I accept Darwin's method of proof . . . only as a first, provisional, incomplete expression of a newly discovered fact."[9] In Engels' opinion,

Darwin's ideas were much too "one-sided and narrow";[10] his method of transferring Hobbesian and Malthusian categories from their social context into the sphere of living nature was nothing but an intellectual "trick"[11] that could not be taken seriously. Early and late, Engels believed, as one of his Russian critics remarked, that oats grow according to Hegel.

Yet in the heat of the battle with the followers of Darwin, Engels occasionally developed comparisons and analogies likely to lead the younger generation of Marxists into some confusion. Engels' eulogy at Marx's funeral (1883) is responsible for much of this difficulty. "Darwin discovered the law of development of organic nature on our planet," declared Engels in Highgate Cemetery; "Marx is the discoverer of the basic law according to which human history moves and develops."[12] This analogy, which has been often quoted, seemed to offer the key to many a thorny problem, and quite a number of the younger generation, above all Mehring, took Engels' rhetorical comparison all too literally. Marx and Engels never doubted the absolute hegemony of history; only in the conception of the younger Marxists was history obliged to yield half its empire to biology and other disciplines.

Marx's conception of the world was dominated by the monolithic principle of history; Mehring, on the other hand, believed that the world was split into two spheres of existence, one of nature and one of history. As a dualist, Mehring ascribed to the natural sciences an axiomatic importance that Marx never would have admitted; in Mehring's view, nature and history, science and history (that is, dialectical materialism), complemented one another in the most satisfactory way, each without ever exceeding its own competence.[13] Without being able to supply any proof, Mehring suggests that "Marx and Engels, in the area of science, were just as much mechanical materialists as they were historical materialists in the area of society."[14] Under the pressure of contemporary Darwinism, G. V. Plekhanov, another young Marxist, was to come to similar dualistic conclusions in his London exile (1895).

After Darwin it is Kant who most clearly provides concepts, above all in the area of aesthetics, that distinguish Mehring's views from those of Engels and Marx. Mehring regards Kant's *Critique of Judgment* (*Kritik der Urteilskraft*), not Hegel's *Lectures,* as the decisive work in the history of aesthetics. "Kant," he stresses, "demonstrated [art] to be a particular and original ability of mankind, and in a deeply thought-out and . . . ramified system, which is, however, rich in open and broad vistas."[15] Following Kant, Mehring believes in an isolated human ability to apprehend the beautiful; like Kant, he, too, is convinced that only a disinterested enjoyment of the work of art assures the experience of beauty. The legacy of Hegel seems to be distinctly ignored; Mehring returns instead to the pre-Hegelian aesthetics of the eighteenth century. As an example it is sufficient to note Mehring's enthusiasm for the Kantian Schiller; his assertion that "basically every creative work of art" produces "its own aesthetics"[16] points the same way.

Finally, Mehring's literary criticism is strongly imbued with his implacable hatred of the Prussian monarchy. This prejudice (to the dangers of which Lukács refers with some justice)[17] restricts Mehring's horizon and turns even his most intelligent pamphlet into a document of provincial disputation; not infrequently he is concerned more with the monarchy than the particular writer he is studying. Yet seen historically, Mehring's Prussian perspective agrees remarkably with the first beginnings of Marxist literary doctrine. Marx, too, develops his criticisms of Hegel, and the first elements of his literary theory, in bitter opposition to Hegel's alleged defense of the Prussian monarchy as the perfect state in the truest sense. In a certain sense, both Marx and Mehring remain disappointed subjects of the Prussian king.

Mehring's Prussian interests appear unmistakably in his powerfully written *Die Lessing-Legende* (1893); it is the first compact book that attempts to interpret literary and critical phenomena according to the as yet rudimentary principles of a Marxist aesthetic. As the title suggests, Mehring concerns himself less with Lessing himself than with the Lessing interpretation of the follow-

ing generations, above all with the Lessing image of the Wilhelminian age. Mehring directs his main argument against the patriotic interpretation, which tries to see Lessing in the most intimate
relationship to Frederick the Great. But between Lessing, the
champion of the rising bourgeoisie, and Frederick, the sterile, if
talented, representative of an enlightened despotism, there was
not the slightest communion; Lessing, declares Mehring, had to
create his works in continuing resistance to Frederick's anti-
intellectual absolutism. Frederick and Lessing had "about as
much [in common] as Kaiser Wilhelm II with Lassalle and
Marx, or even much less."[18] Between the critic and the ruler a
harmony of mind was impossible: "Frederick had nothing but
contempt from the depths of his soul for the commoners (*Roture*)
whose champion Lessing was, and personally expelled . . . every
bourgeois from the ranks of his officers. Lessing, however, full
of the most acid aversion and disdain and in complete agreement
with . . . the native Prussians Herder and Winckelmann, saw
in Frederick's state 'the most slavish country in Europe.' "[19]
Mehring's aim is to trace the optimistic legend of the alliance
between Frederick and Lessing to economic and political causes;
even literary legends, he stresses, are "only the ideological superstructure of an economic and political development."[20] The
Lessing legend, asserts Mehring, was created by the Prussian
bourgeoisie after its defeat in 1848 in an attempt to justify its
compromise with the dynasty by means of a precedent from
literary history; in order to camouflage their own cowardice,
they had to pretend that similar compromises between the bourgeoisie and the dynasty had long been the rule in Prussian history. Above all, the bourgeois professors of literature Wilhelm
Scherer (1841–86) and Erich Schmidt (1853–1913), Mehring
stressed, played a significant role in creating the legend by glori-
fying contemporary bourgeois servility with their "byzantine
sentiments."[21]

In place of the false Lessing legend which he had exposed as
a bourgeois attempt at political self-justification, Mehring had
to substitute his own image of Lessing. But he did not quite

succeed; the portrait remains vague and without a spark of genuine life; Mehring's criticism could not remotely compete with Schmidt's biographical achievement. Mehring's presentation of Lessing suffers from all the inevitable failings of economic determinism. Although he consistently deals with the economic situation of Saxony and devotes an interesting sociological chapter to the Berlin of Frederick the Great, the statistics of the number of French, Jews, and Czechs living in Berlin hardly contribute much that is essential to a finely nuanced portrait of Lessing. There is little connection between the economic description and the writer's psychology; upon a richly documented background of irrelevant social facts Mehring projects a hasty sketch of a bourgeois Lessing whose literary and theoretical achievements remain nearly invisible. Many of Mehring's assertions suffer from the symptomatic blemishes of Marxist dogmatism; Mehring insists that Saxony became Lessing's birthplace with all but historical necessity because it was "economically by far the most developed, and, accordingly, the most cultivated land"[22] among the German states; Lessing's early comedies, Mehring asserts in the same chapter, were just as fragile as the contemporary class consciousness of the German bourgeoisie.[23] This fierce concern with the economic and political causes of literature leaves little room for an investigation of Lessing's literary art. *Minna von Barnhelm* (1767) is disposed of with the simple judgment that it is "a cutting satire upon Frederician rule."[24] Even *Laokoon* (1766), Mehring insists, fulfilled, in its own historical moment, its function on the battlefield of the classes; in *Laokoon* Lessing condemns descriptive poetry that only serves to encourage middle-class inactivity—"the middle-class routine was really finally lulled to sleep by the praise of colorful alpine herbs and the sacred shadows of the forests."[25] But Lessing had to fail, not because he lacked genius, but because the middle classes he represented were incapable of effectively defending their political right of survival.

Mehring's essay on *Schiller* (1905)[26] reveals a growing alienation from the premises of Marxist literary doctrine. In contrast to Marx and Engels, Mehring characterizes Schiller as a most daring conceptual thinker. In Schiller's work the whole secret of German classicism is unfolded; unable to master the narrowness and wretchedness of the contemporary situation, Schiller's pure enthusiasm seeks a richer fulfilment in art. It is true that with Schiller German literature and philosophy ascend to the clouds, but in their ascent they fortunately lose contact with dubious reality; in ascending they rescue the creative spirit from being stained by contemporary servility and preserve its integrity for future generations. Here Mehring's intermediate position between Marx and Kant clearly emerges; he accuses Schiller of a crime that later was to be called the mortal sin of *escapism* and, at the same time, attempts to demonstrate that Schiller was only able to maintain his integrity of spirit by flight into the sphere of autonomous art. A similar discord is visible in Mehring's final judgment upon Schiller; although Schiller is not to be counted among the great German writers, the proletarian masses would be badly advised if they were to disregard Schiller's "outcry against tyrants" and the "elevation of his conviction."[27] Mehring attempts with some success to make his liberal sympathies for Schiller an integral part of the Marxist literary canon; and how far he succeeded was demonstrated not long ago by the Schiller anniversary celebrations supported by the Communist party in the Soviet Union and in Ulbricht's Germany.

Mehring's literary theory finally aims at a prophecy of the *future* possibilities of great literature. In the present every literary effort is condemned to failure; as long as the class struggle poisons men's minds, any pure joy in beauty, any genuine creativity is impossible. "In all revolutionary periods," Mehring asserts, "in all classes fighting for their freedom, taste will always be extensively obscured by logic and morality, which, translated into philosophy, means only that where the capacity for perception and desire are severely strained, aesthetic judgment will always come under pressure."[28] The political desires of the fighting classes destroy any possibility of disinterested enjoyment; and with the destruction of detached joy, the possibility of great art

is demolished. ". . . Molière would not have been a great writer
of comedies if he had not been to a certain degree above the class
struggles of his time."[29] Mehring is sufficiently tolerant to ascribe
the responsibility for the contemporary denigration of art in the
confusion of the class war to both struggling parties; both of
them, the proletariat and the bourgeoisie, have their specific
share in the artistic decay: "If the declining bourgeois class cannot create great art *any more*," Mehring declares, "the rising
working class cannot *yet* create great art, even though a warm
longing for art may live in the depths of its soul."[30] Only the
victory of the proletariat will create the conditions for a new
and glorious development of art; the socialist state will resuscitate
that disinterested enjoyment of beauty out of which an undimmed
and truly autonomous art arises. In matters of aesthetics, the
final battle of the proletariat prepares an ultimate triumph for
none other than Immanuel Kant.

Georgy Valentinovich Plekhanov (1857–1918)

On December 6, 1876, a nineteen-year-old mining student,
G. V. Plekhanov, took part in a radical demonstration in St.
Petersburg's Kazan Square.[31] The tsarist police outlawed him on
the same day. Temporarily he sought refuge in Germany, but
soon decided to return to Russia in order to spread the ideas of
the *Narodniki*, who were trying to find support for their agrarian
socialism, developed from the traditional village communes, among
the peasants of the Don and Saratov regions. In his subsequent
second exile, young Plekhanov began to study Marx and Engels
in order to clarify his thoughts about the program of the *Narodniki*. In contrast to his Russian friends, he came to the conclusion
that a successful radical movement in Russia could no longer
depend on the slogans of the *Narodniki;* the new science of dialectical materialism should instead be introduced into the political
battle. During the eighties Plekhanov was busy firmly establishing
Marxism among the Russian radicals. He first published a series

of essays that defined the differences between Marxism and the theories of the Russian opposition groups; later, in his essay *On the Question of the Development of the Monistic View of History* (1895), he attempted to sketch a compact picture of historical materialism for the educated reader. Plekhanov was the first to plant the seed of Marxist aesthetics in the Russian sphere; most important among his critical writings in this endeavor are his *Letters without an Address* (1899–1900), in which he is concerned with the origins of art; his study of *French Dramatic Literature and French Painting in the XVIIIth Century from the Sociological Standpoint* (1905); and his essays on *Art and Society* (1912–13), *Belinsky* (1897), *Chernishevsky* (1897), and *Tolstoy* (1910).

Plekhanov's discussion of aesthetic questions takes its starting point from Tolstoy's pamphlet *What Is Art* (1898), which excited much interest among the intellectuals of the *fin de siècle*. In contrast to Tolstoy, who stressed above all communication of feeling, Plekhanov emphasized art's rational and social function. "I believe," he declared, "that art begins when the human being recalls within himself feelings *and ideas* that he has had under the influence of the reality surrounding him and *gives them a certain figurative expression.* Naturally he does this in the overwhelming majority of cases with the aim of transmitting what he has re-thought and re-felt to *other people.* Art is a *social phenomenon.*"[32] Plekhanov is primarily interested in locating the social basis of art: he is concerned with the origin of art "under the influence of the reality surrounding [the human being]." According to Plekhanov, idealistic systems of aesthetics are incapable of explaining adequately the social source of art; only dialectical materialism reveals art as a "reflection [of the] social order" as determined "in its historical development by the development of the means of production."[33]

It is important to note that the dogmatic axioms of Plekhanov —like those of his German colleague Franz Mehring—are partly shaped by contemporary Darwinism. The basic intention of Plekhanov's essay *On the Question of the Development of the*

Monistic View of History (1895) is to make Marxist proselytes from among the Russian Darwinists. Plekhanov's main arguments are directed against the Russian writer Nikolai Konstantinovich Mikhailovsky (1842–1904), who in his magazine *Russkoe Bogatsvo* ("Russian Wealth") had dared to compare Darwin and Marx by contrasting Darwin's scientific rigor with Marx's confusing abstractions. Mikhailovsky asserted that Darwin had constructed a logically ordered science of astonishing unity and richness, had, as it were, piled up a Mont Blanc of scientific observations—but where, asked the Russian critic, were the comparable achievements of the Marxists? Plekhanov could not turn a completely deaf ear to this charge; in order to convince the Russian Darwinists of the theoretical validity of Marxism, he declared that Marx was basically the most logical of the Darwinists. Plekhanov insisted that any scientific study of development must build upon Hegelian foundations; both Darwin and Marx had tried in their own way to observe the principle of continuous development in the struggle for existence. Darwin had concentrated upon the origin of plant and animal species; Marx, on the other hand, upon the origin of differing social organizations. Nevertheless, the researches of both moved in essentially the same direction: Plekhanov asserted in conclusion that Marxism, in the last analysis, was Darwinism applied to the social sciences. Plekhanov, who had studied zoölogy and anthropology in Geneva and at the Sorbonne, was not unwilling to fuse Darwinian principles into his Marxist aesthetic.

First, Plekhanov accepted Darwin's belief in a particular instinct that aims at the experience of beauty. "But when we behold," Darwin wrote, "male birds elaborately displaying their plumes and splendid colors before the females, while other birds not thus decorated make no such display, it is impossible to doubt that the females admire the beauty of their male partners."[34] Plekhanov, too, found it impossible to doubt Darwin's idea of a biological instinct for beauty. Without hesitation, the Russian Marxist declared that mankind was gifted with a specific instinct in its organic constitution for the experience of beauty.

For Plekhanov, as for Mehring, admiration for Darwin precedes a definite neo-Kantianism: from Darwin's idea of an *instinct* for beauty it is only a step to acceptance of Kant's rigorous diagnosis of a specific *faculty of the soul* that is directed toward the perception of beauty.

Plekhanov also willingly subscribes to Darwin's biological principle of antithesis. "Certain states of the mind," wrote Darwin, "lead . . . to certain habitual movements which were primarily, or may still be, of service; and we shall find that when a directly opposite state of mind is induced, there is a strong and involuntary tendency to the performance of movements of a directly opposite nature, though these have never been of any service."[35] For Plekhanov the same *biological* principle of antithesis operates in the history of human culture. Darwin restricts himself to the contrary reactions of dogs and cats, while the Russian Marxist points triumphantly to the attitude of the English aristocracy after the Restoration of 1666. In the antithesis of aristocratic cynicism to bourgeois sentimentality, in the clash of Royalist luxury and Puritan austerity, Plekhanov seriously believed that he had discovered "a special case of the Darwinian principle of antithesis in social psychology."[36] A zoölogical nadir of cultural history has been reached: in Plekhanov's perspective, clever writers like the Duke of Buckingham and brilliant stylists like the Earl of Rochester have been reduced, in the name of Darwin, to the level of *canis vulgaris*. But Plekhanov was aware that these zoölogical projections created a set of problems and paradoxes that were troublesome to the dogmatic Marxist. If it is true that biological factors such as the instinct for beauty and the antithesis of reactions govern the origin of art, what is the range of their actual effect? Do not the biological causes clash with the economic determinants that, according to the Marxist view, determine the origin of the arts? Are biological and economic elements effective side by side or does one supervene the other? What group of determinants, the biological or the economic, finally remains truly decisive?

Plekhanov tries to avoid the contradictions arising out of the

unavoidable clash between Darwinism and Marxism by means of
a philosophical distinction borrowed from the Aristotelian-Scho-
lastic tradition. Like the Scholastics of the Middle Ages, the
Russian Marxist distinguishes between the *potentialitas* and the
realitas of being. Biology, he asserts, determines nothing but the
creative possibilities of mankind; economics, on the other hand,
determines in the actual case which of the anticipated possibilities
will become historical reality. Accordingly, the experience of
beauty and with it, taste, rest upon a dual base: "It is because of
the nature of man that he *can have* aesthetic feelings and concepts. The transition from this *possibility* to *reality* comes from
the conditions surrounding him; through them it can be explained
how a particular social being (that is, a particular society, a
particular people, a particular class) must possess *just these*
aesthetic tastes and concepts and *no others*."[37] Plekhanov, like
Mehring, recognizes no contradiction between the demands of
biology and the postulates of dialectical materialism; biology as
the science of human possibilities and dialectical materialism as
the science of historically realized achievements each go their
own way without encroaching upon one another. One must admit,
declares Plekhanov emphatically, "that Darwinism does not in
the slightest contradict . . . the materialistic view of history."[38]

Inevitably, Plekhanov's interest in the biological factors of the
development of art led to a critical confrontation with the literary
doctrine of Hippolyte Taine. Plekhanov describes Taine's theory
of art as a circular argument; the vicious circle arises from
Taine's effort to prove that "the psyche of man, which is determined by its situation . . . is itself the final cause of this situation."[39] It is not too difficult to discover the source of the discomfort Plekhanov felt from Taine. Taine postulates an aggregate
of matter and spirit as the cause of art; besides climate and soil,
he stresses again and again the part played by religion, philosophy, and a particular legal system. To the Marxist Plekhanov
such a plurality of causes appears as an impermissible mixture
that must be broken down again by separating the material elements from the intellectual; therefore he praises Taine's inclina-

tion for the one while sharply condemning his tolerance for the other. "When Taine said that the psyche of man changes as a result of changes in man's situation," asserts Plekhanov, "he was a materialist; when he said that the situation of man is determined by his psyche, he repeated the idealistic view of the eighteenth century."[40] To be sure, Plekhanov is here defending a dogmatic point that had been disposed of some time before. Engels himself in a letter to Hans Starkenburg that appeared in the *Deutscher Akademiker* (1895), a little-known magazine of German socialist students, had explicitly denied this extreme standpoint; unaware of Engels' correspondence, Plekhanov had to defend a point four full years after Engels had changed his mind.

In another respect, however, Plekhanov goes far beyond Marx and Engels. He uses anthropological data in order to support his conception of the origin and development of art out of human labor. Engels was forced by the pressure of science to call upon modern anthropology in his essay on *The Origin of the Family, Private Property, and the State* (*Der Ursprung der Familie, des Privateigentums und des Staats* [1884]), but essentially he was satisfied to cite the researches of the American Lewis Henry Morgan (1818–81). Plekhanov went to work much more thoroughly: in the second and third (1900) *Letters without an Address* he unfolds a vast amount of expert anthropological knowledge. It is clear that he is inclined to take his most important arguments from the works of the German scholar Karl Bücher (1847–1930). He concentrates less on Bücher's essay *On the Primitive Economic Situation* (*Über den wirtschaftlichen Urzustand* [1893]), which allows the principle of play and art to precede the economic organization of natural man, but rather on his later study, *Work and Rhythm* (*Arbeit und Rhythmus* [1896]), in which the German scholar pursues the undeniable connections between musical rhythms, work songs, and simple forms of art. But Plekhanov simplifies Bücher's explorations into a brutal formula of the priority of work over art: Bücher's *Work and Rhythm* proves, says Plekhanov, "that *work is older than art* and that in any case *man first regards objects and phenomena from the utilitarian standpoint and only subsequently comes to an aesthetic standpoint in his relationship to them.*"[41] Despite this extreme simplification, Plekhanov remains conscious of the narrow boundaries of anthropological proof in the aesthetic sphere. He knows that anthropology may be of importance in the investigation of simple art forms but that it quickly loses its usefulness where higher, that is, more intricately organized, works of art are involved. Although, as he says, "the study of the way of life of primitive men" explicitly confirms "the basic thesis of historical materialism,"[42] it is impossible to follow the more complicated development of the arts from the same point of view. In order to observe "the presence of a causal relationship between being and consciousness, between the technology and economics of a society . . . and its art," a new method is required that "sociologically" absorbs and illuminates the anthropological material.

Plekhanov's study *On French Dramatic Literature and French Painting of the XVIIIth Century from the Standpoint of Sociology* illustrates a method of research that claims to be a Marxist sociology of art. Yet it owes a great deal to Taine. Although Plekhanov wanted to explain French art strictly from economic causes, he came, like Taine, to the conclusion that French tragedy was "a child of the courtly aristocracy";[43] like Taine, the Russian Marxist also asserted that a "playwright in whose works the proper conventional dose of courtly, aristocratic 'sublimity' was not present . . . would have waited [in vain] for the applause of the public of that time."[44] The difficulties in such explanations become apparent as soon as Plekhanov attempts to describe the meaning of the dramatic unities in economic terms. In his opinion, the popularity of the three unities correspond "to the increased artistic expectations of the higher classes, for whom the naïve scenic absurdities of the preceding age had become intolerable."[45]

Of greater consequence than these literary exercises in Taine's footsteps was Plekhanov's enthusiasm for Kantian aesthetics. Like Mehring, with whose *Die Lessing-Legende* (1893) he was acquainted, Plekhanov, too, speaks with distinct admiration of

Kant's postulate of disinterested enjoyment of beauty—at least in the case of the individual. "Kant said that the enjoyment that determines the judgment of taste was completely disinterested, and a judgment upon beauty in which the least interestedness were mixed would be very partial and not a pure judgment of taste."[46] Plekhanov admits that the Kantian postulate of disinterested enjoyment of beauty necessarily contradicts a utilitarian theory of the development of art. In order to resolve the contradiction, Plekhanov is forced to return to the psychology of the eighteenth century and to distinguish, in Kant's sense, between the various spiritual capacities of man. The sphere of utility, writes Plekhanov, is that of calculation and intellect; the sphere of beauty, on the other hand, coincides with that of contemplation; furthermore, he concludes, "the area that belongs to contemplation is incomparably larger than the area of the intellect: although the social human being enjoys that which appears beautiful to him, he is almost never conscious of the utility with [which] . . . the notion of this object is connected."[47] To be sure, such an attempt at explanation contributes little to the resolution of the inner paradox: basically, Plekhanov has no other way out than to pass over the contradictions with an apodictic proposition. "The utility," he asserts dauntlessly, "exists nevertheless; it lies nevertheless at the basis of aesthetic pleasure. . . . If the utility were not there, the object would not appear beautiful."[48]

The incompatibility of these philosophical premises appears in Plekhanov's lectures on *Art and Social Life* (1912–13). He characterizes two possible attitudes toward art: the utilitarian standpoint, which tries to force art into the service of outside forces, and another, freer, perspective, which allows art a pure and independent existence. Plekhanov is far from favoring completely either one or the other perspective; surprisingly enough, he shows very little sympathy for utilitarian demands on art and artists. He goes so far as to censure important Russian critics like Chernishevsky and Pissarev for their all too pragmatic demands on the writer; propaganda art, Plekhanov points out, has always enjoyed the undivided support of every political regime, whether of a revolutionary or a reactionary kind. In significant contrast to Lenin, Plekhanov explicitly insists that art shall judge itself. Plekhanov's clarity leaves nothing to be desired: speaking to his comrades, Plekhanov mentions a number of reactionary ministers and rulers who were wrong in demanding subservient art, such as, for example Razumovsky, the tsarist minister of education, Louis XIV, Napoleon Bonaparte, Tsar Nicholas I, and Napoleon III. What would have happened, asks Plekhanov, if the tsars had really succeeded in making important writers like Pushkin or Ostrovsky "into servants of morality as it is understood by the police?"[49] The answer to this question is not without prophetic insight into the future development of Russian literature: "The Muses, subordinated as they were to the artists, had they become Muses of the state, would have shown the clearest signs of decay and would have lost much of their veracity, their strength, and their charm."[50]

This condemnation of subservient art corresponds to Plekhanov's half-hearted defense of the principle of *l'art pour l'art*. The Marxist Plekhanov stresses that every artist who separates himself from his class raises his voice without hope; nevertheless, from time to time an art separated from the fertile soil of its class, being therefore politically indifferent, may fulfil an important task. Even artists like Théophile Gautier and his followers had a revolutionary effect in their protest against the ugly commercialism of the bourgeois world. "The young sons of the bourgeoisie belonged to the Romantic circles," declares Plekhanov, ". . . who . . . were nevertheless outraged by the filth, the desolation, and the insipidness of bourgeois existence. The new art to which they felt so strongly attracted was for them a place of refuge from this filth, this desolation, this insipidness."[51] Even if political indifference limited the vision of the writer, he raised "the value of his literary creations" by preventing them "from taking the part of bourgeois insipidness, sedateness, and literalness."[52] Plekhanov appreciates Gautier and condemns Gorky's novel *The Mothers* (1907), which Lenin liked very much, as mere propaganda. Plekhanov took the position that propaganda for or against Marxism destroys the work of art, because political rhetoric forces "the writer into the role of a preacher." It was, after all, not the task of the artist to speak "primarily the language of logic"; his job was rather to speak "in the language of images."[53] If Gorky wanted to earn the real laurels of the artist, he would have to return immediately to the artist's true tasks.

There is basically no way out of the contradiction in which Plekhanov, as a theoretician of art, became entangled. As a convinced Marxist, he believed in the economic foundation of art and in the overwhelming force of historical development; as an admirer of Kant, however, he was, like Mehring, concerned about the autonomy of pure beauty. Plekhanov undertook a difficult attempt to clear up the contradictions by insisting that in the last analysis *the idea* determines the quality of a work of art; the artist, if he were only wise enough, must give himself up to the great emancipatory impulses of his age and, with them, to the determining forces of history. But this attempt, too, failed to convince his comrades. Lunacharsky charged Plekhanov with "objectivism"; Lenin, who demanded the strictest service from art, accused Plekhanov of disloyalty to the principles of the Bolshevik cause. The bitter end came with the triumph of the Revolution. Hardly had the Soviets taken power when they issued a police ordinance "concerning the security of Citizen G. V. Plekhanov" (November 16, 1917). The man who had transplanted the political and aesthetic theory of Marxism to Russia died as a prisoner of his victorious comrades. He lies buried, not far from Belinsky, in Leningrad.

8

Georg Lukács as a Theoretician of Literature

The political fate of Georg Lukács has not lacked ironic reversals. Twice he stood at the threshold of power, but neither as Bela Kun's people's commissar for education nor as Imre Nagy's minister of culture was he able to stay in office for very long. After the collapse of the Hungarian Soviet regime in 1919, his political opponents drove him into exile in Austria; a generation later it was the political police of his own Russian comrades who deported him, along with the other ministers of the revolutionary Nagy regime (even though he had resigned his office as early as November 3, 1956) to a remote Rumanian spa from which he was not permitted to return home until the spring of the following year. It was about this time that his essays were rediscovered by the younger generation of intellectuals in France, Italy, and West Germany; and if Brecht became a figure of international fame after the visit of his troupe to Paris (1954), Lukács found himself, surely against his will, a political philosopher and critic of wide European influence when he was deported by the Soviets, whose cause he had defended almost all his adult life.

But his ideas had been long in developing; for him, the Hungarian revolution of 1956 marked a late turning point rather than a radical change. Indeed, there is as much continuity as change in his rich intellectual development; as a critic of literature he is always concerned with a historical view of the "forms" created by the human mind and their changing relationship to man's ethical existence; and although for purely pedagogical reasons it is tempting to distinguish at least three distinct periods in his development as a theoretician and critic of literature, he never wavered in his loyalty to his basic concerns. The critic Lukács began as a disciple of German philosophy with a particular talent for responding to art; after absorbing a good deal of *Lebensphilosophie* and Neo-Kantianism, he turned to Hegel for a more total view of human life (1909–17). But a political hiatus of more than a decade separates his early "idealistic" period from his doctrinaire—if not Stalinist—maturity (1931–56); only after he had spent at least ten years elaborating political ideas that provoked Lenin himself did he again return to literary theory and criticism, and, in a climate more favorable to his conservative ideas, developed a theory of realism that he ingeniously identified with the socialist realism imposed upon Communist writers by the political bureaucracy. In the years after Stalin's death, Khrushchev's critique of the "personality cult," and the Hungarian uprising, a third stage in Lukács' literary thought emerged and was confirmed by the first volumes of his *Aesthetik* (1965——). Though still conservative in taste, the octogenarian Lukács has become more tolerant; he unexpectedly praises Aristotle for his pragmatic ways and looks back to the teachers of his early days with renewed sympathy. The wheel has come full circle.

The Heidelberg Period

The critic Lukács, who has a definite claim to the serious attention of even his most determined political opponents, comes from that gifted central European *jeunesse dorée* that, in the wasteland of World War I, sought salvation in the absolutist embrace of the great antiliberal movements. Georgy Szegedy von Lukács, born in Budapest on April 13, 1885, into a family of bankers and diplomats, attended the university first at home and later in Berlin, where he greatly admired the philosopher Georg Simmel. As an editor of the magazine *Nyugat* ("The West"), young Lukács took a lively part in the intellectual life of the Hungarian capital, wrote an important essay on the development of the modern drama (which received a distinguished literary prize), and after a grand tour in Italy, settled in Heidelberg (1912), where he was to be found among the admirers of Max Weber, Friedrich Gundolf, and Stefan George. At that time he was probably thinking seriously of qualifying for a professorship of aesthetics at the University of Heidelberg. His first German books, *The Soul and the Forms* (*Die Seele und die Formen* [1911]), a collection of sensitive soliloquies on the nature of modern art, and his difficult *Theory of the Novel* (*Theorie des Romans*, written in 1914–15, published in 1920) were—quite apart from his later political developments—documents of an artistic and critical talent of the first rank; only now are these early essays, which charm by the power of suggestive poetry rather than by precise philological analysis, coming into their own.

At a time when Shklovsky in Russia and Lubbock in Great Britain were successfully banning metaphysics from literary criticism, Lukács' *Theory of the Novel* appeared as a late and stubborn attempt to reconstruct the most characteristic genre of modern literature from pure thought. To young Lukács, the theory of any genre coincides with its history, which, in true German fashion, he believes begins with the inimitable art of Greece. But young Lukács rejects the "beautiful souls" (*schöne Seelen*)[1] who claim to perceive a characteristic calm in Greek antiquity as decisively as he does those "deep minds"[2] who dissolve the Greek world into ecstatic pessimism. In contrast to Winckelmann and Nietzsche, Lukács strives for his own topography of the Greek mind; like Hegel and the art historian Wölfflin, he conceives of Greece as a world of sculptured depth and harmony that does not yet know any gap between meaning and being, soul and essence, inner and external life. Lukács does not tolerate any history of the mind before that of Greece; the Greeks are the nation whose inevitable destiny in the intellectual development of mankind it was to give birth to the great "forms" of the creative mind: the epic, tragedy, and philosophy. In the dawn of history we perceive the absolute immanence of the heroic age of Homer; as time progresses, however, integral substance withers (*ent-weicht*) more and more until, finally, the irremediable development toward philosophical alienation results in the most rigid opposition of meaning and being confirmed by the unfortunate transcendence of Platonic thought.

Tragedy, according to young Lukács, develops precisely between the time of the great epic and Plato. While the epic is still fortunate enough to be able to deal with the magnificent essence of life, tragedy (in a moment of progressive alienation) has no other chance but to question reality. "The great epic gives form to the extensive totality of life; the drama to the intensive totality of essence."[3] From these assumptions Lukács derives a closed ontology of the epic and tragic genres; unavoidably, the epic is empirical because it aims at the particular, at the given condition of the world; drama, on the other hand, lives in the world of what ought to be, in a tension toward the future. With great emphasis young Lukács (quite in contrast to his later Marxist ideas on the novel) excludes the hero "as he ought to be" from all forms of the epic; Homer's Achilles is epically "more valid" than Vergil's Aeneas, motivated as he is by imperatives; Balzac's figures are more authentic than the programmatic heroes of Zola.

After the epic and tragedy developed, Greek thought ossified in the harsh opposition of idea and being of Platonic philosophy. A great divide is reached; now art, to use Schiller's terminology, constitutes a "created totality"[4] that, detached from real being, must create an illusion to mask its fall from grace. In this "sentimentive" epoch, the novel, as a second possibility of the epic mode, takes the place of the genuine, resplendent genre. But it is by no means the psychology of the individual writers, asserts Lukács, that is responsible for the change in form; in his bitter aversion to a merely psychological explication of literature (to be continued throughout his Stalinist period), young Lukács insists that the change of form is not determined by a metamorphosis of "individual intentions" but rather by the succession of suprapersonal and, as it were, objective "events in the history of philosophy."[5] The epic, as the incarnation of a harmonious life, formed a self-contained totality; in the moment after the great disenchantment it is the task and the cursed fate of the novel that it must go searching for lost integrity.

Unfortunately, the novel, as a late product of the mind, seems more liable to degradation than any other genre. Lukács builds his defense of the "genuine" novel, as well as his condemnation of the "empty" novel, completely upon philosophical criteria of content and ignores literary standards. It is not the writer's craftsmanship that is ultimately decisive but the philosophical basis of the work. The light novel (*Unterhaltungsroman*) is, according to Lukács, inartistic not because it works with inartistic methods but because it lacks definite moorings in the philosophy of history; it is philosophically meaningless and therefore aesthetically invalid. The immanent problem of the genuine novel relates to the equivalent issue of the philosophical moment and is aesthetically justified because of the share it has in "fate."[6] In elevating philosophy to the position of supreme judge of art it hardly occurs to Lukács that the wise judge may be incompetent in this particular case; a fundamental decision has been reached, and although in Lukács' later development the judges will change, the incompetent court remains in session.

But by formulating a philosophical justification of the novel Lukács suggests an inner structure that in principle separates the disharmonious novel from the felicitous integrity of the epic. As a reflection of harmonious life, the epic had "organic continuity," whereas the novel, as an expression of metaphysical tension, merely offers a "heterogeneous, contingent disjunct (*Diskretum*)."[7] In spite of these abstract obsessions, young Lukács does arrive at important insights into the technique of the novel; the elements of the novel, in contrast to the epic, must have a strictly architec-

tonic function whether as a reflection of the theme or as an anticipation of hidden motives important for the conclusion.[8] The way
is open to a judicious interpretation of the literary expedients of
the novel, but philosophical theory once again insists upon its
privileges. Because the novel cannot represent anything but the
search for totality, Lukács stresses that "the external form of the
novel is essentially biographical";[9] and thus the novel as such is
falsely equated with one of its particular forms, the novel of development and education (*Bildungsroman*) that occurs so prominently in German literature. It is not accidental that young Lukács
seems to be thoroughly charmed by the Romantic Novalis; the
norm of the novel that Lukács postulates is ultimately oriented on
Heinrich von Ofterdingen (1802) and must fail when the novel,
as a portrait of manners, concerns itself with a "circle of persons"
(Theodor Fontane).

Lukács cannot avoid the question of how the particular individual whose career appears in the novel can have universal
meaning; he derives his answer, as is to be expected, from German idealism. The individual, in the sense of Hegel (and Taine)
symbolically represents and incarnates an important moment in
the philosophy of history and receives an ontological blessing
from a power far beyond individuality. Inevitably, Lukács has
touched upon the question of the representative type that will
turn into one of the central issues of his middle period.

But young Lukács was aware of the difficulties that arise from
equating the novel with the spiritual history of a select individual.
Aiming at greater variety, he concedes to the novel two main
forms of historical realization: (1) the form of the "narrower
soul," which confronts the world with a rigid *apriority;* and (2)
that of the "wider soul," which is more comprehensively alive
than the experience to which it is subjected by the world. The
narrower soul incarnates a "demonism of abstract idealism"[10]
and moves in pure activity; the world loses its intrinsic value and
turns into the wall of a cave on which, like Platonic shadows, the
visions of the solipsistic soul appear. Ardent soul and emptied

world constitute the structure of a novel with intensive plot and fragmentary psychology (*Don Quixote*).

The wider soul thinks of its individual life as spontaneous truth, enters into self-willed competition with the outer world, and attempts to see itself as the essence of the universe. Necessarily, it must come to grief, and, in failing, provide material for a novel of limited action and extensive psychology (Flaubert's *Education sentimentale*). If the form of the narrower soul is threatened by the danger of abstraction, the opposite case appears in the novel of the wider soul; it is weakened by the danger of too much concreteness. According to young Lukács, only Goethe's *Wilhelm Meister* (1795–96) succeeded in fusing the all too concrete and the all too abstract into a concrete universal; only in *Wilhelm Meister*, Lukács insists, does the individual soul seem finally united with the world, and the world revealed in the individual. For the first time, *Wilhelm Meister*, as though in a mystic revelation, exposes the secret desire of the novel to return home to the epic of lost totality. Goethe's *Wilhelm Meister*, like Dostoevsky's novels later (which derive from a harmonious world of Russian piety), may well anticipate a coming third period of the narrative that will once again mirror harmonious abundance and express a world in which all seeking is transformed into finding again, and all the alienation of the soul from true being will be healed in the solemn unity of meaning and existence.

The Doctrinaire Period

To the author, this theory of the novel must have had an almost spectral appearance when it was finally published in Berlin (1920). During the later years of the war, Lukács returned to Hungary, developed (as he said) by way of a local form of syndicalism into a radical Marxist, and, again according to his own later report, joined the Communist party in the winter of 1918. After the brief interlude of the Hungarian Soviet Republic, he had to escape to Austria from the Horthy regime; in Vienna he edited a Communist party periodical for a time and worked on important political studies. It seems that he had abandoned literary criticism altogether; his writings of the twenties consist of provocative essays in political philosophy, above all *History and Class-Consciousness* (*Geschichte und Klassenbewusstsein* [1923]), *Lenin* (1924), and *Moses Hess and the Problems of Idealist Dialectics* (*Moses Hess und die Probleme der idealistischen Dialektik* [1926]).[11] In Vienna, Lukács was at loggerheads with the other functionaries of the Hungarian party exiled in Moscow; after *History and Class-Consciousness* was published, Lukács was condemned by the Comintern, attacked by his own friends, and deprived of all editorial functions. But he did not return to literary studies immediately; only after he had studied for a year at the Marx-Engels-Lenin Institute in Moscow (1930–31) did he begin to comment on contemporary Communist writers and concern himself with Friedrich Theodor Vischer,[12] whose work is a continuation of Hegel's, and Franz Mehring,[13] the first Marxist literary historian. When Hitler came to power, Lukács, who had been living in Berlin, returned to Moscow once more and began to elaborate his system of realism, which he conveniently identified with the official postulates of the period; it is hard to overlook that during World War II he functioned as a Stalinist watchdog over the unhappy writers among the German anti-Fascist writers in exile. In 1945 he came back to Hungary; he was installed in Parliament and the Academy and elevated to the position of professor of aesthetics at the University of Budapest. Although he did not always enjoy the favor of the political administration, which from time to time accused him of subtle irreverence for the achievements of recent Soviet literature, it became increasingly clear that during the thirties and forties he had earned authoritative importance as the foremost theoretician and literary critic of the entire Stalinist sphere. As was demonstrated by the *Festschrift* ([East] Berlin, 1955) presented to him on his seventieth birthday, shortly before the outbreak of the Hungarian uprising and new Party attacks on him, he was widely quoted by his friends as well as by unsuspecting official admirers as the patriarch of Communist literary studies.

Lukács bases the literary norm of his doctrinaire period on a crude motif from Lenin's epistemology. Like Lenin in his conflict with the philosopher Ernst Mach, Lukács insists upon a fundamental dualism of objective, real, external, and internal worlds that together form a unified and knowable universe. In this dualism, all consciousness of the external world arises as a "reflection of reality that exists independently of our consciousness."[14] Art presents images of being; in order to give an interpretation of artistic processes, Lukács must necessarily revive the age-old metaphor of the mirror, which thus continues to enjoy a latter-day resurrection in Marxist aesthetics. But Lukács does not hesitate in the least to admit that the image of the work of art as a mirror derives from Platonic idealism; the trouble is that in his aesthetics the function of the mirror as well as the range of the mirrored reality is not less restricted a priori than in the Renaissance. Genuine literature results only when the mirror reflects a circumscribed segment of reality; the decision between what is too little and what is too much is unfortunately made not by the artist himself but by the socially committed philosopher. Whenever the reflection shows too much of the unformed expanse of reality, "naturalism" threatens; when the mirror fulfils only its technical function and irresponsibly neglects external reality for the sake of its own egotistic glory, art degenerates into "formalism." In "naturalism" there arises "abstract objectivity";[15] a multitude of "superficial details"[16] appears: the raw material that the passive writer formlessly gathers together. In "formalism," on the other hand, the writer is able to offer nothing but "abstract subjectivity";[17] the image of objective reality is obscured by the false glare of the poetic subject himself, who places in the foreground the refined but empty ego and the hubris of self-involved techniques.

Lukács' characterization of the false extremes of artistic practice—"naturalism" and "formalism"—derives methodically from German classical philosophy and possesses a certain relevance outside his thought as well. "Naturalism," as Lukács understands it, corresponds to the predominance of the material over the idea that should inform and permeate it; his concept of "formalism" refers to the completely dematerialized idea that seeks vainly for the sensory mode in which it is to be made visible. "Naturalism" is blind because it lacks intellectual form; "formalism" empty because it lacks material appeal to the senses. Most of Lukács' questionable value judgments derive from this axiom. He finds the false extremes represented in western European literature by the naturalist Zola and the symbolist Maeterlinck; in Germany the corresponding aesthetically invalid pair is made up of Hauptmann and Rilke. Hauptmann serves as a representative example to Lukács because in *Hannele's Ascension* (*Hanneles Himmelfahrt* [1893]), "naturalist" art, true to Hegel's concept, suddenly turns into a "formalist" opposite of insubstantial symbolism. Rilke's overrefined ego, according to Lukács, can turn just as easily into the antithesis of brutality and anticipates the crimes of the Nazi Storm Troops. To demonstrate this astonishing assertion, Lukács quotes a section from Rilke's poem "Charles XII of Sweden Rides in the Ukraine" ("Karl der Zwölfte von Schweden reitet in der Ukraine" [1900]), completely ignores the fact that the poem is written from the perspective of the Swedish king's fictional persona, and naïvely identifies Rilke with his speaker.[18]

Lukács continues to assert that the work of art is an intermediate phenomenon (*Mittelding*) in the truest sense of the word; standing equidistant from a conglomeration of mere materials and an empty idea, it strives "for the specifically artistic reflection of reality in a dialectical way."[19] Unfortunately, the criteria of the "specifically artistic" as well as of the "dialectic" are beyond rational control; being inaccessible to further analysis, they merely conceal the absolute demand that the artist must aim for the typical—not the typical that appears on the surface of transient things but "in the elements and tendencies of reality that recur according to regular laws, although changing with the changing circumstances."[20] The type in literature is by no means identical with the mere hero; literary heroes only turn into genuine types when they correspond to a series of philosophical stipulations. According to Lukács, the literary type is to be defined by the four criteria of breadth (*Breite*), essentiality (*Wesentlichkeit*), enhancement (*Steigerung*), and self-awareness (*Selbstbewusstheit*).

Lukács defines *breadth* as the "formed connection between Weltanschauung and the personal being of the character."[21] This means that the writer must equip his hero with a number of tangible details and specific character traits. The literary characteristic of breadth corresponds to the philosophical category of singularity. For Lukács, exactly as for Hegel and his disciple Friedrich Engels, the literary type must be a *Dieser*, that is, a richly determined individual whose development takes place while remaining constantly rooted in the soil of history. Schiller's heroes, asserts Lukács, lack literary breadth and are therefore far inferior to Shakespeare's characters—an observation at least as old as the corresponding passages in Hegel's *Lectures on Aesthetics*.

In order to be *essential*, the literary type must, in its individuation, substantially represent the dominant forces of changing society. The type has universality as well as singularity; it is, exactly as a German idealist would demand, the literary form of the concrete universal. The danger lies in the potential degradation of what is "essential"; here the substantial idea is no longer defined by an enthusiast of the divine like Schelling or by a believer in the absolutely free *Weltgeist* like Hegel. Lukács quite intolerantly defines the essential out of the political postulates of a narrow power group in a temporary situation of conflict. His massive and unrefined idea of the essential clearly emerges in his criticism of Döblin's brilliant novel *Berlin Alexanderplatz* and in his polemic against the liberal authors of the German emigration (1933). Franz Biberkopf, Döblin's hero, can make no claim to be a type, for, asks Lukács, "what has . . . the psychological fate of such a character [a pimp and criminal] to do with the fate of the German working class in the post-war period and through it with that of the German people of this period?"[22]

By means of the criteria of *enhancement* and *self-awareness*, the concept of the literary type is bound even more tightly to the political apriority. Literary enhancement appears as an "amplification of individual dimensions"[23] or as the "perceptible unfolding of [those] . . . dormant possibilities"[24] that in real life appear only in incomplete form. This concept of the type does not attempt to capture ordinary or average phenomena near at hand, but rather the potential or latent character of a situation that has not yet developed and is only remotely suggested in present reality. By requiring an anticipation of what is going to happen, Lukács' concept of the type—like that of Engels—rejoins the theological tradition. Lukács, too, reasserts its messianic implications when he quotes Paul Lafargue and speaks of the type as a "prophetic figure."[25]

Finally, the fourth category, which completes the philosophical definition of the literary type, is that of *self-awareness.* "The 'rank' of the main character [of a literary work]," asserts Lukács, "arises essentially from the degree of his consciousness of his fate, from his ability to *consciously* raise the personal and accidental quality of his fate to a definite, concrete level of generality."[26] In other words, the type must clearly articulate his connection with the essential and make himself a sounding board for universal propositions. Again some dubious criteria for practical literary criticism are implied: Lukács unavoidably condemns all works whose heroes are slow-witted and inarticulate. Büchner's *Woyzeck* barely escapes this condemnation because of the political activity of its author; all the more implacable is Lukács' judgment on Hauptmann, who dared to put inarticulate heroes, in the Hegelian sense, on the stage. Hauptmann's work shows nothing but "the impossibility of solving even a relatively simple situation because all possibility of communication has ceased among these people who have become completely isolated, because each one is solipsistically and egoistically imprisoned in his own world."[27] *Rose Bernd*, the most deeply moving plebeian figure in modern German drama, is swept from the stage with a wave of the hand because the theoretician of proletarian aesthetics finds that she suffers below the level of Hegelian self-awareness.

The theory of the literary type, which does not attempt to conceal its origins in German idealism and nineteenth-century traditions, provides Lukács with critical insights into contemporary literature that are distinctly different from those of his own political allies as well as from the critical temperament of the age. Lukács' angry rejection of the leitmotiv technique, which seems to have prevailed since "Wagner and others"[28]—Thomas Mann's name is politely suppressed—sounds completely Hegelian. Quoting a critical remark of Balzac on James Fenimore Cooper, Lukács battles tirelessly against a literary method that damages the solidity of characters by circumventing the legitimate structuring of the type; instead of concrete "breadth," the leitmotiv presents a "merely abstract, mechanical, and schematic 'unity' of the character."[29] With a harshness that is as surprising as it is consistent, Lukács, who as a good classicist insists upon the sharp differentiation of literary genres, condemns any modern attempt to construct an epic drama. Any combination or mixture of genres is anathema to him; the doctrinaire Lukács has never hesitated to join the Stalinist critics of Brecht in accusing the epic theater of being a misleading experiment. "The failure to acknowledge the inner laws of the [genre] has lately produced a clever, empty, and void collection of substitutes for the absence of drama on the stage."[30] Only the aging Lukács grudgingly concerns himself with the implications of Brecht's artistic achievements and tries to reinterpret Brecht in his own way.

The connection Lukács establishes between the theory of reflection and the concept of the literary type must finally end in rationally insoluble contradictions. How can a work of art as a mirror reflect the present *and* the future simultaneously? How is the writer to find access to the required type? Lukács has no other choice but to stand the aesthetics of objective realism on its head (or, as he would say himself, on its feet). It is, Lukács asserts, primarily historical reality itself that leads the writer to the discovery of the essential, and as soon as the essential has been discovered and isolated, it must immediately be clothed in sensory detail in order to make the type apparent as "communicated directness" (*vermittelte Unmittelbarkeit*).[31] However, this by no means resolves the original paradox but only sharpens it; it is still true that the work of art as a mirror must reflect "the currents hidden under the surface."[32] Whenever necessary, the mirror has to function as an X-ray machine or as a divining rod.

In the historical movement of reality that reveals itself to the writer, the materialistic element of Marxism finally triumphs. Type and genre are torn away from the intent of the writer and declared to be a function of historical reality itself. It is history itself that immediately brings forth epic and drama out of epic situations and dramatic conflicts. With a highly questionable denial of the poetic mind (reminiscent of Lukács' earliest work), he claims that the genres arise "out of the material of life."[33] In a book surprisingly rich in legitimate literary insights, *The Historical Novel* (Russian ed., 1938; German ed., 1955), Lukács for a moment succumbs to the temptation of suggesting epic and dramatic periods of world history as the foundation of distinct genres; it is no accident, he says, "that the great periods of tragedy coincide with the great historical revolutions in human society."[34] But such periodizing of literary genres can only be purchased at the price of gross oversimplifications. Lukács believes that the zenith of Greek tragedy coincides with the rise of the democratic city-state and the decay of the original Greek tribal community; Shakespearean tragedy, in turn, grows out of the collision of declining feudalism with the vanguard of the new bourgeoisie. Yet the particular economic basis for French and German classical tragedy is lacking; Lukács must therefore quickly modify his hypothesis. "An obstinate insistence upon great revolutions"[35] would be false, for the inner contradictions of social existence are "a universal fact of life."[36] Perhaps the reason why Lukács does not push his historical theory of genres too far is to avoid obscuring the more comprehensive historical conception of literature that powerfully permeates his work. History and literature appear to be driven by a mysterious force that, in three great fulfilments, carries art from the noble glory of Greece across the intermediate peaks of German classicism and its lesser ranges to the renewed glory of the Communist age. Lukács follows Hegel and the idealist tradition in his belief that Greece possessed as the secret of its art the "unity of the sensorially realistic form of the particular with the clear working-out of the universally essential."[37] Although Winckelmann, Goethe, and Hegel preserved a reflection of Greek splendor, the Greek heritage was ruined by the capitalist age, which destroys the integrity of human existence by the brutal and progressive division of labor and thus, even in the realm of the intellectual superstructure, forces idea and sensuous abundance, content and form, mind and reality into unfortunate opposition. The economic division of labor, in its own dialectic, creates two characteristic bourgeois types, who, even in the realm of literature, passionately pursue their singular possibilities. On the one hand, the *bourgeois* strives for mastery of the purely material and degenerates into gathering superficial details, plebeian opposition, and "naturalism"; on the other, the *citoyen* embraces too enthusiastically the pure idea and ends, by proudly accentuating his own ego, with empty technique and insubstantial "formalism."[38] To be sure, the best among the *bourgeois* and *citoyens* are aware of the lost greatness and strive vainly for its renewal, but it is impossible to fight the economic situation. The *bourgeois* Zola inevitably ends in passive description of reality; the noble *citoyens* Milton, Alfieri, and Hölderlin create works of the highest ideal purity and yet the greatest poverty in substance. In this conception of history, the German *Klassik* occupies a peculiarly intermediate position; it develops midway between the already lost and not yet rewon paradise of the concrete universal. Schiller, in his theory far more than in his works, attempts to unite aesthetic theory with history and thus anticipates Hegel; Goethe in his *Faust* embodies the whole human history of genres and creates a poetic analogy to Hegel's *Phenomenology of the Spirit*. Lukács' heroes of the nineteenth century are Scott, Balzac, Gottfried Keller, and Tolstoy: Scott was the first to aim consciously at a typology of the historical novel; Balzac (here Lukács follows Marx and Gutzkow) recognized the economic foundation of social processes; Keller symbolically demonstrated what heights German literature might have reached if the revolution of 1848 had been successful in Germany; Tolstoy masterfully united popular substance with the height of representative typology. Baudelaire is tolerated in the history of literature because he revealed "the ugliness of capitalist life";[39] Flaubert, on the other hand, once a favorite of the young Lukács, retreats into obscurity because he tried artificially to force a "formalistic" system of words upon life that is always changing. At times Nietzsche appears in a surprisingly bright light; although Lukács discusses him as the "forerunner of Fascist aesthetics," behind the camouflage of such slogans there appears high praise for a "thinker of quality and rank"[40] who preserved the classical and rationalist heritage of the Germans in the imperialist age. The October Revolution of 1917 constitutes the prologue to a new period of literary history; Lukács long believed that with the Soviet state the millennium of a reinterpreted human existence had dawned, for the proletarian revolution negates the capitalist division of labor, and, in the negation of the negation, reunites truth and beauty. It will be the task of Communist writers and poets, Lukács asserts in his doctrinaire period, to found the third age of the concrete universal.

Idealist and Doctrinaire: Some Continuities

In one of the works of his middle period, Lukács calls his *Theory of the Novel* (1920) "a reactionary work in every respect, full of idealistic mysticism, wrong in all its estimates of historical development."[41] This ritual self-condemnation—one of many in Lukács' life—has the purpose of bringing the reader to the quick conclusion that his conversion to Marxism was an epoch-making event in his development that completely revolutionized his world view and his aesthetic theory. Politically, Lukács may have undergone a considerable metamorphosis since his Berlin and Heidelberg days, when his attention was concentrated on Georg Simmel, Max Weber, Friedrich Gundolf, and Stefan George; in his literary theory the conversion to Marxism was much less revolutionary. Lukács never left the territory of classical aesthetics; in a certain sense he is the last Hegelian in the grand style who still succeeded —even if under widely differing circumstances—in restoring the basic conceptions of classical German aesthetics.

A basic continuity appears first of all in the dichotomy of content and form, to which Lukács remained equally devoted in his doctrinaire as in his idealistic period. A radical conversion was not at all necessary; the objective idealist looks at the individual work of art just as condescendingly from the heights of the absolute spirit as does the Marxist from his standpoint of absolute history; both, idealist and doctrinaire Marxist, are first of all devoted to their ideological truth and therefore all too inclined to judge the work of art according to those non-aesthetic elements that are misused to define the artistic character of the work. In the *Theory of the Novel* it is essentially the philosophy of history that is realized in the novel; in the Marxist theory it is the social movement of a material kind that comes to light in the individual achievement. Therefore Lukács can speak in his *Theory of the Novel* of those "empty shells of dead forms"[42] that do not house the spirit of the age; in his Marxist period, without having to change his fundamental attitude, he speaks of the *formal-artistic* and the *content* elements of literature. The hegemony of content is almost absolute; first it is the Hegelian *Weltgeist,* then material history, which proves in its development "that the formal problems of art must grow out of problems of content, that the formal problems are determined by problems of content."[43] Necessarily Lukács succumbs (at least occasionally) to the temptation of regarding artistic form as decoration that can be intentionally added to the work or abstracted from it. "One need only" he once wrote, "turn [Croce's] theory of history into verse in order to get a poem of Hofmannsthal or of Henri de Régnier."[44]

Like the division between content and form, the concept of the typical constitutes one of Lukács' major concerns throughout his intellectual development. In his idealistic period the typical is a quality that elevates the fate of the particular, of the individually formed hero, to philosophical universality by illuminating the concrete with the aura of the universal; it is the only way in which the individual hero may gain significance, as he is turned into a typical representative "of that system of ideas and experienced ideas that determines and defines the internal and external world of the novel."[45] In the Marxist period, this definition of the type, which survives from the *Theory of the Novel,* retains its methodological importance unchanged: it is sufficient to replace "idea" and "experienced idea" with the concepts of "history" and "experienced history" (thus radically historicizing the Hegelian *Geist*) in order to make the idealistic categories usable for a political age.

There is a strange coincidence between Lukács' development as a literary critic and the advent of socialist realism as the official doctrine of the Communist party in 1932–34. As long as Russian communism favored a number of brilliant groups of avant-garde poets or the radical proletarian writers' school (RAPP), Lukács, with his aesthetics nourished from the spirit of German classicism, hardly had a chance within the establishment; at the very moment, however, when the Russian discussion revived the nineteenth-century concept of the type, the way was again open for him. The prearranged Moscow art discussions of 1932–34 did not, to be sure, look back to German idealism as Lukács did but proceeded from Russian assumptions found in the radical literary criticism of Belinsky, Dobrolyubov, and Pissarev. But in these Russian beginnings the concept of the typical was of basic importance; Belinsky, who knew Hegel at second- and third-hand, occupied himself with the typical as much as his successors did. The Russian concern with the typical was basically a distant reflection of Hegelian and Young Hegelian theories; perhaps this is one of the reasons why Lukács may have found it easy to be of one mind with the new line, cheerfully declaring his private aesthetics to be identical with the new doctrine and more often than not supporting the official line with arguments taken from his authentic study of Hegelian sources.

The third unchanging element in Lukács' idealistic and doctrinaire periods may be discerned in his tripartite conception of literary history. It is a rhythm that obviously goes back to the

visions of German Romanticism, as it appears for example in
Novalis, and farther to mystic sources in antiquity; Lukács secu-
larizes the ancient Christian vision of the world process into a
concept of an ordered development of literature. In his idealistic
period he equates pre-Platonic Greece with Paradise, interprets
the post-Platonic age of disunited thinking as the fall of man and
hopes for Paradise regained from an indefinite but near future as
it seemed to be suggested in Goethe's *Wilhelm Meister* and in the
mystical novels of Dostoevsky. The doctrinaire Marxist Lukács
clings to the same tripartite structure of literary history. As before, Greece is the sphere of original blessedness, while the Fall
and Redemption appear in new guises. Satan now wears the
striped trousers of the greedy textile manufacturer, and the angels
of the new redemption the plainer tunic of the political commissar. Of greater consequence than this new masquerade for old
concepts are the ominous blind spots that result from the application of a preconceived scheme to the exuberant richness of literature. Since the three decisive peaks of literary art are a priori to
be found in Greece, in German classicism, and in the Russia of the
future, the remaining landscape of literature appears as a "Waste
Land," the contours of which are defined by ideological precon-
ceptions. A dangerous atomization of literary history appears;
Lukács recognizes neither Roman poetry nor the literature of the
Middle Ages nor that of the Renaissance as independent and
meaningful phenomena; whatever happens between the peaks is,
in order to save the total philosophical conception, quickly assigned to groups of heralds, forerunners, or imitators. Lost in
admiration for the three grand peaks, Lukács turns a blind eye to
the many ranges and colorful valleys beyond.

The Octogenarian Lukács: On the Way to Aristotle

During the mid-fifties Lukács went through his own private
"thaw." After Stalin had died and Khrushchev had criticized the
"personality cult," the critics, too, joined those who reconsidered
the experience of the past years and asked themselves whether

they had not failed in insight and judgment. But the conservative Lukács found himself in a difficult position; while favoring a new latitude, he was clearly concerned with rescuing as much as possible of tradition. His little book *Realism in Our Time* (*Wider den missverstandenen Realismus* [1958] constitutes a rearguard action against the desires of the younger generation; written a few months before the Hungarian uprising, it is an earnest plea for retaining traditional realism as the most productive middle course between the aberrations of "naturalism" (here related to Heidegger's *Angst*) and the degeneration of socialist realism into the schematic propaganda literature furthered by Zhdanov and his henchmen. Politically, Lukács tried to reformulate the pre-Stalinist Party line of 1925; collaboration with middle-class authors who at least forego active opposition to "socialism" should be welcomed and a new invitation to the European liberals and Neo-Marxists is issued to join the ranks of the victorious proletarian artists. The hesitating should follow Thomas Mann, the great critical realist in the nineteenth-century tradition, rather than Franz Kafka, who, in spite of his undoubted talent, "objectively" tends to abet the imperialists because he never escaped the dangerous *Angst;* critical realists have a legitimate place next to socialist writers although, as Lukács clearly and ominously says, after the victory of "socialism" critical realism will "wither away."

These polemic ideas mark but the beginning of Lukács' private "thaw." After he had been a member of the Nagy government, deported, and some time later, permitted to return to his Budapest apartment, his change of mind emerged in his late and voluminous discussions of history and aesthetics. In his salad days in Florence and Berlin, Lukács wrote his essays on *The Soul and the Forms* (1911); as an old man, as fascinated as ever by the tension between the world and the "objective" forms of the mind, he rewrote his first essays. The early book grew into a systematic aesthetic whose most intimate problems are suggested in the revealing subtitle, *The Particularity of the Aesthetic* (*Die Eigenart des Aesthetischen*). The *Aesthetik,* still incomplete today, is the summing-up of an aging revolutionary traditionalist who defends a middle way against his comrades on the left as well as his most illustrious opponents of the right; his Marxism, finally relieved of official obligations, has come to rest in a persuasive syncretism of ideas that stresses the unifying elements of intellectual tradition rather than its contradictions, and tends to by-pass Hegel and Marx in the quest for an unexpected and belated alliance with Aristotle. Following Lessing and the important critics of the Renaissance, the aging Lukács is essentially determined to model himself on Aristotle, "the true discoverer of the particular quality (*Eigenart*) of the aesthetic";[46] and where Lukács cannot make the idea truly Aristotelian, he at least uses (and often misuses) traditional Greek terminology. Of course, he does not doubt the "continuity and coherence of the aesthetic thought"[47] of Marx and Engels, but the once customary quotations from the Marxist "classics" appear much less frequently than in the earlier works; indeed, Lukács cheerfully admits "that at the same time there is and there is not a Marxist aesthetics"; it "may be ideally present,"[48] but it is to be "realized by independent research." Blessed dialectic! After making the customary obeisance to Marx and Engels one is permitted to prevail upon Aristotle for any justification of artistic efforts; and while talking less and less about substratum and superstructure one can rely on mimesis and catharsis as other traditional critics do.

But the descriptive insights of the pragmatic Greek and the grand visions of Hegelianism are not easily combined. The fundamentals of Lukács' late thought remain thoroughly German, but where more than a generation before it was the *soul* that generated intellectual forms, it is now the powerful, boundless, variegated, and irritating power of *Life* (with a capital *L*) that provokes different human needs to which, as differentiated answers, objectified forms of the human mind (arts and sciences) correspond. The philosophy of vitalism was not at all alien to the young Lukács, and his new concept of Life (more implied than defined) as well as his central metaphor are equally revealing. Science and the arts, the intellectual waters, he says, spring from the earth of comprehensive and luxuriant Life and gather in separate rivulets, currents, and streams until they return to Mother Earth in sudden activating falls urging on to new fulfilment and fertility. Lukács still believes, as did Plekhanov at the turn of the century, that work alone (not play) provokes the first objectifications of the human mind. Yet, in sharp contrast to Hegelian tradition, art and science no longer appear as historically sequential stages of the *one* stream in which the mind returns to itself; rather, they constitute two synchronous answers of the mind to two different (co-existing) needs of human existence. Arts and sciences are constantly determined by two sets of principles: science, which seeks to grasp the objective proportions of reality, requires verification, whereas art, which creates its own structures, aims at catharsis. Science is interested in being in itself, art in the nature of being as it is relevant for us. Science removes man from the center of the universe; art remains anthropomorphic and sensual: it "may never lose direct contact with sensory apperception of the world . . . if it is to remain aesthetic."[49] A first important breach has been forced in Hegelian uniformity; the way is open for the rich plurality of artistic forms, whose contradictory autonomy can dispense with purely scientific legitimation.

But in the category of reflection (*Widerspiegelung*) one of the most familiar norms of tradition as well as of militant socialist realism continues to survive in the new system. If in the thirties Lukács was concerned to derive reflection, as the substance of realism, from Lenin's naïve theory, he now tries to sanction reflection as mimesis in the Aristotelian sense; and the Greek term with its traditional translation as imitation (*Nachahmung*) replaces earlier terminology step by step. Imitation remains, as in Aristotle, "an elementary fact of every highly organized life";[50] but if Aristotle stresses the joy in the act of imitation (*Poetics* 1448*b*), Lukács is satisfied with its function "for the particular action";[51] he was never much interested in joy. Within the area of the mimetic Lukács grants a good deal of room to the organizing power of form; mimesis appears to be the "qualitative formation" of the "material of life, which attempts to raise the abundance of life into evocative effect,"[52] indeed, to sharpen "the human unity of the content by . . . constructing forms in an intensified unity."[53] For long stretches the old principle of the typical coincides with form and formation, but it is clear that the connection is becoming increasingly loose. The reflected image, appearing in the arts, is no longer obligated to a localized moment of history (he who tests the historical exactitude of a work of art sees it merely from the outside, Lukács wisely remarks) but to the progressive development of all human history, or the ever-moving cause of humanity. "Out of the infinite number . . . of particular possible characters, traits, deeds, collisions," Lukács says, "those are chosen and compositionally so ordered that their assemblage makes something apparent that is worthy of living on in the memory of mankind and that man can experience at great distances in space and time, under completely different circumstances, with the feeling: *nostra causa agitur*."[54] Both the disadvantages and the virtues of such an expanded concept of imitation are quickly obvious: the work of art is removed from the individual historical moment, and the critical judgment freed from the pressure of a particular hour and its immediate necessities; nevertheless, political interest in the work of art persists undiminished in "the long run." And who is to say, in the concrete case, what the *causa nostra* is that, with the blessing of the critic, is to be communicated to the audience? As far as Lukács' practice is concerned, the "cause," which was seldom ours, was unfortunately all too narrowly determined and, during the long winter of Stalinism, definitely opposed to the interests of humanity.

Fundamentally, Lukács unrestrainedly terrorizes genres and arts from a mimetic point of view and elevates the norm of reflection to a hegemony that it may have possessed only in the thought of the lesser Renaissance critics. Lukács admires "the matter-of-fact manner of Aristotle"[55] but stretches the principle of imitation beyond its possible boundaries. Lukács is still convincing when he declares the art of the cinema to be a double mimesis (shooting as its first stage, cutting as its second); but his interpretation of architecture as twofold imitation requires painful digressions, and when he attempts to assert that music doubly reflects human nature, he wipes out more than two centuries of expressive theory with a stroke of the pen. It is not surprising that he compares Bartók, because of his use of folklore elements, to Thomas Mann's Adrian Leverkühn (as though Leverkühn ever composed anything but ingenious verbal collages from Adorno and Schönberg) and praises folk song and folk dance "because the reality they reflect . . . was, despite all narrow limitations, human society in which essential problems of human life were worked out."[56] The musical elements seem here thoroughly ignored in favor of an idea of *Volksgemeinschaft* left over from the bourgeois and pseudo-Romantic German Youth Movement.

It is when applied to lyric poetry that this mimetic terrorism reveals its most obvious vices. Aristotle avoided subjecting lyric poetry (insofar as he mentioned it at all in his *Poetics*) to the category of imitation—perhaps because in his time lyric poetry did not attain the quality of tragedy or because he was hesitant to subsume the intimately musical quality of poetry under the concept of μίμησις τῶν πραξέων (imitation of deeds). Lukács ignores the nuances and falls victim to his own stubborn postulates. For his theory of the poem he suddenly returns to an unsuccessful older essay (1952) on the Communist poet Johannes R. Becher, in which he had defined lyric poetry as a particular process of mirroring in which subjectivity itself becomes visible; this is the reason why he attacks, with some asperity, the young British Marxist Christopher Caudwell, who dared to sense remains of ancient magic attitudes in poetry. Lukács' ear had always been more closely attuned to the massive substance of the novel and the metaphysical qualities of tragedy than to the fragile connotations of verse, but it is paradoxical that, contrary to his usual procedure, he now differentiates between the "correctness" and the "truth" of ideas articulated in a poem and ascribes to the lyric form a power of transformation that he would never have admitted for the structure of a novel or a play. Whenever his system goes to pieces, he becomes more tolerant: the thought that has been turned into a poem may be "true" even if it is not "correct"; in spite of its ideological deficiencies, it may have "a significant, positive function in the development of mankind."[57] And Lukács continues: "The development of human thought has surpassed the conceptual world of Lucretius Carus and Dante but not their poetic power."[58]

These are very significant and highly welcome concessions to poetry; nowhere else does Lukács come so close to subscribing to certain reflections of T. S. Eliot concerning the "wisdom" of many poems; the categories of "truth" and "correctness" seem to correspond almost exactly to Hans Egon Holthusen's differentiation of "the true" from "truth" in a poem. Yet Lukács' late ideas on poetry cannot really be compared to Theodor W. Adorno's more perceptive thoughts on the social implications of poetry; Lukács' relationship to poetry remains, on the whole, unrefined and wavers irresolutely between an attempt to explain verse "mimetically" and a surrender of the questionable idea to the sacred power of poetry.

It is form that separates the aesthetic reflection from life (art is art and life is life, the German realist Theodor Fontane once remarked in his dry way). But form also refines the reflection in a resolute dialectic so sharply and effectively that it actually enables the work of art to have a fruitful effect on life. We are approaching the core of Lukács' late thought; nowhere is he more illuminating, more passionately engaged, than in explicating aesthetic form as something separating and yet also unifying, as an "arrangement" that isolates the work from the stream of history and yet (because of the effectiveness of the form) successfully forces its way back into the historical flow and the practical affairs of men. As soon as Lukács touches upon the almost self-sustained work of art in the context of time, the tension of the "objectified" mind and time inspires him to brilliant flashes of insight; and because he now believes that the "separate" character of the form furthers its ethical function in changing society, he feels obliged to stress the particularity of the work of art more decisively than ever before. The work has its own cosmos; not only the individuality of the author but the law of the genre essentially contributes to its definite form; it is the genre that finally determines what aspects of the totality of the world are to be reflected in the epic, dramatic, or lyric mode. The work of art, Lukács occasionally asserts with the fervor of a New Critic, "[is] a qualitatively unique world containing a closed system of decisive determinants."[59] This dialectic remains aware of the most attractive temptations of "formalism" but resolutely retracts, balances, and finally annihilates them because it does not cease to believe that form is something extremely useful in the complex process of making decisions of ethical relevance. The ultimate denial of form as form (independent of the social needs of mankind) again demonstrates that Lukács is constantly trying to proceed on two tracks at once; socialist realism and Aristotelian tradition turn out to be uncomfortable bedfellows. The quondam lawgiver of socialist realism insists on the hypothesis that different ages, because of historical causation, articulate in particular dominant genres, and he continues to demand a linear, if not naïve, congruence between historical periods and poetic genres. The Aristotelian neophyte, convinced that differentiated answers to different needs of life exist contemporaneously, neutralizes the dangers of form by declaring it to be the true spur of ethical effectiveness, the basis of universal catharsis. The more significant the form, the Puritan Lukács hopes, the more effective will be its ethical intervention in the world; he, too, believes in Apollo *Katharsios*, the purifying God of art.

Lukács' idea of "purification," which turns up as a central motif in his late thought, has little more in common with its Aristotelian model than its name; the specific is dissolved and expanded into the universal. Lukács does not suffer from philological doubts; the age-old argument about the interpretation of the catharsis sentence and the difficulties with its genitive and its pronoun ($\tau\grave{o}\nu$ $\tauο\iotaο\hat{u}\tauο\nu$ $\pi\alpha\theta\acute{\eta}\mu\alpha\tauο\nu$) do not bother him; and although he gratefully refers to Lessing's interpretation, he follows Lessing only in moral concern, not in philological involvement. The difficult concept is transformed into a colorful and kaleidoscopic idea; the term does not refer to particular passions or emotions, as does Aristotle's or Lessing's, but to a fundamental convulsion of the whole man. Catharsis occurs through an awareness of "the most extreme fulfilment of . . . definite human possibilities";[60] the experience thrusts man before "a mirror that shames him with its greatness, that shows his fragility, his superficiality, his incapacity for self-perfection";[61] faced with this image, man is inspired to "affirm what is essential in his own life" and to create "the earthly perfection of the human soul."[62] The picture of the world becomes clearer, new perceptions crystallize, and as though under Brecht's alienation effect, the familiar appears in a new light: "Catharsis is not limited to showing new facts of life in a completely new light, but the qualitative clearness of the vision achieved in this way alters the perception . . . , makes it into an apperception of new things, familiar objects in a new illumination."[63] Lukács may not have been well-disposed to expressionist art, but his idea of catharsis strangely corresponds to the dramatic transformations that the new Adam experienced on the German expressionist stage of the twenties. The individual surface crumbles away, and the ego begins to expand in the sphere of man and society; "this lifts man out beyond his immediately given particularity, shows him wide and deep perspectives, connections of his narrowly personal, limited fate with the essence of the world around him . . . and through [them] binds him with the destiny of the whole race."[64] Thus Lukács combines ethical appeal, intense affirmation of life, urge to perfection, renewed insight into the totality of the world, freedom from the narrowness of individuality, and euphoric entrance into a realm beyond selfishness; if mystical ecstasies are possible in a world without transcendence, then surely they are found here.

But these ecstasies deeply satisfy the materialist and man of political affairs; the stream of art, alienated from its earthly sources, turns back to society once more—not immediately but "afterward," when man transformed by the catharsis, having, as it were, taken a moment's respite in the aesthetic realm, once more begins to communicate with his world. Lukács admits that even Kant's requirement of disinterestedness has its element of truth; but it is limited in time, reduced to a momentary "suspension of interest" that is to be followed by increased commitment. Lukács not only argued against Kant but also, no less energetically, against his own allies on the left who demand from the work of art an immediately relevant, hasty, breathless intervention in the contemporary world. He emphatically rejects the Stalinist "practicism" that degrades every work of art, without any suspension of interest, to an instrument of a political program; and he is no less skeptical of Bertolt Brecht, whose alienation effect he prefers to transform into a "rational convulsion"[65] of total man. It is not surprising that he conjures up Rainer Maria Rilke ("You must change your life") as his chief witness against an epic drama that impatiently demands political action. Lukács obviously wants the aesthetic transformation of man to humanity; and it is difficult to say what distinguishes his late desires from Friedrich Schiller's hopes for an aesthetic education of mankind. Homer, Goethe, and Tolstoy continue to appear as significant educators, guiding men to what is "high, deep, pure" (Lukács' norms occasionally sound quite bourgeois and professorial); he still prefers the classical to the "naturalistic," Goethe's *Iphigenie* to Hauptmann's *Rose Bernd;* he likes the humane and touching better than the gloomy, Chaplin better than Kafka. But even in his old age Lukács has remained a youthful reader; new names from American and English literature occupy him: Melville, but also Joseph Conrad, receives high praise; Beckett and Robbe-Grillet are sarcastically condemned, at a level of criticism, however, that is beneath any serious consideration.

Unfortunately, Lukács often continues to judge many works of art on the basis of their author's theories and dulls his sensitivity to the possibility that the work may contradict theoretic intent; it is certainly not sufficient to cite Flaubert's conversation with Maupassant to criticize *Madame Bovary* (the novel lacks "typicality"); Zola's *Germinal* remains, with or without the theory of naturalism, one of the great works of world literature. It is a sad sight to watch Lukács dress down the humanist Zola, the archrepublican, socialist, defender of Dreyfus, friend of the workingman. Zola was unable to create a single living character, Lukács disparagingly remarks, and it does not occur to him that Zola's Mère Maheu (in *Germinal*) might have more in common as an emblematic figure of stubborn life with Brecht's Mother Courage than his robust theory would ever suspect.

It is revealing that Lukács always takes great pains to elucidate Plato's ambivalent attitude toward the arts; it is part of his self-analysis. Lukács is at his best when he speaks about Scott, Balzac, Stendhal, and Tolstoy in their context of social history; in other spheres of art, he is blinded by his ideological assumptions, decrees entire worlds of the imagination out of existence, and substantially misrepresents others; his is a sophisticated perception tuned to the massive narrative revealing historical developments rather than to the inaudible connotations of the text. There can be little doubt that Lukács is followed more in the western part of the world than in the country of his birth; the younger intellectual generation in Germany, Italy, and, above all, France, uses his stubborn insights and his political vigor to fight against the entrenched critical and academic establishments: Lucien Goldmann to oppose the positivism of the French universities; Paolo Chiarini to counteract the heritage of Croce; young West Germans to attack their elders, who, after faithfully serving Hitler, in 1945 suddenly discovered the "work of art itself." Because of his wide horizon, firm value judgments, and political passion, Lukács (if one chooses to disregard the darker side of his genius) proves to be an ally of stature and importance. It may be his hidden tragedy that the younger generation in the Communist countries continues to turn away from him; as the recent Kafka Conference (Prague, 1963) demonstrated, the younger Communist intellectuals prefer Kafka, not Thomas Mann, have little use for nineteenth-century traditions, and are more deeply aware than their colleagues in the West of Lukács' involvement in the Stalinist policies of the past. Lukács might be a father figure, as Irving Howe suggests, but his Communist sons more and more prefer those intellectual nourishments he has ignored or cursed.

9

Marxist Criticism: Past and Present

In my analysis of Plekhanov's and Georg Lukács' literary theories, I am beginning to exceed the original boundaries of the present study, which has concentrated on the central issues of the nineteenth century, and it may be appropriate to review a few results, fragmentary though they may be. I have attempted to show that Marx and Engels arrived at their explanations of literary phenomena by way of oblique, personal, and often diverging paths. Following Feuerbach and Moses Hess, young Marx at first formulated an almost religious vision of the alienated and then reconciled world, and only somewhat later did he decide to declare the state, and with it, literature, a product of the economically determined social order. Engels learned his lessons in industrial Lancashire: the English social situation, Carlyle's grim cries of protest, and the suffering of the English workingmen convinced him that economics was of an importance undreamed of by the Young Germans and the Young Hegelians in their cafés and university seminars. The Marxist image of the poet was intimately fused with its image of man; yet the concept of the functional place of the writer was defined differently at different times. In the alienated world as described by young Marx in the *Economic-Philosophical Manuscripts*, even the writer appears as a pitiable "specialist" who only in the reconciled world of the future will yield to the whole, restored, integrated man who also, if he chooses, will know how to write poetry. In a later concept of the world, Marx and Engels locate the writer on the surface of the economic universe and press his ear against the pounding machines; only the aging Engels, with more respect for the dignity of creative achievements, releases the poet into other spheres, where he can sense the rhythm of economic production and reproduce it, in accordance with the immanent laws of poetry, in his own language. But even here—to remain within the musical metaphor—the ground-bass of economics continues to be audible even if somewhat muted.

In the development of Marxist literary doctrine, the early vision of the alienated world (1843–44) and the energetic dogmatism of the next few years (1845–49) no longer appear so forcibly in Engels' later interpretations (1890–94); even though Marx in his "Introduction" (1857) questioned his own theory, it remained for Engels to relax the rigid dogmatism of his friend by suggesting a limited mutual interaction between the material foundation and the intellectual superstructure as well as by sketching a more complex and stratified idea of reality.

But even Engels' effort at a solution quickly turned out to be inadequate. With the progressive development of Marxist literary theory, literature demanded more and more explicitly the restoration of its lost authority. Franz Mehring and G. V. Plekhanov attempted to solve the problem in their own way and fled into an ontological dualism in order to grant to art more of its old dignity. In their definition of the economic foundation they combined the results of recent economics with those of Darwin's researches and of anthropology; in their discussion of higher forms of art they moved ever more unambiguously toward the Kantian concept of a world of art independent of the class struggle and partisan propaganda. Georg Lukács, with whom a systematic development of Marxist aesthetics commences, wants no part of such concessions; rather he is concerned to return to Hegel and, at least in his late work, to combine the spirit of dialectics with an Aristotelian respect for artistic form.

German literary theory, from whose radical elements Marxist

aesthetics was derived generations ago, contributed little to its development in the first decades of the twentieth century. In Germany, Marxist aesthetics was for a long time the property of the Social Democratic or Communist outsider, who all too willingly subordinated himself to the tactical requirements of his political organization; meanwhile, academic research, ignoring Walter Benjamin and Theodor W. Adorno, followed the prescribed and traditional paths of *Geistesgeschichte*.

Elsewhere there was a more persistent concern with the possibilities of a Marxist theory of literature. In England, where during the depression of the thirties writers like W. H. Auden, Stephen Spender, and Louis MacNeice were to be found among the Marxist critics, the gifted essayist Christopher Caudwell attempted to carry on the efforts of Plekhanov and combine Marxism and anthropology into a new theory of the origins of literature. In his study *Illusion and Reality* (1937), Caudwell declared that the actual source of literature is primitive tribal ritual; in the tribal celebrations and harvest festivals collective labor and collective poetry were mystically united, before the progressive division of labor separated the poet as an individual from society and forced him to seek to recover the lost unity.

American criticism of the thirties, too, was under the impact of Marxist doctrine; within a decade, however, social concerns were displaced by the artistic interests of the "New Criticism." In Michael Gold's robust articles in the *New Masses* and in V. F. Calverton's *The Liberation of American Literature* (1932), Marxist doctrine appeared in its most intolerant forms; as a leavening yeast, sociological concepts are to be found in the early work of the philosopher Kenneth Burke and in F. O. Matthiessen's masterly *American Renaissance* (1941). It was Edmund Wilson who undertook a consistent effort to develop Marxist motifs further. In *Axel's Castle* (1931), he made political demands upon the contemporary generation of American writers; of the moderns, including Proust and Joyce, Rimbaud alone was to be praised for having renounced poetry in favor of deeds with a relevance for the future. In his essay "The Historical Interpretation of Literature" (1941), Wilson tries to weave Marxist motifs more closely into psychoanalytic theories: holding fast to the theory of the superstructure, Wilson argues that the work of art arises from the socially determined trauma in the early childhood of the writer. Wilson's studies on Dickens and Kipling (1941) demonstrate the surprising fruitfulness of such a method.

From the first appearance of formalism (1914–15), whose spokesmen stressed the linguistic self-sufficiency of art, until Stalin's consolidation of power (1932–34), Russian critics discussed the possibilities of Marxist aesthetics with passionate commitment and some important results. The victory of the October Revolution was by no means synonymous with an immediate hegemony of Marxist aesthetics. In the years of civil war and foreign intervention (1917–21), Soviet leaders were still flexible enough to recognize art, in Plekhanov's sense, as a particular activity of the human mind and (insofar as the artist professed the principle of the Revolution) not to draw too narrowly the permissible limits of artistic method. Lenin, whose personal taste was quite conservative and who by his own admission did not understand the expressionists and futurists, even tolerated the noisy and highly talented Moscow disciples of Marinetti; Trotsky spoke with admiration of their daring language experiments; and Gorky continued to extol his idea of a "revolutionary romanticism." Only the beginning of the New Economic Policy (1921–27), with its re-establishment of some private publishing and the creation of a new cosmopolitan reading public, led to violent debates about the true relative merit of Marxist and formalist literary theory. But even these conflicts, in which Trotsky and Lunacharsky had their part, still took place in an atmosphere in which one could call for a possible synthesis of Marxism and formalism; and critics like Zeitlin and Levidov insisted that the causal derivation of art as postulated by Marxism must be reconciled with the formal analysis of aesthetic structure. This peculiar period of suspense ended with the total consolidation of Stalin's power. On April 23, 1932, the relatively independent left-radical writers' organization (RAPP), to which the fate of Russian literature and criticism had been entrusted during the first Five-Year Plan (1928–32), was dissolved by an official decree and replaced by a Soviet writers' organization directly subordinate to the Party. At the same time Plekhanov was degraded to the position of a heretic and Lenin's casually formulated principle of the total partisanship of literature was elevated to an official axiom;[1] the long winter of socialist realism began.

But Stalin and his spokesman Zhdanov did not succeed in silencing the steadily continuing discussion of Marxism and formalism with one blow. At the first All-Soviet Writers' Congress (1934), Bukharin once again raised his warning voice, lamented the negative attitude of Marxism to art, and declared again that Soviet literary theory ought not to be afraid of supplementing the Marxist aspects of research with the important results of a structural analysis. A few years later he was silenced by the firing squad.

In the last decades, two divergent attitudes toward the unity and substance of nineteenth-century Marxist literary doctrine have developed. On the one side, the orthodox functionaries (including Georg Lukács in his Stalinist period) claim that the utterances of Marx and Engels on literature form a carefully thought-out whole that can easily stand comparison with Hegel's aesthetics; on the other side, a more skeptical view (as formulated, for example, by the American Slavist Ernest J. Simmons) sharply points out that Marxist aesthetics consists merely of "shreds and patches." After my examination of the accessible texts, I have come to a third view that takes rather a middle position between partisan assertion and unphilosophical skepticism. I am rather convinced that nineteenth-century Marxist literary doctrine possesses a relatively solid core of economic principles, to which are joined (often with some measure of inconsistency) Marx's and Engels' specific judgments on individual writers, which in turn reflect the distinct inclinations of their respective tastes. Even though the divergent judgments of taste markedly compromise the substance of the economic core, it would be difficult to deny a basic structure of doctrine that is grounded in a social derivation of literary phenomena.

My historical perspective, which tries to encompass more than a century, shows Marxist literary doctrine as a strange bedfellow of the historicism that began to develop in the second half of the eighteenth century after the collapse of classical poetics. Marx and Engels are distant cousins of Vico, Winckelmann, Herder, and Madame de Staël; in a certain sense they are the black sheep of the Romantic herd. But it would be irrelevant to accuse Marx and Engels of having occupied themselves too exclusively with the genealogy and the extraliterary sources of art; in this respect they share the inclinations and prejudices of whole generations of important critics. The specific defect of Marxist aesthetics results from the ruthless limitations it sets upon the historical perspective; whereas the Romantics recognized a whole chain of various elements (religion, philosophy, *Volksgeist,* geography) as motive principles for art, Marx and Engels isolate a single (the economic) element and insist with varying degrees of stress on its determining hegemony.

More recent theories of literature oriented on Hegel and Marx try to avoid these limitations: Hans Mayer excels in the combination of methods; Lucien Goldmann inquires how the world view of the individual work of art may be bound in a complex way to a collective consciousness; Theodor W. Adorno wants to comprehend the social implications of literary forms. Hans Mayer (who in the late summer of 1962 left the Karl Marx University in Leipzig to continue his work in West Germany) is more concerned with the practice of critical confrontation than with a systematic theory of literature; for him, as for every Hegelian, history is always an issue in literature. "In his own sphere," he says, "[the literary historian] constantly runs up against connections to the material area of existence"; therefore "literary history is a component, a highly independent and to a large extent autonomous component, of historical scholarship (*Geschichtswissenschaft*)."[2] In many studies Mayer demonstrates with great sensitivity how literature and social history are "tied" and "woven together,"[3] or how literature "corresponds" to history;[4] in other essays, sociological discussions are combined in sophisticated ways with exact textual analyses (on Brecht), the analysis of epic time structures (E. T. A. Hoffmann), concrete investigations of narrative techniques (in his book on Thomas Mann), and an exemplary interest in the achievements of world literature not usually shown by German professors. Lucien Goldmann in France is more explicitly a follower of Georg Lukács than Mayer, although, to be sure, it is *young* Lukács' theory of the novel that Goldmann attempts to continue in his "dialectical aesthetics" and the "structural-genetic method" of literary history. Goldmann seeks for the coherence of a world view (*vision du monde*), not in the personal philosophy of the author, but in the individual literary text; recalling the Hegelian Taine, he declares the "vision of the world" to be a function of a historically changing collective consciousness, that is, an articulation "of that totality of aspirations and ideas that binds the members of a group or, rather, of a social class, with one another and distinguishes them from other groups."[5] Goldmann knows the problem of the hermeneutic circle and proceeds from his text (reading it in the manner of the American "New Critics") to the idea and then returns from the idea to the individual text. His studies try to relate *Weltanschauung*, collective consciousness, and political and social processes meaningfully with one another; in his difficult book on Pascal and Racine, he persuasively demonstrates how the ideas of ascetic Jansenism were conceived in the milieu of those jurists and administrators of the *noblesse de la robe* who lost their power and influence through the transformation of the French state into an absolute monarchy. In other studies, as, for example, in his analyses of the development of the modern novel[6]—he claims that the three stages of the novel correspond exactly to three stages of European economics—the loose connections are unfortunately reduced to a rigid nexus. The French critic Roland Barthes is right in saying that Goldmann does not always succeed in escaping the "ghost of causality" and the intellectual pressures of the nineteenth century.[7]

Theodor W. Adorno may be better known to American audiences as the co-author of a seminal sociological work on *The Authoritarian Personality* (1950) than as a critic of music and literature. He is above all concerned with the social implications of artistic forms; and it is characteristic that he does not regard highly the traditional metaphor of literature as a mirror of society. The cliché is shattered; the historico-philosophical element "is deposited (*sedimentiert*)," or "precipitated,"[8] and the form of a work of art "reminds of, and converges to"[9] sociological relationships. A desirable refinement of method seeks ultimately to allow the aesthetic structure to speak for itself without ignoring the structure of the real world; "it is better," Adorno justly observes, "to look three times at what has been written, than over and over again . . . at what it symbolizes."[10]

As against the subjective intention of the writer, Adorno chooses rather the "objective meaning" (*Gehalt*) of what has been written; it preserves and liquidates the writer's personal intent. But the interpretation never proceeds deductively; as soon as he determines a significant element in the language of the text, the interpreter shifts gears and defines the society and times of the writer in an individual way; his philological observations correspond to sociological analysis as meaningfully as the positive pole of a battery to the negative one. But Adorno does not completely break with tradition. Art remains mimetically related to social concerns; by insisting upon an *ontological* realism, the critic destroys any *literary* realism that depends upon the reproduction of a continual process of action and highly individualized central figures. The modern realist has no other choice than to be a "formalist," Adorno says, if he still wants to describe social reality; "if . . . the time continuum collapses in Joyce . . . , [his] literary procedure converges to the collapse of the time continuum in reality, and to the dying of experience, which ultimately goes back to the process of the production of material goods codified regardless of time."[11] From here Adorno leads directly to a defense of programmatically "pure" art; in an age defiled by alienation, consumers' markets, and mass media, it is just such an art that offers asylum to the free mind in which it is not necessary for it "to stoop to vileness (*sich zu encanaillieren*)."

It is hard to ignore the fact that sociological literary criticism, somewhat belatedly, but with refined methods, is in the process of emancipating itself from the nineteenth century. The "classical" source texts and more recent methods are beginning to diverge; a world of development separates Franz Mehring's *Die Lessing-Legende* (1893) from Lucien Goldmann's *Le Dieu caché* (1955) or Adorno's *Noten zur Literatur* (1962–65). In the previous century critics were concerned with seeking instruction in the dogmatic writings; today they are more inclined to return to Marx's *Economic-Philosophical Manuscripts* and to Engels' late correspondence, which defend a relative autonomy of the poetic sphere. The center of attention has shifted: in the last century one spoke of foundation and superstructure, of cause and effect; in recent decades interpretations have emerged that are trying to place economics and the world of literature in a complicated and oblique relationship. The sociological background of the author and his political opinions are ignored, and critics concentrate on questions of the inner structure of the work of art, the social implications of its form, or the development of genres in the stream of historical processes. American criticism should not hesitate to respond to these new developments as productively as it did, in the "New Criticism," to the massive literary sociology of the thirties; if American critics were to abandon their isolationism (so inconsistent with American politics), the fruitful tension of literature and society might again become of legitimate interest to enlightened research.

Notes

MEGA   *Karl Marx—Friedrich Engels. Historisch-kritische Gesamtaus-*
         gabe, ed. C. B. Ryazanov and V. Adoratsky (Moscow: Marx-
         Engels-Lenin-[Stalin-] Institute, 1927–35).

ÜKL   Karl Marx and Friedrich Engels, *Über Kunst und Literatur,* ed.
         Michail Lifschitz (German ed., ed. Kurt Thöricht and Roderich
         Fechner; Berlin, 1949).

CHAPTER 1   YOUNG FRIEDRICH ENGELS AS A CRITIC

1. *MEGA,* I, Pt. II, 23–41.

2. The "Letters from the Wuppertal" imitated not only Heine but an imitation of Heine as well, namely, Gustav Kühne's *Weibliche und männ-liche Charaktere* (Leipzig, 1838) ("Female and Male Characters"), a much-read book that, among other things, also treated the situation in Barmen-Elberfeld. Arnold Ruge wrote an important review of this book and made a thorough analysis of the Wuppertal chapter. See *Hallische Jahrbücher,* I (1838), cols. 1720–36.

3. *MEGA,* I, Pt. II, 41.

4. The accomplished Engels scholar Gustav Mayer demonstrated this fact beyond any doubt in exhaustive and penetrating detail. See "Ein Pseudonym von Friedrich Engels," *Archiv für die Geschichte des Sozialis-mus und der Arbeiterbewegung,* IV (1914), 86–89.

5. *MEGA,* I, Pt. II, 465.

6. *Ibid.,* p. 480.

7. *Ibid.,* p. 41.

8. *Ibid.,* pp. 7–8.

9. See Reinhold Seeger, *Friedrich Engels als Junger Deutscher* (disser-tation, University of Halle, 1935).

10. Letter of April 8–9, 1839 (*MEGA,* I, Pt. II, 502).

11. *Ibid.,* p. 503.

12. Karl Gutzkow, *Götter, Helden, Don Quichote* (Hamburg, 1838), pp. 159–60.

13. *MEGA,* I, Pt. II, 111–18.

14. *Ibid.,* pp. 126–27.

15. Friedrich Engels, *Schriften der Frühzeit* (hereinafter cited as Engels, *Schriften*), ed. Gustav Mayer (Berlin, 1920), p. 75; *MEGA,* I, Pt. II, 536.

16. *MEGA*, I, Pt. II, 60–61.
17. Engels, *Schriften*, p. 54; *MEGA*, I, Pt. II, 516.
18. Gustav Mayer, *Friedrich Engels* (Berlin, 1920), I, 40.
19. *Karl Gutzkows Werke*, ed. Reinhold Gensel (Berlin, 1912), VIII, 93.
20. Karl Gutzkow, *Das Leben Ludwig Börnes* (Hamburg, 1840), pp. 14–15.
21. Ludwig Börne, *Dramaturgische Blätter* (Hamburg, 1835), I, xiii.
22. *Ibid.*, p. xv.
23. *Ibid.*, p. 2.
24. *Ibid.*, p. 29.
25. *MEGA*, I, Pt. II, 49–56.
26. *Ibid.*, p. 49.
27. *Ibid.*
28. *Ibid.*, p. 55.
29. *Ibid.*, pp. 53–54.
30. *Ibid.*, p. 54.
31. *Ludwig Börnes Werke*, ed. Ludwig Geiger (Berlin, 1913), VII, 392.
32. *Ibid.*, p. 386.
33. Engels, *Schriften*, p. 86; *MEGA*, I, Pt. II, 547.
34. Engels, *Schriften*, p. 144; *MEGA*, I, Pt. II, 101.
35. Engels, *Schriften*, p. 89; *MEGA*, I, Pt. II, 550.
36. *MEGA*, I, Pt. II, 83–87.
37. *Ibid.*, p. 83.
38. *Ibid.*, p. 84.
39. *Ibid.*, p. 86.
40. Letter of December 9, 1839–February 5, 1840 (*MEGA*, I, Pt. II, 556).
41. "Zur Einführung," *Hallische Jahrbücher*, I (1838), cover.
42. Cf. Else von Eck, *Die Literaturkritik in den "Hallischen" und den "Deutschen Jahrbüchern"* (Germanische Studien, No. 42 [Berlin, 1926]). See also Douglas Alick Joyce, "Arnold Ruge as a Literary Critic" (Ph.D. dissertation, Harvard University, 1952).
43. Karl Biedermann, "Gutzkows 'Götter, Helden, Don Quichote,'" *Hallische Jahrbücher*, II (1839), col. 698.
44. *MEGA*, I, Pt. II, 326.
45. *Hallische Jahrbücher*, II (1839), cols. 1913–2480, 2113–64, 2401–80.
46. Karl Gutzkow, *Das Leben Ludwig Börnes*, pp. 14–15.
47. *Hallische Jahrbücher*, III (1840), cols. 2417–33, 2424–28, 2438–83.
48. *Ibid.*, II (1839), cols. 627–75, 681–88, 689–96, 697–99.
49. *Ibid.*, III (1840), col. 2424.
50. Engels, *Schriften*, p. 192; *MEGA*, I, Pt. II, 328.
51. Engels, *Schriften*, p. 192; *MEGA*, I, Pt. II, 327.
52. Engels, *Schriften*, p. 193; *MEGA*, I, Pt. II, 328.
53. *MEGA*, I, Pt. II, 121–23.
54. K., "'Richard Savage' in Leipzig," *Hallische Jahrbücher*, III (1840), cols. 756–60.

55. For biographical details, see Adolf Frisé, *Alexander Jung* (dissertation, Heidelberg University, 1932).

56. Alexander Jung, *Vorlesungen über die moderne Literatur der Deutschen* (Danzig, 1842), p. 156.

57. *Ibid.*, p. 157.

58. *MEGA*, I, Pt. II, 324.

59. *Ibid.*

60. *Ibid.*, p. 330.

61. Cf. Gustav Mayer, "Ein Pseudonym von Friedrich Engels," *Archiv für die Geschichte des Sozialismus und der Arbeiterbewegung*, IV (1914), 86–89.

CHAPTER 2 ECONOMICS AND INTELLECT: THOMAS CARLYLE

1. *MEGA*, I, Pt. II, 76–82.

2. *Ibid.*, pp. 80–81.

3. *Ibid.*, pp. 287–89.

4. *Ibid.*, pp. 351–76.

5. Cf. Friedrich von Raumer, *England in 1841*, trans. H. Evans Lloyd (London, 1842), II, 300.

6. Cf. William H. Gilman, *Melville's Early Life and Redburn* (New York, 1951), chaps. iii–iv.

7. *MEGA*, I, Pt. II, 365.

8. *Ibid.*, pp. 405–31.

9. *Ibid.*, p. 424.

10. *Ibid.*, p. 425.

11. *Ibid.*, p. 408.

12. *Ibid.*, I, Pt. IV, 279 n.

13. Cf. George L. Nesbitt, *Benthamite Reviewing: The First Twelve Years of the Westminster Review: 1824 till 1836* (New York, 1934); René Wellek, "Social and Aesthetic Values in Russian Nineteenth Century Criticism," in *Continuity and Change in Russian and Soviet Thought*, ed. E. J. Simmons (Cambridge, Mass., 1955), pp. 381–97.

14. Cf. Frederick William Roe, *Thomas Carlyle as a Literary Critic* (New York, 1910); Alfredo Obertello, *Carlyle's Critical Theories* (Genoa, 1948).

15. Thomas Carlyle, *Critical and Miscellaneous Essays* (Library ed.; London, 1896), I, 60–61.

16. *Ibid.*, p. 66.

17. *Ibid.*, p. 244.

18. *Ibid.*, II, 40.

19. Carlyle, *Past and Present* (Library ed.; London, 1870), p. 201.

20. *MEGA*, I, Pt. II, 330.

21. Carlyle, *Past and Present*, p. 210.

22. *MEGA*, I, Pt. II, 407.
23. *Ibid.*, pp. 407–8.
24. *MEGA*, I, Pt. IV, 227.
25. As has been shown in detail by Sylvia Norman in her study *The Flight of the Skylark: The Development of Shelley's Reputation* (Norman, Okla., 1954), pp. 143–45, 149–53, it was the English radical publishers, for example, Henry Hetherington, who misused Shelley's works for personal political machinations.
26. Carlyle, *Past and Present*, p. 70.
27. *Ibid.*
28. See Luise Sigman, *Die englische Literatur (1800–1850) im Urteil der zeitgenössischen deutschen Kritik* (Heidelberg, 1918); Ellis N. Gummer, *Dickens' Work in Germany* (Oxford, 1940).
29. Gummer, *Dickens' Work in Germany*, pp. 17–18.
30. *MEGA*, I, Pt. II, 455.
31. *ÜKL*, p. 231.
32. Carlyle, *Sartor Resartus* (Library ed.; London, 1870), p. 50.
33. Carlyle, *Past and Present*, p. 27.
34. *Ibid.*, p. 199.

CHAPTER 3   ON THE WAY TO ECONOMIC DETERMINISM: KARL MARX

1. *MEGA*, I, Pt. I (2), 183.
2. *Ibid.*
3. *Ibid.*, p. 176.
4. See *Allgemeine Deutsche Biographie*, XLII (Leipzig, 1897), 228–31.
5. *Karl Marx: Abriss seines Lebens in Einzeldaten*, ed. E. Czóbel (Moscow, 1934), p. 3. The references to Geibel and others are based upon M. Carrière's "Lebenserinnerungen," *Archiv für hessische Geschichte und Altertumskunde*, N.S. X (1914), 165.
6. *MEGA*, I, Pt. I (2), 189.
7. *Ibid.*
8. *Ibid.*, p. 194.
9. *Ibid.*, p. 226.
10. Reprinted in *ibid.*, pp. 4–58.
11. *Ibid.*, p. 187.
12. *Ibid.*, p. 220.
13. *Ibid.*
14. Reprinted in *ibid.*, pp. 41–42.
15. See *ibid.*, pp. 76–89.
16. *Ibid.*, p. 204.
17. *Ibid.*
18. Reprinted in *ibid.*, pp. 59–75.
19. *Ibid.*, pp. 68–69.
20. *Ibid.*, p. 60.

21. *Ibid.*, p. 63.
22. *Ibid.*, p. 69.
23. *Ibid.*, I, Pt. I (1), 607.
24. See *ÜKL*, p. 478.
25. *MEGA*, I, Pt. I (2), 210–11.
26. *Ibid.*, p. 211.
27. See Marx's letter of November 10, 1837, in *ibid.*, pp. 215–16.
28. *Ibid.*, p. 218.
29. *Ibid.*, p. 219.
30. See the excerpts in *ibid.*, pp. 114–18.
31. See Georg Lukács, "Karl Marx und Friedrich Theodor Vischer," in *Beiträge zur Geschichte der Ästhetik* (Berlin, 1954), pp. 217–84.
32. Karl Marx, *Frühe Schriften*, Vol. I, ed. Hans Joachim Lieber und Peter Furth (Stuttgart, 1962), p. 23.
33. *Ibid.*, p. 104.
34. *Ibid.*
35. *Ibid.*, p. 103.
36. *Ibid.*
37. *Ibid.*, p. 650.
38. *Ibid.*
39. *Ibid.*, p. 410.
40. *Ibid.*, p. 363.
41. *Ibid.*, p. 262.
42. *Ibid.*, p. 293.
43. Ludwig Feuerbach, *Das Wesen des Christentums* (Leipzig, 1841), pp. 6–7.
44. *Ibid.*, p. 146.
45. Robert C. Tucker, *Philosophy and Myth in Karl Marx* (Cambridge, England, 1961), pp. 114–17.
46. Marx, *Frühe Schriften*, p. 505.
47. *Ibid.*, pp. 561–62.
48. *Ibid.*, p. 594.
49. *Ibid.*, p. 593.
50. *Ibid.*
51. *Ibid.*
52. *Ibid.*, p. 595.
53. *Ibid.*
54. *Ibid.*
55. *Ibid.*, p. 601.
56. *Ibid.*
57. Feuerbach, *Das Wesen des Christentums*, p. 7.
58. Marx, *Frühe Schriften*, p. 599.
59. *Ibid.*
60. *Ibid.*
61. *Ibid.*
62. *Ibid.*
63. *Ibid.*

64. *Ibid.*, p. 601.
65. *Ibid.*
66. Feuerbach, *Das Wesen des Christentums*, p. 265.
67. *Ibid.*
68. *Ibid.*
69. *ÜKL*, p. 173.
70. *MEGA*, I, Pt. II, x.
71. *Ibid.*, I, Pt. V, 15 (5*a*).
72. *Ibid.*, para. 5*b*.
73. Karl Marx, "Einleitung" [to the *Kritik der politischen Ökonomie*, ed. Karl Kautsky], in *Die Neue Zeit* (1902–3), pp. 710–18, 772–81.
74. *Ibid.*, p. 779.
75. *Ibid.*
76. *Ibid.*, p. 780.
77. *Ibid.*
78. *Ibid.*
79. *Ibid.*
80. *Ibid.*, pp. 780–81.
81. As one might expect, the Introduction (1857) and Foreword (1859) to the *Critique of Political Economy* caused some confusion among Marx's disciples. It is to be noted that Marx never published the so-called Introduction and demonstratively began his book with the Foreword. By confusing the two pieces or intentionally neglecting one or the other of them, Marx can be represented either as an uncommonly sensitive friend of literature (Introduction) or as a dogmatic theoretician (Foreword). Thus, for example, the excellent American critic Stanley Edgar Hyman, in *The Armed Vision* (New York, 1948), p. 185, seems to take the Introduction for the actual Foreword to the *Critique of Political Economy* with some quite doubtful results; similarly, although presumably with diametrically opposed intent, Georg Lukács, *Beiträge zur Geschichte der Ästhetik*, p. 202, cites the Introduction without ever admitting that it is a fragment that Marx himself had rejected or at least never published. In the Soviet Union, sometimes the Introduction and at other times the Foreword has been in vogue, depending on shifts in the political climate: with every "thaw" the Introduction, of course, is quoted, and with every new "frost," the Foreword.
82. Karl Marx, *Zur Kritik der politischen Ökonomie*, ed. Karl Kautsky (Stuttgart, 1897), p. xi.

CHAPTER 4 CONFLICTS AND DISCUSSIONS

1. The more recent East German publications are none too ready to admit these nuances. Cf. Werner Ilberg, *Unser Heine* (Berlin, 1952), and Walter Victor, *Marx und Heine: Tatsachen und Spekulationen in der Darstellung ihrer Beziehungen* (Berlin, 1952).

2. *MEGA*, I, Pt. II, 72.

3. *Ibid.*, p. 331.

4. *Ibid.*, p. 535 (letter of July 30, 1839). Ludwig Marcuse, in "Heinrich Heine und Marx," *Germanic Review*, XXX (1955), 110–24, points out that Engels uses the same expression again in his letter of December 21, 1866.

5. *MEGA*, I, Pt. II, 96.

6. Karl Marx and Friedrich Engels, *Werke*, ed. Institut für Marxismus-Leninismus beim ZK der SED ([East] Berlin, 1956–63), II, 512–13.

7. *Ibid.*, p. 513.

8. *Ibid.*

9. *Ibid.*

10. *Ibid.*, XXVII, 441. The letter is here correctly dated for the first time.

11. Jeanette Strauss-Wohl's book was entitled *Ludwig Börne's Urtheil über H. Heine. Ungedruckte Stellen aus den Pariser Briefen* (Frankfurt, 1840).

12. *ÜKL*, p. 361 (Gustav Mayer, "Drei Briefe von Karl Marx an Heinrich Heine," *Archiv für die Geschichte des Sozialismus und der Arbeiterbewegung*, ed. Carl Grünberg, IX [1921], 132–33).

13. *Ibid.*

14. *Ibid.*

15. *Heinrich Heines Sämtliche Werke*, ed. Ernst Elster (Leipzig [1887–90]), VI, 254.

16. *Ibid.*, p. 149.

17. *Ibid.*, p. 348 (letter of March 20, 1843).

18. *Ibid.*, p. 230 (letter of November 6, 1840).

19. *Ibid.*, p. 279 (letter of December 11, 1841).

20. *Ibid.*, p. 230 (letter of November 6, 1840).

21. *Ibid.*

22. *Ibid.*, p. 392 (letter of May 7, 1843).

23. *Ibid.*

24. *Ibid.*, p. 393.

25. *Ibid.*

26. Marcuse, "Heinrich Heine und Marx," pp. 115–16.

27. *Heinrich Heines Sämtliche Werke*, II, 169–73.

28. See *Die Neue Zeit*, XIV (1896), 15.

29. *Ibid.*

30. Marx and Engels, *Werke*, XXVII, 434 (letter of January 12, 1845).

31. *ÜKL*, p. 362 (letter of February 1, 1845).

32. See Engels' report to the Communist Committee of Correspondence of September 16, 1846; Partly reprinted in *ÜKL*, p. 363. Further material *ibid.* in *ÜKL* and *MEGA*, III, Pt. I, 93 (letter of January 14, 1848).

33. See Marcuse, "Heinrich Heine und Marx," p. 116.

34. *ÜKL*, p. 364; *MEGA*, III, Pt. II, 73.

35. *ÜKL* p. 364; *MEGA*, III, Pt. II, 135 (letter of May 8, 1856).

36. *ÜKL*, p. 365; *MEGA*, III, Pt. III, 371 (letter of December 21, 1866).

37. *Ibid.*
38. *Ibid.*
39. See *Heinrich Heines Sämtliche Werke,* VII, 520.
40. *Ibid.,* VI, 572. Heine's French text reads: ". . . ce n'est qu'avec horreur et effroi que je pense à l'époque où ces sombres iconoclastes parviendront à la domination: de leurs mains calleuses ils briseront sans merci toutes les statues de marbre de la beauté, si chères à mon cœur; ils fracasseront toutes ces babioles et fanfreluches fantastiques de l'art, qu'aimait tant le poëte; ils détruiront mes bois de lauriers et y planteront des pommes de terre . . . les rossignols, ces chanteurs inutiles, seront chassés, et hélas! mon LIVRE des CHANTS servira à l'épicier pour en faire des cornets où il versera du café ou du tabac à priser pour les vieilles femmes de l'avenir."
41. *Ibid.*
42. *Ibid.,* VII, 519–20.
43. *Ibid.,* p. 520.
44. *Ibid.,* VI, 573 (March 30, 1855).
45. *Ibid.,* p. 53.
46. *Ibid.*
47. *Ibid.*
48. *Ibid.*
49. *Ibid.*
50. *ÜKL,* p. 366 (Marx's communication to Herwegh is dated Brussels, July 27, 1847).
51. *Ibid.,* p. 368 (August 1, 1859); *MEGA,* III, Pt. II, 410.
52. See Arnold Ruge's article in the *Hallische Jahrbücher* of February 16, 1842.
53. *Ferdinand Freiligraths Sämtliche Werke* (New York, 1859), VI, 13–17.
54. Reprint and commentary in *Um Einheit und Freiheit,* ed. Ernst Volkmann (Leipzig, 1936), pp. 166–67. For the genesis and subsequent effect of the poem, see pp. 302–6.
55. *Ibid.,* p. 305, quoted from Karl Glossy, *Literarische Geheimberichte des Vormärz* (Jahrbücher der Grillparzer-Gesellschaft; Vienna, 1912), II, 270.
56. Quoted by Ernst Baldinger, *Georg Herwegh: Die Gedankenwelt der "Gedichte eines Lebendigen"* (dissertation, University of Berne, 1917), p. 107.
57. *Ibid.,* p. 109.
58. *Ibid.*
59. *Deutsch-Französische Jahrbücher* (1844), pp. 149–51.
60. See *Arnold Ruges Briefwechsel und Tagebuchblätter,* ed. Paul Nerrlich (Berlin, 1886), I, 349–51 (Ruge's letter of May 19, 1844).
61. *Ibid.,* I, 350.
62. Quoted by Baldinger, *Georg Herwegh,* p. 110.
63. *Ibid.*

64. Wilhelm Buchner, *Ferdinand Freiligrath: Ein Dichterleben in Briefen* (Lahr, 1882), II, 88.

65. *Ferdinand Freiligraths Sämtliche Werke*, VI, ix.

66. Buchner, *Ferdinand Freiligrath*, II, 120.

67. *Ibid.*

68. *Ferdinand Freiligraths Sämtliche Werke*, VI, 173–97.

69. *Ibid.*, VI, 183–87.

70. *Ibid.*, VI, 185–86.

71. *ÜKL*, p. 269; *MEGA*, I, Pt. VI, 106.

72. Buchner, *Ferdinand Freiligrath*, II, 234.

73. *Ferdinand Freiligraths Sämtliche Werke*, VI, 177.

74. *Ibid.*, pp. 278–80.

75. Buchner, *Ferdinand Freiligrath*, II, 234.

76. *ÜKL*, p. 400.

77. *Ibid.*, p. 372.

78. *Ibid.*, p. 373.

79. *Ibid.*, p. 372 (letter of May 28, 1851).

80. *Ibid.*, p. 377; *MEGA*, III, Pt. II, 350 (letter of December 11, 1858).

81. *ÜKL*, p. 383; *MEGA*, III, Pt. II, 432 (letter of November 5, 1859).

82. *ÜKL*, p. 382; *MEGA*, III, Pt. II, 429 (letter of November 3, 1859).

83. *ÜKL*, p. 388.

84. *Ibid.*, p. 394; *MEGA*, III, Pt. II, 471 (letter of February 9, 1860).

85. *ÜKL*, p. 394; *MEGA*, III, Pt. II, 452 (letter of January 11, 1860).

86. *ÜKL*, p. 395 (letter of February 23, 1860).

87. *Ibid.*, p. 397 (letter of February 23, 1860).

88. *Ibid.*, p. 395; *MEGA*, III, Pt. II, 471 (letter of February 9, 1860).

89. *ÜKL*, p. 395 (letter of February 23, 1860).

90. See Franz Mehring, "Freiligrath und Marx in ihrem Briefwechsel," *Die Neue Zeit*, XXX (1912), Suppl., p. 40.

91. *Ibid.*

92. See Nora Atkinson, *Eugène Sue et le roman-feuilleton* (Nemours, 1929); Georges Jarbinet, *Les mystères de Paris d'Eugène Sue* (Paris, 1932).

93. Eugène Sue, *Les mystères de Paris* (Paris, 1843), I, 1.

94. Sainte-Beuve, *Causeries du lundi* (Paris, 1857–62), II, 361.

95. See J. E. Dresch, *Le roman social en Allemagne* (Paris, 1913), pp. 3–9.

96. V. G. Belinsky, *Polno'e sobrani'e sochineniĭ*, VIII (Moscow, 1956), 167–85.

97. Théophile Gautier, *Histoire de l'art dramatique* (Paris, 1858–59), III, 161.

98. This Young Hegelian monthly, edited by Bruno Bauer, is not to be confused with the famous *Allgemeine Literatur-Zeitung* (1785–1848), which was published first in Jena and Weimar, later in Halle and Leipzig.

99. See *Biographisches Jahrbuch und Deutscher Nekrolog* (Berlin, 1903), V, 272–73.

100. *MEGA*, I, Pt. III, 238.
101. *Ibid.*
102. *Ibid.*, p. 239.
103. *Ibid.*, p. 246.
104. *Ibid.*, p. 245.
105. *Ibid.*, p. 387.
106. *Ibid.*, p. 382.
107. See René Wellek, "Social and Aesthetic Values in Russian Nineteenth Century Criticism," in *Continuity and Change in Russian and Soviet Thought*, ed. E. J. Simmons (Cambridge, Mass., 1956), p. 393.
108. See Victor Erlich, "Soviet Russian Criticism," in *Continuity and Change in Russian and Soviet Thought*, pp. 415–16.
109. Marx's and Engels' remarks on tragedy generated a lively controversy a few years ago. Georg Lukács defended the dogmatic standpoint, and Ludwig Marcuse a more liberal way of thinking. See Georg Lukács, "Marx und Engels über dramatische Fragen," *Aufbau*, IX (1953), 407–24, and Ludwig Marcuse, "Die marxistische Auslegung des Tragischen," *Monatshefte*, XLVI (1954), 241–48.
110. Reprinted in *Ferdinand Lassalle: Gesammelte Schriften und Reden*, ed. Eduard Bernstein (Berlin, 1919), I, 150–345.
111. *Ibid.*, p. 345.
112. *ÜKL*, pp. 119–25; also in *Ferdinand Lassalle: Gesammelte Schriften und Reden*, pp. 137–48.
113. *ÜKL*, pp. 116–19.
114. *Ibid.*, pp. 110–13.
115. *Ibid.*, pp. 113–16.
116. *Ibid.*, p. 113.
117. *Ibid.*, p. 111.
118. *Ibid.*
119. *Ibid.*, p. 112.
120. *Ibid.*, p. 114.
121. Hegel, *Vorlesungen über die Ästhetik*, XIV (iii), 569.
122. *Ibid.*
123. *ÜKL*, p. 114.
124. *Ibid.*, p. 112.
125. *Ibid.*, p. 111.
126. *Ibid.*, p. 115.
127. *Ibid.*
128. *Ibid.*
129. *Ibid.*, pp. 126–46.
130. *Ibid.*, p. 138.
131. *Ibid.*, p. 140.
132. *Ibid.*, p. 127.
133. *Ibid.*, p. 140.
134. *Ibid.*, p. 141.
135. *Ibid.*

136. *Ibid.*, p. 134.
137. *Ibid.*, p. 135.
138. *Ibid.*
139. Marcuse, "Die marxistische Auslegung des Tragischen," pp. 241–48.
140. *ÜKL*, p. 119.
141. *Ibid.*, p. 121.
142. *Ibid.*, p. 135.
143. *Ibid.*, p. 128.

CHAPTER 5   THE LATER ENGELS AS A CRITIC
OF MARXIST LITERARY DOCTRINE

1. Georg Lukács, *Beiträge zur Geschichte der Ästhetik* (Berlin, 1954). On p. 206 Lukács quotes, for example, Engels' letter to Minna Kautsky and continues: "But the type is, according to Marx and Engels . . . ," although the context has nothing to do with Marx.
2. Victor Erlich, "Soviet Literary Criticism," in *Continuity and Change in Soviet and Russian Thought*, ed. E. J. Simmons (Cambridge, Mass., 1955), p. 412: "Marx and Engels had a distinct bias in favor of 'realistic' literature."
3. *ÜKL*, p. 479 (*Die Neue Zeit*, XXXI [1913], 856).
4. *MEGA*, I, Pt. II, 517.
5. Letter of June 20, 1860 (*ÜKL*, pp. 169–71; *MEGA*, III, Pt. II, 491–92).
6. *ÜKL*, pp. 240–41; originally in *Der Social-Demokrat* (Berlin), May 11, 1865.
7. *ÜKL*, p. 168 (Friedrich Engels, *Der Ursprung der Familie, des Privateigentums und des Staates* [Zurich-Hottingen, 1884], p. 18 n.).
8. *ÜKL*, p. 174 (*New York Daily Tribune*, April 4, 1853).
9. *ÜKL*, p. 171 (Engels, *Ursprung der Familie . . .*, p. 41).
10. *Ibid.*
11. *Ibid.*, p. 173.
12. *Ibid.*
13. Published by Marx-Engels-Lenin-[Stalin-] Institute (Moscow, 1935).
14. Letter of June 6, 1853 (*ÜKL*, p. 152; *MEGA*, III, Pt. I, 481).
15. *ÜKL*, p. 15 (*Das Kapital* [2d ed.; Hamburg, 1872], I, 343).
16. *ÜKL*, p. 153 (Engels, *Ursprung der Familie . . .*, p. 67).
17. *ÜKL*, p. 152 (Engels, *Ursprung der Familie . . .*, p. 13).
18. Letter of June 26, 1869 (*ÜKL*, pp. 180–81; *MEGA*, III, Pt. IV, 197).
19. Letter of April 15, 1869 (*ÜKL*, p. 185; *MEGA*, III, Pt. IV, 183).
20. See G. F. W. Hegel, *Phänomenologie des Geistes*, ed. H. Glockner (Stuttgart, 1927), pp. 401–2.

21. Hegel quoted in *ÜKL*, p. 185; *MEGA*, III, Pt. IV, 183.

22. *ÜKL*, p. 185; *MEGA*, III, Pt. IV, 184.

23. *Ibid.*

24. *ÜKL*, p. 193; *MEGA*, III, Pt. IV, 409.

25. Hegel, *Vorlesungen über die Philosophie der Geschichte*, ed. H. Glockner (Stuttgart, 1928), p. 149.

26. *Ibid.*

27. Gustav Mayer, *Friedrich Engels* (London, 1936), pp. 145–46.

28. *ÜKL*, pp. 232–33; *MEGA*, III, Pt. II, 121–22.

29. *ÜKL*, p. 233.

30. Letter of March 7, 1856 (*ÜKL*, p. 233; *MEGA*, III, Pt. II, 121).

31. *Ibid.*

32. *Ibid.*

33. *ÜKL*, p. 234 (*New York Daily Tribune*, July 25, 1854).

34. *ÜKL*, p. 234; Karl Marx and Friedrich Engels, *Briefe an Danielson*, ed. K. Mandelbaum (Leipzig, 1929), p. 54.

35. *ÜKL*, p. 238; Marx and Engels, *Briefe an Danielson*, p. 12.

36. *ÜKL*, p. 235 (*Der Volksstaat* [Leipzig], October 6, 1874).

37. *ÜKL*, p. 232.

38. Franz Mehring, *Karl Marx*, trans. Edward Fitzgerald (New York, 1935), p. 410.

39. George Reavey, *Soviet Literature Today* (New Haven, Conn., 1947), pp. 19–20. See also Edward J. Brown, *The Proletarian Episode in Russian Literature* (New York, 1953).

40. Reavey, *Soviet Literature Today*, pp. 19–20.

41. Minna Kautsky, *Die Alten und die Neuen* (Leipzig, 1885), I, 58.

42. *Ibid.*, I, 36.

43. *ÜKL*, p. 102.

44. *Ibid.*

45. *Ibid.*

46. *Ibid.*

47. *Ibid.*

48. *Ibid.*

49. Cf. Hippolyte Taine, *Lectures on Art*, trans. John Durand (New York, 1875), I, 76.

50. The Library of the British Museum is the only place where a copy of this rare book is available. The officials of the British Museum were kind enough to permit me to have a microfilm of the text made.

51. *ÜKL*, p. 103.

52. *Ibid.*

53. *Ibid.*

54. *Ibid.*

55. My brief survey develops suggestions from René Wellek's *A History of Modern Criticism* (New Haven, 1955), Vol. II. A more thorough investigation of the concept would have to consider also Leo Spitzer's essay in *Essays in Historical Semantics* (New York, 1948), pp. 147–70.

56. See Erich Auerbach, *Neue Dantestudien* (Istanbul, 1944).

57. Wellek, *A History of Modern Criticism*, II, 257.

58. Discussed a few years ago by Heinrich Henel in "Type and Proto-Phenomenon in Goethe's Science," *PMLA*, LXXI (1956), 651–68. See also Emil Staiger, *Goethe* (Zurich, 1956), II, 104–27.

59. See *Grimms Wörterbuch*, XI, Sec. 1, Pt. 2 (Leipzig, 1952), cols. 1961–67.

60. *Œuvres complètes de Honoré de Balzac* (Paris, 1869), I, 1–16.

61. *Ibid.*, p. 1.

62. *Ibid.*, p. 5.

63. A series of references will be found in *Grimms Wörterbuch*, XI, Sec. 1, Pt. 2, cols. 1961–67; and in *OED*, X, cols. 555–57.

64. Aristotle, *Poetics* (S. H. Butcher, ed.), 1460*b*.

65. *Ibid.*

66. George Sand, *Indiana* (Paris, 1923), p. 7.

67. George Sand, "Notice," *Le compagnon du tour de France* (Paris, 1869), I, 1.

68. *Ibid.*

69. *Ibid.*

70. *Ibid.*

71. V. G. Belinsky, *Polno'e sobrani'e sochineniǐ* (Moscow, 1956), X, 307. Miss Harkness also speaks in one of her novels, *In Darkest London* (London, 1871), p. 92 n., about types: ". . . The principal characters . . . are all types not real men and women. Captain Lobe is a type of a Salvation Army captain. . . . I hope that my English readers will understand this."

72. See F. A. Sorge, "Zum 14. März," *Die Neue Zeit*, XXI (1903), 722.

73. *Ibid.*

74. *ÜKL*, p. 8 (*Sozialistische Monatshefte*, XXVI [1920], 796–97).

75. *Ibid.*

76. *Ibid.*

77. *Freie Bühne für das moderne Leben*, I (1890), 366.

78. *Ibid.*, pp. 423–26.

79. *Ibid.*, p. 423.

80. *Ibid.*

81. *Ibid.*, p. 424.

82. *Ibid.*, p. 426.

83. *Ibid.*, pp. 469–72.

84. *Ibid.*, p. 471.

85. *Ibid.*, p. 469.

86. *Ibid.*

87. *ÜKL*, p. 15.

88. *Ibid.*

89. See the letter to J. Bloch of September 21, 1890, in *ÜKL*, p. 8 (*Der sozialistische Akademiker*, I [1895], 353).

90. *UKL*, p. 6 (*Der sozialistische Akademiker*, I [1895], 352).

91. In his letter to Conrad Schmidt on October 27, 1890, quoted in Gustav Mayer, *Friedrich Engels* (The Hague, 1934), II, 448.

92. *ÜKL*, pp. 7–8 (*Sozialistische Monatshefte*, XXVI [1920], 874–75).
93. *Dokumente des Sozialismus*, ed. Eduard Bernstein, II (1903), 73–75.
94. Sholom Kahn, *Science and Aesthetic Judgement* (London, 1953), p. 105.
95. *MEGA*, I, Pt. IV, 122.
96. W. C. Taylor, *Notes of a Tour in the Manufacturing Districts of Lancashire* (London, 1842), p. 160.
97. Marx, "Einleitung," *Die Neue Zeit*, XXI (1903), 779.
98. *Das Kapital*, I, 534.

CHAPTER 6   THREE INTERPRETATIONS: SHAKESPEARE,
GOETHE, BALZAC

1. Donald Morrow, *Where Shakespeare Stood* (Milwaukee, 1935), p. 15.
2. A. A. Smirnov, *Shakespeare*, trans. by the Critics Group (New York, 1936), p. 85.
3. Reprinted in *ÜKL*, p. 476.
4. *MEGA*, I, Pt. III, 146.
5. If we accept the chronology suggested by Robert Tucker, *Philosophy and Myth in Karl Marx* (Cambridge, Eng., 1961), p. 111.
6. *Ibid.*, p. 298; *MEGA*, I, Pt. I (1), 601, 603.
7. *MEGA*, I, Pt. III, 149.
8. Roderich Benedix, *Die Shakespearomanie* (Stuttgart, 1873), p. 445.
9. *Ibid.*, p. 436.
10. *Ibid.*, p. 264.
11. *Ibid.*, p. 272.
12. *ÜKL*, p. 178; *MEGA*, III, Pt. IV, 413.
13. *Ibid.*
14. Letter of December 11, 1873; *ÜKL*, p. 178; *MEGA*, III, Pt. IV, 414.
15. This section is a revised version of my article, "Young Germany and Soviet Goethe Interpretation," *German Life and Letters*, IX (1956), 181–88. I am grateful to the editors of *German Life and Letters* for permission to reprint.
16. Miss Shaginian's writings include a novel, *The Power Plant* (1931), and two volumes of travel sketches, *Life and People in Armenia* (1947) and *A Journey Through Soviet Armenia* (1950).
17. I quote the West German edition available to me: Marietta Shaginian, *Goethe* (Essen, 1952).
18. *Ibid.*, p. 15.
19. *Ibid.*, p. 144.
20. *Ibid.*, p. 217.
21. Miss Shaginian prefers to forget the fact that Ryazanov, the editor of *MEGA*, corrected Mehring's version almost a generation ago. But Ryazanov was executed by a firing squad and and so it seems more wholesome to forget about his edition.

22. Shaginian, *Goethe*, p. 219.

23. *Ibid.*, p. 221.

24. I tried to stress some forgotten links in "The Early Beginnings of Marxist Literary Theory," *Germanic Review*, Columbia Bicentennial Issue (1954), pp. 201–13.

25. Wolfgang Menzel, *German Literature*, trans. Cornelius Felton (Boston, 1840), III, 20, in *Specimens of Foreign Standard Literature*, ed. George Ripley (Boston, 1840), Vol. VIII.

26. Ludwig Börne, *Gesammelte Schriften* (Leipzig, 1912), I, 573.

27. *Heinrich Heines Sämtliche Werke*, ed. Ernst Elster (Leipzig and Vienna, [1887–90]), V, 253.

28. *Ibid.*, p. 254.

29. Details in Viktor Schweitzer, *Ludolf Wienbarg—Beiträge zu einer jungdeutschen Ästhetik* (Leipzig, 1897).

30. *MEGA*, I, Pt. II, 335

31. *Ibid.*, p. 539.

32. *Ibid.*, p. 540.

33. *Ibid.*

34. *Ibid.*, p. 330.

35. *Ibid.*, p. 112.

36. Ludolf Wienbarg, *Ästhetische Feldzüge* (Hamburg, 1834).

37. *MEGA*, I, Pt. II, 505–25.

38. Karl Grün, *Über Göthe vom menschlichen Standpunkte* (Darmstadt, 1846).

39. No. 1 (November 21, 1847), No. 2 (November 25), No. 3 (November 28), No. 4 (December 4), No. 5 (December 5), No. 6 (December 9).

40. *MEGA*, I, Pt. II, 35.

41. *Ibid.*, p. 52.

42. *Ibid.*, pp. 487–88.

43. *Ibid.*, p. 606.

44. *Ibid.*, p. 601.

45. Wienbarg, *Ästhetische Feldzüge*, pp. 257–58.

46. *Ibid.*, p. 265.

47. *Ibid.*, pp. 271–72.

48. *MEGA*, I, Pt. VI, 56–57.

49. Wienbarg, *Ästhetische Feldzüge*, p. 255.

50. *MEGA*, I, Pt. VI, 57.

51. Wienbarg, *Ästhetische Feldzüge*, p. 273.

52. *MEGA*, I, Pt. VI, 57.

53. Wienbarg, *Ästhetische Feldzüge*, p. 274.

54. *MEGA*, I, Pt. VI, 57.

55. *MEGA*, IV, 171–74.

56. Georg Lukács, *Balzac und der französische Realismus* (Berlin, 1952), pp. 39–43.

57. Vladimir Grib, *Balzac: A Marxist Analysis*, trans. S. Bloomfield (New York, 1937), p. 85.

58. Karl Gutzkow, *Beiträge zur neuesten Literatur* (Stuttgart, 1836), II, 36–37.

  59. See *ÜKL*, p. 229.

  60. *Ibid.*, p. 230.

  61. *Ibid.*; *MEGA*, III, Pt. IV, 141.

  62. *Œuvres complètes de Honoré de Balzac* (Paris, 1869), XV, 291.

  63. *Ibid.*

  64. *ÜKL*, p. 230.

  65. *Œuvres complètes de Honoré de Balzac*, XV, 317.

  66. *Ibid.*

  67. *Ibid.*

  68. *Ibid.*, p. 328.

  69. See *ÜKL*, p. 477.

  70. From the original English version. See *ÜKL*, pp. 105–6.

  71. See *ÜKL*, p. 106.

  72. "[Balzac] était d'opinions aristocratiques. Rien de plus étrange, d'ailleurs, que ce soutien de pouvoir absolu, dont le talent est essentiellement démocratique, et qui a écrit l'œuvre la plus révolutionnaire qu'on puisse lire." (Émile Zola, *Les œuvres complètes*, ed. Maurice Le Blond and Eugène Fasquelle [Paris, 1927–29], XXXXIV, 47.)

  73. "Il y aurait là une étude curieuse à faire, que je poserai ainsi: comment le génie d'un homme put aller contre les convictions de cet homme." (*Ibid.*)

  74. *Ibid.*, XII, 807.

  75. This identification and spelling of the place is the correct one rather than that given by Engels.

  76. "Ainsi au milieu de cette cité de plus d'un million d'inhabitants, dans le quartier le plus populeux de Paris, à la face du soleil, on vît soixante citoyens défier un gouvernement, tenir en échec un armée, parlementer, livrer bataille." (Louis Blanc, *Histoire de dix ans* [Paris, 1846], III, 303.)

  77. *Heinrich Heines Sämtliche Werke*, V, 143–48; 167–89.

  78. *Œuvres complètes de Honoré de Balzac*, VII, 326.

  79. *Ibid.*, IX, 520.

CHAPTER 7   THE FIRST DISCIPLES

  1. See *Deutsches Biographisches Jahrbuch* (Berlin, 1928), II, 446–53; and also Georg Lukács' "Franz Mehring," *Beiträge zur Geschichte der Ästhetik* (Berlin, 1954), pp. 313–403, a polemical essay, but argued at a high level.

  2. See Lukács, "Franz Mehring," p. 322.

  3. The expression is probably derived from F. A. Lange's *Geschichte des Materialismus* (Iserlohn, 1876), p. 55.

  4. Mehring, "Über den historischen Materialismus," *Die Lessing-Legende* (Stuttgart, 1893), p. 446.

5. *MEGA*, III, Pt. II, 447–48.

6. *Ibid.*, p. 533.

7. See V. L. Komarov, "Marx and Engels on Biology," *Marxism and Modern Thought*, ed. N. I. Bucharin (New York, 1935).

8. *MEGA*, III, Pt. III, 355–56.

9. Quoted in Gustav Mayer, *Friedrich Engels* (The Hague, 1934), II, 319–20.

10. *Ibid.*

11. *Ibid.*

12. *Ibid.*, p. 352.

13. Franz Mehring, *Gesammelte Schriften und Aufsätze* (hereinafter cited as Mehring, *Gesammelte Schriften* (Berlin, 1929), VI, 260. The whole question is discussed by Lukács, "Franz Mehring," pp. 354–55.

14. Mehring, *Gesammelte Schriften*, I, 337.

15. *Ibid.*, p. 243.

16. *Ibid.*, p. 242.

17. Lukács, "Franz Mehring," p. 384.

18. Mehring, *Die Lessing-Legende*, pp. 63–64.

19. *Ibid.*, p. 64.

20. *Ibid.*, p. 9.

21. *Ibid.*, p. 199.

22. *Ibid.*, p. 218.

23. *Ibid.*, p. 244.

24. *Ibid.*, p. 322.

25. *Ibid.*, p. 325. The reference is to a well-known passage in Lessing's work attacking the Enlightenment poet Albrecht von Haller's (1708–77) description of the gentian in his poem *Die Alpen* (1729).

26. Mehring, *Gesammelte Schriften*, I, 117–276.

27. *Ibid.*, p. 266.

28. *Ibid.*, II, 263. See also Lukács, "Franz Mehring," pp. 370–71.

29. Mehring, *Gesammelte Schriften*, II, 305.

30. *Ibid.*, p. 299.

31. See Leopold H. Haimson, *The Russian Marxists and the Origins of Bolshevism* (Cambridge, Mass., 1955), chap. ii.

32. G. V. Plekhanov, *Kunst und Literatur*, ed. N. F. Belchikov (Berlin, 1955), p. 42; G. V. Plekhanov, *Sochineni'a* (Moscow, 1920–28), XIV, 2.

33. Plekhanov, *Kunst und Literatur*, p. 44; Plekhanov, *Sochineni'a*, XIV, 4.

34. Plekhanov, *Kunst und Literatur*, p. 45; Plekhanov, *Sochineni'a*, XIV, 4. The Darwin quotation is from *The Descent of Man and Selection in Relation to Sex* (New York, 1871), I, 61.

35. See Plekhanov, *Kunst und Literatur*, p. 55; Plekhanov, *Sochineni'a*, XIV, 14–15. The Darwin quotation is from *The Expression of the Emotions in Man and Animals* (New York, 1873), p .50.

36. Plekhanov, *Kunst und Literatur*, p. 58; Plekhanov, *Sochineni'a*, XIV, 17.

37. Plekhanov, *Kunst und Literatur*, p. 52; Plekhanov, *Sochineni'a*, XIV, 11.
38. Plekhanov, *Kunst und Literatur*, p. 50; Plekhanov, *Sochineni'a*, XIV, 9.
39. Plekhanov, *Kunst und Literature*, p. 77; Plekhanov, *Sochineni'a*, XIV, 36.
40. *Ibid.*
41. Plekhanov, *Kunst und Literatur*, p. 114; Plekhanov, *Sochineni'a*, XIV, 72.
42. Plekhanov, *Kunst und Literatur*, p. 172; Plekhanov, *Sochineni'a*, XIV, 95.
43. Plekhanov, *Kunst und Literatur*, p. 176; Plekhanov, *Sochineni'a*, XIV, 99.
44. *Ibid.*
45. Plekhanov, *Kunst und Literatur*, p. 175; Plekhanov, *Sochineni'a*, XIV, 98.
46. Plekhanov, *Kunst und Literatur*, p. 196; Plekhanov, *Sochineni'a*, XIV, 118.
47. Plekhanov, *Kunst und Literatur*, p. 196; Plekhanov, *Sochineni'a*, XIV, 119.
48. Plekhanov, *Kunst und Literatur*, p. 197.
49. Plekhanov, *Kunst und Literatur*, p. 247; Plekhanov, *Sochineni'a*, XIV, 136.
50. Plekhanov, *Kunst und Literatur*, p. 248.
51. *Ibid.*, p. 239.
52. Plekhanov, *Kunst und Literatur*, p. 253; Plekhanov, *Sochineni'a*, XIV, 141.
53. The criticism of Gorky appears in the popular anthologies, such as, for example, *Kunst und Literatur*, pp. 228–29, symptomatically abridged. The unabridged text on which I have based my discussion here appears in the Russian edition of Plekhanov (*Sochineni'a*, XIV, 227). This volume of the complete edition appeared in 1926.

CHAPTER 8   GEORG LUKÁCS AS A THEORETICIAN
OF LITERATURE

1. Georg Lukács, *Die Theorie des Romans* (Berlin, 1920), p. 12.
2. *Ibid.*
3. *Ibid.*, p. 31.
4. *Ibid.*, p. 20.
5. *Ibid.*, p. 44.
6. Cf. *ibid.*, pp. 65–68.
7. *Ibid.*, p. 69.
8. *Ibid.*
9. *Ibid.*, p. 70.
10. *Ibid.*, p. 95.

11. *Georg Lukács zum 70. Geburtstag* (Berlin, 1955), p. 228. Cf. Morris Watnick, "Georg Lukács: An Intellectual Biography," *Soviet Survey*, No. 23 (January–March, 1958), pp. 60–65; No. 24 (April–June, 1958), pp. 51–57; No. 25 (July–September, 1958), pp. 61–68; No. 27 (January–March, 1959), pp. 75–81.

12. Georg Lukács, "Karl Marx und Friedrich Theodor Vischer," *Beiträge zur Geschichte der Ästhetik* (Berlin, 1954), pp. 217–85.

13. Georg Lukács, "Franz Mehring," *ibid.*, pp. 318–403.

14. Georg Lukács, "Johannes R. Becher," *Schicksalswende* (Berlin, 1956), p. 230.

15. Georg Lukács, "Marx und das Problem des ideologischen Verfalls," *Marx und Engels als Literaturhistoriker* (Berlin, 1948), p. 163.

16. *Ibid.*

17. *Ibid.*

18. *Ibid.*, p. 133.

19. Georg Lukács, "Objektive Dialektik und die Schranken des Idealismus," *Beiträge zur Geschichte der Ästhetik*, p. 205.

20. Georg Lukács, "Einführung in die ästhetischen Schriften von Marx und Engels," *ibid.*, p. 205.

21. Georg Lukács, "Die intellektuelle Physiognomie der künstlerischen Gestalten," *Essays über Realismus* (Berlin, 1948), p. 28.

22. Georg Lukács, *Der historische Roman* (Berlin, 1955), p. 309.

23. *Ibid.*, p. 31.

24. *Ibid.*

25. Georg Lukács, "Es geht um den Realismus," *Essays über Realismus*, p. 153.

26. Georg Lukács, "Die intellektuelle Physiognomie der künsterischen Gestalten," *ibid.*, p. 33.

27. *Ibid.*, p. 65.

28. Georg Lukács, "Balzac als Kritiker Stendhals," *Balzac und der französischer Realismus* (Berlin, 1952), p. 76.

29. Lukács, "Die intellektuelle Physiognomie der künsterischen Gestalten," *Essays über Realismus*, p. 57.

30. Lukács, *Der historische Roman*, p. 136.

31. Lukács, "Es geht um den Realismus," *Essays über Realismus*, p. 143.

32. *Ibid.*, p. 155.

33. Lukács, *Der historische Roman*, p. 106.

34. *Ibid.*, p. 97.

35. *Ibid.*, p. 98.

36. *Ibid.*, p. 99.

37. Georg Lukács, "Schillers Theorie der modernen Literatur," *Goethe und seine Zeit* (Berlin, 1950), p. 143.

38. *Ibid.*, pp. 123–35.

39. Georg Lukács, "Zur Ästhetik Schillers, *Beiträge zur Geschichte der Ästhetik*, p. 84.

40. Georg Lukács, "Nietzsche als Vorläufer der faschistischen Ästhetik," *Beiträge zur Geschichte der Ästhetik,* p. 299.
41. Lukács, "Es geht um den Realismus," *Essays über Realismus,* p. 157.
42. Lukács, *Die Theorie des Romans,* p. 101.
43. Lukács, "Zur Ästhetik Schillers," *Beiträge zur Geschichte der Ästhetik,* p. 42.
44. Lukács, *Der historische Roman,* p. 191.
45. Lukács, *Die Theorie des Romans,* p. 77.
46. Georg Lukács, *Aesthetik* (Neuwied am Rhein, 1965), II, 669.
47. *Ibid.,* I, 17.
48. *Ibid.*
49. *Ibid.,* p. 246.
50. *Ibid.,* p. 362.
51. *Ibid.,* p. 369.
52. *Ibid.,* p. 609.
53. *Ibid.*
54. *Ibid.,* p. 610.
55. *Ibid.,* p. 689.
56. *Ibid.,* p. 401.
57. *Ibid.,* p. 168.
58. *Ibid.*
59. *Ibid.,* p. 620.
60. *Ibid.,* II, 687.
61. *Ibid.*
62. *Ibid.*
63. *Ibid.,* I, 838.
64. *Ibid.,* II, 777.
65. *Ibid.,* I, 825.

CHAPTER 9 MARXIST CRITICISM: PAST AND PRESENT

1. November 26, 1905; *Novaya Zhizn,* No. 12.
2. Hans Mayer, *Von Lessing bis Thomas Mann* (Pfullingen, 1960), p. 135.
3. *Ibid.,* p. 402.
4. Hans Mayer, *Georg Büchner* (2d ed.; Wiesbaden, 1960), p. 126.
5. Lucien Goldmann, *Le Dieu caché* (Paris, 1955), p. 27.
6. Lucien Goldmann, *Pour une sociologie du roman* (Paris, 1966).
7. Roland Barthes, *Essais critiques* (Paris, 1965).
8. Theodor W. Adorno, *Noten zur Literatur* (Frankfurt, 1962–65), I, 52.
9. *Ibid.,* III, 144.
10. *Ibid.,* III, 20.
11. *Ibid.,* II, 144–45.

Bibliography

I. PRIMARY SOURCES

1. Works by Marx and Engels

ENGELS, FRIEDRICH. *Frankskŭ dialekt.* Moscow, 1935.

———. *Schriften der Frühzeit.* Edited by GUSTAV MAYER. Berlin, 1920.

———. *Der Ursprung der Familie, des Privateigentums und des Staats.* Zurich-Hottingen, 1884.

MARX, KARL. "Einleitung" [zur *Kritik der politischen Ökonomie*]. Edited by KARL KAUTSKY. In *Die Neue Zeit*, XXI (1902–3), 710–18, 741–45, 772–81.

———. *Frühschriften.* Vol. I. Edited by HANS JOACHIM LIBER and PETER FURTH. Stuttgart, 1962.

———. *Das Kapital.* 2d ed. Hamburg, 1872.

———. *Zur Kritik der politischen Ökonomie.* Edited by KARL KAUTSKY. Stuttgart, 1897.

MARX, KARL, and ENGELS, FRIEDRICH. *Briefe an Danielson.* Edited by K. MANDELBAUM. Leipzig, 1929.

———. *Historisch-kritische Gesamtausgabe.* Edited by D. B. RYAZANOV and W. ADORATSKY. Moscow, 1927–35. (*MEGA*)

———. *Über Kunst und Literatur.* Edited by MICHAIL LIFSCHITZ. German ed. edited by KURT THÖRICHT and RODERICH FECHNER. Berlin, 1949. (*ÜKL*)

Marx-Engels Ausgabe. Edited by INSTITUT FÜR MARXISMUS-LENINISMUS BEIM ZK DER SED. Berlin, 1956–63.

2. Other Primary Sources

ADORNO, THEODOR W. *Noten zur Literatur.* 3 vols. Frankfurt, 1963–65.

AVELING, EDWARD, and MARX-AVELING, ELEANOR. "Shelley und der Sozialismus," *Die Neue Zeit*, X (1891–92), 581 ff., 609 ff.

BALZAC, HONORÉ DE. *Œuvres complètes.* Paris, 1869.

BELINSKY, V. G. *Polno'e sobrani'e sochinenü.* Moscow, 1956.

BENEDIX, RODERICH. *Die Shakespearomanie.* Stuttgart, 1873.

BENJAMIN, WALTER. *Ursprung des deutschen Trauerspiels.* Berlin, 1928.

BÖRNE, LUDWIG. *Dramaturgische Blätter.* Hamburg, 1835.

———. *Gesammelte Schriften.* Edited by LUDWIG GEIGER. Leipzig, 1912.

BONALD, LOUIS DE. *Œuvres complètes de M. de Bonald.* Edited by L'ABBÉ MIGNE. 3 vols. Paris, 1859.

CARLYLE, THOMAS. *Critical and Miscellaneous Essays.* Library ed. London, 1869.

———. *On Heroes, Hero-Worship and the Heroic in History.* Library ed. London, 1869.

———. *Past and Present.* Library ed. London, 1870.

———. *Sartor Resartus.* Library ed. London, 1870.

COLERIDGE, SAMUEL TAYLOR. *The Complete Works of Samuel Taylor Coleridge.* Edited by W. G. T. SHEDD. New York, 1884.

DIDEROT, DENIS. *Le neveu de Rameau.* Critical ed. Geneva, 1950.

L'estetica e la poetica in Russia. Edited by ETTORE LO GATTO. Florence, 1947.

FEUERBACH, LUDWIG. *Sämtliche Werke.* Edited by W. BOLIN and F. JODL. Stuttgart, 1903–11.

FREILIGRATH, FERDINAND. *Sämmtliche Werke.* New York, 1858–59.

GOLDMANN, LUCIEN. *Le Dieu caché.* Paris, 1955.

———. *Recherches dialectiques.* Paris, 1959.

———. *Pour une sociologie du roman.* Paris, 1964.

GRÜN, KARL. *Über Göthe, vom menschlichen Standpunkte.* Darmstadt, 1846.

GUTZKOW, KARL. *Werke.* Edited by REINHOLD GENSEL. Leipzig, 1912.

HARKNESS, MARGRET. *See* LAW, JOHN.

HEGEL, GEORG WILHELM FRIEDRICH. *Sämtliche Werke.* Edited by H. GLOCKNER. Stuttgart, 1927–40.

HEINE, HEINRICH. *Sämtliche Werke.* Edited by ERNST ELSTER. Leipzig, [1887–90].

HERWEGH, GEORG. *Gedichte eines Lebendigen.* Zurich, 1848.

HETTNER, HERMANN. *Schriften zur Literatur.* Berlin, 1859.

JONES, RICHARD. *Textbook of Lectures on the Political Economy of Nations.* London, 1852.

JUNG, ALEXANDER. *Vorlesungen über die moderne Literatur der Deutschen.* Danzig, 1842.

KAUTSKY, MINNA. *Die Alten und die Neuen.* Leipzig, 1885.

————. *Stephan von Grillenhof.* Leipzig, 1881.

LASSALLE, FERDINAND. *Gesamtwerk.* Edited by E. SCHIRMER. Leipzig, 1899–1909.

LAW, JOHN [*pseud.* for MARGRET HARKNESS]. *The City Girl.* London, 1887.

————. *In Darkest London.* London, 1891.

LENIN, V. I. *Sochineni'a.* 4th ed. Moscow, 1941–50.

————. *Stati o Tolstom.* Moscow, 1939.

LUKÁCS, GEORG. *Aesthetik.* 2 vols. Neuwied am Rhein, 1965————.

————. *Balzac und der französische Realismus.* Berlin, 1952.

————. *Beiträge zur Geschichte der Ästhetik.* Berlin, 1954.

————. *Deutsche Literatur im Zeitalter des Imperialismus: Eine Übersicht ihrer Hauptströmungen.* Berlin, 1946.

————. *Deutsche Realisten des 19. Jahrhunderts.* Berlin, 1951.

————. *Essays on Thomas Mann.* Translated by STANLEY MITCHELL. London, 1964.

————. *Essays über Realismus.* Berlin, 1948.

————. *Goethe und seine Zeit.* Bern, 1947.

————. *Gottfried Keller.* Berlin, 1946.

————. *The Historical Novel.* Preface to the American ed. by IRVING HOWE. Boston, 1963.

————. *Der junge Hegel. Über die Beziehungen von Dialektik und Ökonomie.* Vienna, 1948.

————. *Karl Marx und Friedrich Engels als Literaturhistoriker.* Berlin, 1947. 2d ed. Berlin, 1952.

————. *The Meaning of Contemporary Realism.* Translated by JOHN and NECKE MANDER. London, 1963.

————. *Realism in Our Time: Literature and the Class Struggle.* Preface by GEORGE STEINER. New York, 1965.

————. *Der russische Realismus in der Weltliteratur.* Berlin, 1949. 3d ed. Berlin, 1953.

————. *Schicksalswende. Beiträge zu einer neuen deutschen Ideologie.* Berlin, 1948. 2d rev. ed. Berlin, 1956.

Lukács, Georg. *Schriften zur Literatursoziologie.* Edited by Peter Ludz. Neuwied am Rhein, 1961. 2d ed. Neuwied am Rhein, 1963.

––––––. *Die Seele und die Formen.* Berlin, 1911.

––––––. *Skizze einer Geschichte der neueren deutschen Literatur.* Berlin, 1953.

––––––. *Studies in European Realism: A Sociological Survey of the Writings of Balzac, Stendhal, Zola, Tolstoy, Gorki, and Others.* London, 1950.

––––––. *Studies in European Realism.* With an Introduction by Alfred Kazin. New York, 1964.

––––––. *Die Theorie des Romans: Ein geschichtsphilosophischer Versuch über die Formen der grossen Epik.* Berlin, 1920. 2d rev. ed. Neuwied am Rhein, 1963.

––––––. *Thomas Mann.* Berlin, 1949.

––––––. *Wider den missverstandenen Realismus.* Hamburg, 1958.

––––––. *Die Zerstörung der Vernunft.* Berlin, 1954. 2d ed. Berlin, 1963.

Mayer, Hans. *Ansichten zur Literatur der Zeit.* Reinbek bei Hamburg, 1962.

––––––. *Bertolt Brecht und die Tradition.* Pfullingen, 1961.

––––––. *Deutsche Literatur und Weltliteratur. Reden und Aufsätze.* Berlin, 1957.

––––––. *Zur deutschen Klassik und Romantik.* Pfullingen, 1963.

––––––. *Dürrenmatt und Frisch. Anmerkungen.* Pfullingen, 1963.

––––––. *Georg Büchner und seine Zeit.* Wiesbaden, 1946. 2d ed. Berlin, 1960.

––––––. *Heinrich von Kleist: Der geschichtliche Augenblick.* Pfullingen, 1962.

––––––. *Das Ideal und das Leben. Rede gehalten aus Anlass der Schiller-Ehrung der Stadt Leipzig am 9. Mai 1955.* Leipzig, 1955.

––––––. *Leiden und Grösse Thomas Manns. Zwei Reden.* Berlin, 1956.

––––––. *Von Lessing bis Thomas Mann. Wandlungen der bürgerlichen Literatur in Deutschland.* Pfullingen, 1959.

––––––. *Platon und die finsteren Zeiten. Über die Möglichkeiten einer Akademie im heutigen Deutschland.* Berlin, 1965.

––––––. *Richard Wagner in Selbstzeugnissen und Bilddokumenten.* Hamburg, 1959.

————. *Schiller und die Nation.* Berlin, 1953. 2d ed. Düsseldorf, 1955.

————. *Studien zur deutschen Literaturgeschichte.* "Neue Beiträge zur Literaturwissenschaft," No. 2. Berlin, 1953. 2d ed., Berlin, 1955.

————. *Thomas Mann: Werk und Entwicklung.* Berlin, 1950.

MAYER, HANS, and HERMLIN, STEPHAN. *Ansichten über einige neue Schriftsteller und Bücher.* Wiesbaden, 1947.

MEHRING, FRANZ. *Gesammelte Schriften und Aufsätze.* Berlin, 1929.

————. *Gesammelte Schriften.* Edited by T. HOEHLE, HANS KOCH, and JOSEF SCHLEIFSTEIN. Berlin, 1960————.

————. *Die Lessing-Legende.* Stuttgart, 1893.

MELVILLE, HERMAN. *Mardi.* Constable ed. London, 1922.

————. *Redburn.* Constable ed. London, 1922.

PLEKHANOV, G. V. *Kunst und Literatur.* Edited by N. F. BELCHIKOV. Berlin, 1955.

————. *Sochineni'a.* Moscow, 1920–28.

Problems of Soviet Literature: Reports and Speeches at the First Soviet Writers' Congress. New York, 1934.

RUGE, ARNOLD. *Briefwechsel und Tagebuchblätter.* Edited by PAUL NERRLICH. Berlin, 1886.

————. *Aus früher Zeit.* Berlin, 1862–67.

————. *Gesammelte Schriften.* Mannheim, 1846.

SAND, GEORGE. *Le compagnon du tour de France.* Paris, 1869.

————. *Indiana.* Paris, 1869.

STAËL-HOLSTEIN, ANNE-LOUISE-GERMAINE DE. *De la littérature con-sidérée dans ses rapports avec les institutions sociales.* 2d ed. Paris, 1801.

SUE, EUGÈNE. *Les mystères de Paris.* Paris, 1843.

TAINE, HIPPOLYTE. *Honoré de Balzac, sa vie et ses œuvres.* Brussels, 1858.

————. *De l'idéal dans l'art.* Paris, 1867.

————. *Philosophie d l'art.* Paris, 1909.

TROTSKY, LEON. *Literatura i revolutsi'a.* 2d ed. Moscow, 1924.

WEERTH, GEORG. *Sämtliche Werke.* Edited by BRUNO KAISER. Berlin, 1957.

WIENBARG, LUDOLF. *Ästhetische Feldzüge.* Hamburg, 1834.

3. Periodicals

Dokumente des Sozialismus, edited by EDUARD BERNSTEIN. Berlin, 1902–3.

Hallische Jahrbücher für Wissenschaft und Kunst, edited by ARNOLD RUGE and THEODOR ECHTERMEYER (January, 1838–January, 1841); continued as *Deutsche Jahrbücher für Wissenschaft und Kunst,* edited by ARNOLD RUGE (February, 1841–January, 1843).

Neue Rheinische Zeitung: Organ der Demokratie. Cologne, 1848–49; reprinted, Berlin, 1928.

II. SECONDARY SOURCES

ADAMS, HENRY PACKWOOD. *Karl Marx in His Earlier Writings.* London, 1940.

ADLER, MAX. *Engels als Denker.* Berlin, 1925.

ALBRECHT, MILTON C. "The Relationship of Literature and Society," *American Journal of Sociology,* LIX (1953–54), 425–36.

ALTHAUS, KURT. *Georg Lukács oder Bürgerlichkeit als Vorschule einer marxistischen Ästhetik.* Bern, 1962.

ASMUS, W. "Marxismus und Kulturtradition," *Unter dem Banner des Marxismus,* II (1928), 213–21.

ATKINSON, NORA. *Eugène Sue et le roman-feuilleton.* Nemours, 1929.

AUERBACH, ERICH. *Neue Dantestudien.* Istanbul, 1944.

BALDENSPERGER, FERNAND. "Ist die Literatur der Ausdruck der Gesellschaft?" *Deutsche Vierteljahrsschrift,* VII (1929), 17–28.

BALDINGER, ERNST. *Georg Herwegh: Die Gedankenwelt der "Gedichte eines Lebendigen."* Bern, 1917.

BARZUN, JACQUES. *Darwin, Marx, Wagner: Critique of a Heritage.* Boston, 1941.

BELOW, GEORG ANTON HUGO VON. *Die deutsche Geschichtsschreibung von den Befreiungskriegen bis zu unseren Tagen.* Munich, 1924.

BERLIN, ISAIAH. *Karl Marx—His Life and Environment.* London, 1948.

BESENBRUCH, WALTER. *Zum Problem des Typischen: Versuch über den Zusammenhang der Grundkategorien der Ästhetik.* "Beiträge zur deutschen Klassik," Vol. III. Edited by Nationale Forschungs- und Gedenkstätten der klassischen deutschen Literatur in Weimar. Weimar, 1956.

BLOCH, ERNST. "Der Student Marx," *Sinn und Form*, III (1951), 12–17.

BOBER, MANDELL MORTON. *Karl Marx's Interpretation of History.* Cambridge, 1948.

BÖHME, SIEGFRIED. *Grundlagen und Methodik der Literaturbetrachtung bei Karl Marx und Friedrich Engels.* Dissertation, University of Berlin, 1954.

BORLAND, HARRIET. *Soviet Literary Theory and Practice during the First Five-Year Plan.* New York, 1950.

BOWMAN, HERBERT. *Vissarion Belinski: Social Criticism in Russia.* Cambridge, Mass., 1955.

BRAMSTED. See KOHN-BRAMSTEDT.

BRAUN, MILTON W. "The Marxist Approach to Literature," *Dialectics*, II (1937), 23–31.

BRETT, VLADIMIR. "K otáce vzniku a vývoje socialistickéno realismu ve Francii," *Časopis pro moderní filologii*, XXXVII (1955), 224–35.

BUCHNER, WILHELM. *Ferdinand Freiligrath: Ein Dichterleben in Briefen.* Lahr, 1882.

CALDER, GRACE J. *The Writing of Past and Present.* New Haven, 1949.

CASELMANN, AUGUST. *Karl Gutzkows Stellung zu den religiös-ethischen Problemen seiner Zeit.* Augsburg, 1900.

CORNU, AUGUSTE. *La jeunesse de Karl Marx.* Paris, 1934.

———. *Karl Marx: L'homme et l'œuvre.* Paris, 1934.

———. *Karl Marx: Die Ökonomisch-Philosophischen Manuskripte.* Berlin, 1955.

———. *Karl Marx et Friedrich Engels.* Vol. I. Paris, 1955.

———. *Moses Hess et la gauche hégélienne.* Paris, 1934.

CZÓBEL, ERNST. "Rjazanow als Marx-Forscher," *Unter dem Banner des Marxismus*, IV (1930), 401–17.

———. (ed.), *Karl Marx: Chronik seines Lebens in Einzeldaten.* Moscow, 1934.

DAHNKE, HANS DIETRICH. *Karl Marx und die politische Lyrik des Vormärz.* Berlin, 1953.

DAICHES, DAVID. *Literature and Society.* London, 1938.

DEMETZ, PETER. "Early Beginnings of Marxist Literary Theory," *Germanic Review*, XXIX (1954), 201–13.

———. "Geschichtsvision und Wissenschaft: Über einige Arbeiten Hans Mayers," *Merkur*, XV (1961), 677–87.

DEMETZ, PETER. "The Uses of Lukács," *Yale Review,* LIV (1965), 435–40.

———. "Young Germany and Soviet Goethe Interpretation," *German Life and Letters,* IX (1956), 181–88.

DIETZE, WALTER. *Junges Deutschland und deutsche Klassik.* 2d ed. Berlin, 1958.

DRESCH, J. E. *Gutzkow et la Jeune Allemagne.* Paris, 1904.

———. *Le roman social en Allemagne.* Paris, 1913.

DUNCAN, HUGH D. *Annotated Bibliography on the Sociology of Literature with an Introductory Essay on Methodological Problems in the Field.* Chicago, 1947.

DUVIGNAUD, JEAN. "*Problèmes de sociologie de la sociologie des arts,*" *Cahiers Internationaux de Sociologie,* VI (1959), 137–48.

ECK, ELSE VON. *Die Literaturkritik in den Hallischen und Deutschen Jahrbüchern.* "Germanische Studien," No. 42. Berlin, 1926.

ELVIN, H. L. "Marx and the Marxists as Literary Critics," *Journal of Adult Education,* X (1938), 260–76.

ERLICH, VICTOR. "Social and Aesthetic Criteria in Soviet Russian Criticism," in *Continuity and Change in Russian and Soviet Thought.* Edited by ERNEST J. SIMMONS. Cambridge, Mass., 1955. Pp. 398–416.

ESCARPIT, ROBERT. *Sociologie de la littérature.* Paris, 1958.

FAUCCI, DARIO. "L'estetica del Marxismo," *Del Romanticismo al Novecento.* Part IV of *Momenti e problemi di storia dell' estetica.* Edited by CARLO MARZONATI. Milan, 1961.

FARNAM, HENRY W. *Shakespeare's Economics.* New Haven, 1931.

FISCHER, ERNST. *Von der Notwendigkeit der Kunst.* Dresden, 1959.

FISHER, J. O. "Některé problémy západoevropského kritického realismu v díle kritických realistů francouzských," *Časopis pro moderní filologii,* XXXVIII (1956), 76–91.

FLEURY, VICTOR. *Le poète Georges Herwegh.* Paris, 1911.

FOOTMAN, DAVID. *Ferdinand Lassalle: Romantic Revolutionary.* New Haven, Conn., 1947.

FOX, RALPH. "The Relation of Literature to Dialectical Materialism," in *Aspects of Dialectical Materialism.* London, 1934.

FRANCKE, KUNO. *A History of German Literature as Determined by Social Forces.* 4th ed. New York, 1901.

FREIBURG-RÜTER, KLEMENS. *Der literarische Kritiker Karl Gutzkow.* Leipzig, 1930.

FRISÉ, ADOLF. *Alexander Jung*. Dissertation, Heidelberg University, 1932.

FROST, WALTER. *Hegels Ästhetik*. Munich, 1928.

FUEGEN, HANS NORBERT. *Die Hauptrichtungen der Literatursoziologie und ihre Methoden*. Bonn, 1964.

GEIGER, L. *Das Junge Deutschland und die preussische Censur*. Berlin, 1900.

Georg Lukács zum 70. Geburtstag. Festschrift. Berlin, 1955.

GILMAN, WILLIAM H. *Melville's Early Life and Redburn*. New York, 1951.

GLICKSBERG, CHARLES I. "The Aberrations of Marxist Criticism," *Queens Quarterly*, LVI (1949), 479–90.

―――. "Literature and the Marxist Aesthetic," *University of Toronto Quarterly*, XVIII (1949), 76–84.

GOITEIN, IRMA. *Probleme der Gesellschaft und des Staates bei Moses Hess*. Beihefte zum *Archiv für die Geschichte des Sozialismus und der Arbeiterbewegung*, Vol. V. Leipzig, 1931.

GOLD, MICHAEL (ed.). *Proletarian Literature in the United States*. New York, 1935.

GRAHAM, WALTER. *Tory Criticism in the "Quarterly Review."* New York, 1921.

GREINER, MARTIN. "Literatur und Gesellschaft: Literatursoziologie als Wirkungsgeschichte der Dichtung," *Deutsche Universitäts-Zeitung*, XII (1957), 14–17.

―――. "Politik und Dichtung 1830–1850," *Sammlung*, II (1956), 289–95.

―――. *Zwischen Biedermeier und Bourgeoisie*. Göttingen. 1953.

GROETHUYSEN, BERNARD. "Les Jeunes Hégéliens et les origines du socialisme contemporain en Allemagne," *Revue Philosophique*, XLVIII (1923), 379–402.

GUÉRARD, ALBERT LÉON. *Literature and Society*. Boston, 1935.

GUMMER, ELLIS N. *Dickens' Work in Germany*. Oxford, 1940.

HAMBURGER, KÄTHE. "Zwei Formen literatursoziologischer Betrachtung," *Orbis Litterarum*, VII (1949), 142–60.

HARROLD, C. F. *Carlyle and German Thought*. New Haven, Conn., 1934.

HENFOLD, KARL. *Georg Herwegh und seine deutschen Vorbilder*. Ansbach, 1916.

266 Bibliography

HERRMANN, MAX. *Die bürgerliche Literaturgeschichte und das Prole-tariat*. Berlin, 1922.

HIRSCH, ARNOLD. "Soziologie und Literaturgeschichte," *Euphorion*, XXIX (1928), 74–82.

HIRTH, FRIEDRICH E. "Heine und Marx," in *Heinrich Heine: Bausteine zu einer Biographie*. Mainz, 1950. Pp. 117–31.

HONIGSHEIM, PAUL. "Soziologie der Kunst, Musik und Literatur," in *Die Lehre von der Gesellschaft*. Edited by G. EISERMANN. Stuttgart, 1958. Pp. 338–73.

HOOK, SIDNEY. *From Hegel to Marx: Studies in the Intellectual Development of Karl Marx*. New York, 1950.

HRÚŠOVSKÝ, IGOR. *Engels ako filozof*. Bratislava, 1946.

HYMAN, STANLEY EDGAR. *The Armed Vision*. New York, 1948.

———. "The Marxist Criticism of Literature," *Antioch Review*, VII (1947), 541–68.

IBEN, HARRY. *Karl Gutzkow als literarischer Kritiker*. Greifswald, 1928.

ILBERG, WERNER. *Unser Heine*. Berlin, 1952.

ISKOWICZ, MARC. *La littérature à la lumière du matérialisme historique*. Paris, 1926.

JACKSON, T. A. "Marx and Shakespeare," *International Literature*, VI (1936), 75–97.

JARBINET, GEORGES. *Les mystères de Paris d'Eugène Sue*. Paris, 1932.

JENS, WALTER. "Sozialistische Germanistik," *Die Zeit*, January 23, 1959.

JOYCE, DOUGLAS ALICK. "Arnold Ruge as a Literary Critic." Unpublished Ph.D. dissertation, Harvard University, 1953.

KAHN, LUDWIG W. *Social Ideas in German Literature, 1770–1830*. New York, 1938.

KAHN, SHOLEM. *Science and Aesthetic Judgement*. London, 1953.

KAUTSKY, KARL. "Gustav Mayers Engels-Biographie," *Archiv für die Geschichte des Sozialismus und der Arbeiterbewegung*, IX (1921), 342–55.

KAYSER, RUDOLF. "Ludolph Wienbarg und der Kampf um den Historismus," *German Quarterly*, XXIX (1956), 71–74.

KEDNEY, J. S. *Hegel's Aesthetics*. Chicago, 1897.

KLINGENDER, F. D. *Marxism and Modern Art*. New York, 1945.

KOCH, HANS. *Georg Lukács und der Revisionismus. Eine Sammlung von Aufsätzen*. Berlin, 1960.

KOFLER, LEO. *Theorie der modernen Literatur: Der Avantgardismus in soziologischer Sicht.* Neuwied am Rhein, 1962.

KOHN-BRAMSTEDT, ERNST. *Aristocracy and the Middle Classes in Germany.* London, 1937. Rev. ed., Chicago, 1964, published under the name Ernest K. Bramsted.

————. "Probleme der Literatursoziologie," *Neue Jahrbücher für Wissenschaft und Jugendbildung,* VII (1931), 719–31.

KOIGEN, DAVID. *Zur Vorgeschichte des modernen philosophischen Sozialismus in Deutschland.* "Berner Studien zur Philosophie und ihrer Geschichte," No. 21. Bern, 1901.

KRAUSS, WERNER. "Literaturgeschichte als geschichtlicher Auftrag," *Sinn und Form,* II (1950), 65–126.

KUCZYNSKI, JÜRGEN. "Über die unterschiedliche Entwicklung der Teile des Überbaus," *Sinn und Form,* IV (1952), 130–50.

LASKINE, EDMOND. "Zur Geschichte des sozialen Toryismus," *Archiv für die Geschichte des Sozialismus und der Arbeiterbewegung,* V (1915), 39–88.

LEHMANN-HAUPT, H. *Art under a Dictatorship.* New York, 1954.

LIFSCHITZ, MIKHAIL. "Marx on Aesthetics," *International Literature,* III (1933), 75–91.

————. *The Philosophy of Art of Karl Marx.* Translated by RALPH T. WINN. New York, 1938.

LIFSCHITZ, MIKHAIL, and SCHILLER, F. *Marx i Engels o isskustve i literature.* Moscow, 1933.

LOCKWOOD, HELEN D. *Tools and the Man: A Comparative Study of the French Workingmen and English Chartists in the Literature of 1830–1848.* New York, 1927.

LÖWENTHAL, LEO. *Literature and the Image of Man: Sociological Studies of the European Drama and Novel, 1600–1900.* Boston, 1957.

LÖWITH, KARL. *Von Hegel bis Nietzsche.* Zurich, 1941.

McCAULEY, ELIZABETH. "Karl Gutzkow as Literary Critic." Unpublished Ph.D. dissertation, University of Chicago, 1941.

MACHÁČKOVÁ, VĚRA. *Der junge Engels und die Literatur.* Berlin, 1961.

MAENNER, LUDWIG. *Karl Gutzkow und der demokratische Gedanke.* Munich, 1921.

MAGILL, C. P. "Young Germany: A Re-evaluation," *German Studies Presented to L. A. Willoughby.* Oxford, 1952.

MARCUSE, HERBERT. *Reason and Revolution: Hegel and the Rise of Social Theory.* London, 1941.

MARCUSE, LUDWIG. *Heine.* 2d ed. Hamburg, 1951.

————. *Ludwig Börne: Das Leben eines Revolutionärs.* Berlin, 1931.

————. "Die marxistische Auslegung des Tragischen," *Monatshefte,* XLVI (1954), 241–48.

MARTIN, JOHN R. "Marxism and the History of Art," *College Art Journal,* II (1951), 3–9.

MASARYK, THOMAS. *Die philosophischen und soziologischen Grundlagen des Marxismus.* Vienna, 1899.

MATHEWSON, RUFUS W. *The Positive Hero in Russian Literature.* New York, 1958.

MATTHIESSEN, F. O. *American Renaissance.* New York, 1941.

MAYER, GUSTAV. "Briefe Ferdinand Lassalles an Ferdinand Freiligrath," *Archiv für die Geschichte des Sozialismus und der Arbeiterbewegung,* VII (1916), 431–45.

————. *Friedrich Engels.* The Hague, 1934.

————. *Friedrich Engels in seiner Frühzeit 1820–1851.* Berlin, 1920.

————. "Ein Pseudonym von Friedrich Engels," *Archiv für die Geschichte des Sozialismus und der Arbeiterbewegung,* IV (1914), 86–89.

————. "Der Untergang der 'Deutsch-Französischen Jahrbücher' und des 'Pariser Vorwärts,'" *Archiv für die Geschichte des Sozialismus und der Arbeiterbewegung,* III (1913), 415–37.

MEINECKE, FRIEDRICH. *Die Entstehung des Historismus.* Munich, 1936.

MENSCHENFREUND, DAVID. *Ferdinand Freiligrath.* Dissertation, Dijon University, 1935.

MOOG, WILLY. *Hegel und die Hegelsche Schule.* Munich, 1930.

MOORE, CARLISLE. "Thomas Carlyle and Fiction: 1822–1834," in *Nineteenth Century Studies.* Ithaca, 1940.

MORTIER, ROLAND. *Diderot en Allemagne.* Paris, 1954.

MYASNIKOV, A. "Lenin and the Problem of Literature," *Soviet Literature,* XIX (1949), 107–16.

NEEDHAM, H. A. *Le développement de l'esthétique sociologique en France et en Angleterre au XIXe siècle.* Paris, 1926.

NEHER, WALTER. "Arnold Ruge als Politiker und politischer Schriftsteller," in *Heidelberger Abhandlungen zur mittleren und neueren*

Geschichte. Edited by ERICH MARCKS and DIETRICH SCHAEFER. Heidelberg, 1933.

NESBITT, GEORGE L. *Benthamite Reviewing: The First Twelve Years of the Westminster Review, 1824–1836.* New York, 1934.

NESCHKINA, M. "Shakespeare in Karl Marx' 'Kapital,' " *International Literature,* V (1935), 75–81.

NEUMANN, F. W. "Die formale Schule der russischen Literaturwissenschaft und die Entwicklung der russischen Literaturtheorien," *Deutsche Vierteljahrsschrift,* XXIX (1955), 99–121.

———. "Sowjetrussische Literaturtheorien seit 1917," *Europa-Archiv,* VII (1952), 5333–36.

NOÉ, ADOLF CARL VON. *Das Junge Deutschland und Goethe.* Chicago, 1910.

NOVÁK, ARNE. *Menzel, Börne, Heine a počátkové kritiky mladoněmecké.* Prague, 1906.

OBERTELLO, AFREDO. *Carlyle's Critical Theories.* Genoa, 1948.

OLLIVIER, M. "Marx poète," *Mercure de France,* April 15, 1933.

PANNONICUS [pseud.]. "Une nouvelle affaire Lukács," *Les Temps Modernes,* CXLIII–CXLIV (1958), 1429–35; CXLIV (1958), 1715–17.

POPITZ, HEINRICH. *Der entfremdete Mensch: Zeitkritik und Geschichtsphilosophie des jungen Marx.* Basel, 1953.

PROSS, HARRY. "Romantik und Revolution (Georg Weerth)," *Deutsche Rundschau,* LXXXII (1956), 755–61.

RAS, G. *Börne und Heine als politische Schriftsteller.* The Hague, 1926.

REAVEY, GEORGE. *Soviet Literature Today.* New Haven, Conn., 1947.

REIMANN, PAUL. *Hauptströmungen der deutschen Literatur: 1750–1848.* Berlin, 1956.

———. "Herder und die dialektische Methode," *Unter dem Banner des Marxismus,* III (1929), 52–77.

———. "Legendenbildung und Geschichtsfälschung in der deutschen Literaturgeschichte," *Unter dem Banner des Marxismus,* IV (1930), 264–75, 376–400.

RILLA, PAUL. *Literatur: Kritik und Polemik.* Berlin, 1953.

ROE, FREDERICK WILLIAM. *Thomas Carlyle as a Critic of Literature.* New York, 1910.

ROHRMOSER, GÜNTER. "Literatursoziologie," *Handwörterbuch der Sozialwissenschaften,* VI (Göttingen, 1959), 636–39.

Rosca, Dumitru D. *L'influence de Hegel sur Taine.* Paris, 1928.

Rose, William. "Heine's Political and Social Attitude," *Heinrich Heine: Two Studies of His Thought and Feeling.* Oxford, 1956.

Schanck, Nikolaus. *Die sozialpolitischen Anschauungen Coleridges und sein Einfluss auf Carlyle.* "Bonner Studien zur englischen Philologie," No. 16. Bonn, 1924.

Schiller, F. "Friedrich Engels on Literature," *International Literature,* III (1933), 122–28.

———. "Marx and Engels on Balzac," *International Literature,* III (1933), 113–24.

Schlosser, Rudolf. *Rameau's Neffe: Studien und Untersuchungen zur Einführung in Goethes Übersetzung.* Berlin, 1900.

Schmitt-Weissenfels, Wilhelm. *Ferdinand Freiligrath.* Leipzig, 1877.

Schücking, Levin L. *Die Soziologie der literarischen Geschmacksbildung.* Leipzig and Berlin, 1931.

Schulte-Kemminghausen, Karl. "Annette von Droste-Hülshoff und Fr. Engels," *Wissenschaftliche Zeitschrift der Friedrich-Schiller-Universität Jena. Gesellschafts- und sprachwissenschaftliche Reihe,* V (1955–56), 439–43.

Schweizer, Viktor. *Ludolf Wienbarg als jungdeutscher Ästhetiker und Kunstkritiker.* Leipzig, 1896.

———. *Ludolf Wienbarg: Beiträge zu einer jungdeutschen Ästhetik.* Leipzig, 1897.

Seeger, Reinhart. "Friedrich Engels als Junger Deutscher." Dissertation, Halle University, 1935.

———. *Friedrich Engels: Die religiöse Entwicklung des Spätpietisten und Frühsozialisten.* Halle, 1935.

Sell, Friedrich C. *Die Tragödie des deutschen Liberalismus.* Stuttgart, 1953.

Sengle, Friedrich. "Voraussetzungen und Entwicklungsformen der deutschen Restaurationsliteratur," *Deutsche Vierteljahrsschrift,* XXX (1956), 268–94.

Siebenschein, Hugo. "Z Leninovy německé četby," *Časopis pro moderní filologii,* XXXV (1953), 25–27.

Sigman, Luise. *Die englische Literatur (1800–1850) im Urteil der zeitgenössischen deutschen Kritik.* Heidelberg, 1918.

Smith, Horatio S. "Relativism in Bonald's Literary Doctrine," *Modern Philology,* XXII (1924–25), 193–210.

SORGE, F. A. "Zum vierzehnten März," *Die Neue Zeit*, 1903, p. 772.

SPAEMANN, ROBERT. *Der Ursprung der Soziologie aus dem Geist der Restauration: Studien über L. G. A. de Bonald*. Munich, 1959.

STAHR, ADOLF. *Kleine Schriften zur Literatur und Kunst*. Berlin, 1871.

STEINER, GEORG. "Mit Engels und Marx gegen Lenin: Über die paramarxistische Schule der Literaturkritik," *Forum: Österreichische Monatsblätter für kulturelle Freiheit*, V (1958), 357 ff.

STRACHEY, JOHN. *Literature and Dialectical Materialism*. New York, 1934.

STRAUSS, E. *Bernard Shaw: Art and Socialism*. London, 1942.

TEMPLIN, ERNEST H. *The Social Approach to Literature*. "University of California Publications in Modern Philology," XXVIII/1. Berkeley and Los Angeles, 1944.

THALHEIM, HANS-GÜNTHER. "Kritische Bemerkungen zu den Literaturauffassungen Georg Lukács' und Hans Mayers: Zur Frage der Untersuchung der Rolle der Volksmassen in der Literatur," *Weimarer Beiträge: Zeitung für deutsche Literaturgeschichte*, IV (1958), 138–71.

THOMSON, GEORGE. *Marxism and Poetry*. New York, 1946.

TIMOFYEYEV, L. "Karl Marx on Literature," *International Literature*, XIII (1943), 63–66.

TROSHENKO, E. "Marx on Literature," *International Literature*, IV (1934), 138–48.

TUCKER, ROBERT. *Philosophy and Myth in Karl Marx*. Cambridge, Eng., 1964.

ULLRICH, HORST. *Der junge Engels*. Berlin, 1961.

ULRICH, JOHANN. *Heinrich Laubes politischer Entwicklungsgang bis 1834*. Berlin, 1934.

VICTOR, WALTER. *Marx und Heine: Tatsachen und Spekulationen in der Darstellung ihrer Beziehungen*. Berlin, 1952.

VIËTOR, KARL. "Programm einer Literatursoziologie," *Volk im Werden*, II (1934), 35 ff.

VOIGT, GÜNTHER. "Friedrich Engels und die deutschen Volksbücher," *Deutsches Jahrbuch für Volkskunde*, I (1955), 65–108.

VOZNESENSKY, A. "Die Methodologie der russischen Literaturforschung in den Jahren 1910–1925," *Zeitschrift für slavische Philologie*, IV (1927), 145–62; V (1928), 175–99.

WARREN, AUSTIN. "Literature and Society," in *Twentieth Century English*. New York, 1946. Pp. 304–14.

WATNIK, MORRIS. "Georg Lukács: An Intellectual Biography," *Soviet Survey*, No. 23 (January–March, 1958), pp. 60–65; No. 24 (April–June, 1958), pp. 51–57; No. 25 (July–September, 1958), pp. 61–68; No. 27 (January–March, 1959), pp. 75–81.

WEIGAND, HERMANN J. "Heine's Return to God," *Modern Philology*, XVIII (1919–20), 77–110.

WEINBERG, BERNARD. *French Realism: The Critical Reaction 1830 to 1870*. New York, 1937.

WELLEK, RENÉ. "Carlyle and the Philosophy of History," *Philological Quarterly*, XXIII (1944), 55–76.

———. *A History of Modern Criticism: 1750–1950*. Vols. I–IV. New Haven, 1955–65.

———. "Social and Aesthetic Values in Russian Nineteenth Century Criticism," in *Continuity and Change in Russian and Soviet Thought*. Edited by ERNEST J. SIMMONS. Cambridge, Mass., 1955. Pp. 381–97.

WENDEL, HERMANN. *Heinrich Heine*. Dresden, 1916.

———. (ed.). *Heinrich Heine und der Sozialismus*. Berlin, 1919.

WHITE, JOHN S. "Taine on Race and Genius," *Social Research*, X (1943), 76–99.

WILSON, EDMUND. *To the Finland Station*. New York, 1940.

WÜNSCHE, WALDEMAR. *Die Staatsauffassung S. T. Coleridges*. Dissertation, Leipzig University, 1934.

ZIEGLER, THEOBALD. *Die geistigen und sozialen Strömungen des 19. Jahrhunderts*. Berlin, 1899.

ZITTA, VICTOR. *Georg Lukács' Marxism: Alienation, Dialectics, Revolution: A Study in Utopia and Ideology*. The Hague, 1964.

ZLOCISTI, THEODOR. "Ein Brief von Moses Hess an Berthold Auerbach über Karl Marx," *Archiv für die Geschichte des Sozialismus und der Arbeiterbewegung*, X (1921–22), 411–12.

———. *Moses Hess*. Berlin, 1921.

Index

Adorno, Theodor W., v, 181, 222, 223, 230, 233, 235–36
Aeschylus, 68, 119, 127–28, 129
Agoult, Marie de Flavigny, Comtesse d', 88
Alfieri, Vittorio, 161, 213
Allgemeine Literatur Zeitung, 105
Allgemeine Zeitung, 5–6
Altenstein, Baron Karl, 24
Alton, Eduard d', 50
Annenkov, Pavel Vassilievich, 75
Aristophanes, 129
Aristotle, 3–4, 57, 59, 136, 146, 153, 181, 200, 219, 220, 221, 222, 224, 229
Athenäum, 51
Auden, W. H., 230
Auerbach, Erich, 133

Bahr, Hermann, 141
Bakunin, Mikhail A., 117
Balzac, Honoré de, 102, 104, 128, 129, 131, 135, 169–77, 202, 211, 213–14, 227
Barthes, Roland, 234
Bartók, Bela, 222
Baudelaire, Charles, 214
Bauer, Bruno, 40, 82, 105, 245 (n. 98)
Bauer, Edgar, 105
Bauer, Egbert, 105
Becher, Johannes R., 222
Beck, Karl, 14
Beckett, Samuel, 226
Belinsky, Vissarion, 41, 104, 125, 127, 136–38, 190, 198, 216
Benedix, Roderich, 157–59
Benjamin, Walter, 230
Bernstein, Eduard, 179
Bettziech, Heinrich, 99
Beyle, Marie Henri, 227
Biedermann, Karl, 29
Bismarck, Otto von, 181
Blanc, Louis, 76, 176
Bloch, Ernst, 181

Bloch, Joseph, 139, 142–43
Börne, Ludwig, 5, 6, 15, 16–23, 27, 29–30, 33, 42, 74, 75, 128, 161, 162, 163, 165–66, 170
Bonald, Louis-Gabriel-Ambroise de, 3
Brecht, Bertolt, 153, 199, 211, 225, 226, 227, 234
Brontë, Charlotte, 45
Brunswick, Duke of, 48
Bücher, Karl, 194–95
Büchner, Georg, 17, 114–15
Bürger, Gottfried August, 50, 51
Bürgers, Heinrich, 91
Buffon, Georges-Louis Leclerc, 135
Bukharin, Nikolai Ivanovich, 232
Bulwer-Lytton, Edward George, 43
Burke, Kenneth, 230
Burns, Lizzy, 117
Burns, Mary, 36, 117
Burns, Robert, 41–42
Burschenschaft, 2, 5, 7
Butler, Samuel, 134
Byron, George Gordon Byron, Lord, 14, 44, 161

Calderon, Pedro, 18, 21, 23
Calverton, V. F., 230
Campe, Julius, 13, 19–20
Carlsbad Decrees, 2
Carlyle, Thomas, 37–46, 61, 132, 228
Casaubon, Isaac, 134
Caudwell, Christopher, 179, 222
Cervantes Saavedra, Miguel de, 129, 204–5
Chamisso, Adalbert von, 51, 95
Chaplin, Charles, 226
Chateaubriand, François René, Vicomte de, 123
Chernishevsky, Nikolai Gavrilovich, 125–26, 171, 190, 196
Chiarini, Paolo, 227
Coleridge, Samuel Taylor, 42

273

Congress of Vienna, 17
Conrad, Joseph, 226
Cooper, James Fenimore, 211
Cornu, Auguste, v
Croce, Benedetto, 215, 227
Cuvier, Georges, 135

Dana, Charles Anderson, 58
Danielson, Nikolai Frantsevich, 125
Dante Alighieri, 120, 129, 161, 223
Darwin, Charles, 179, 183–85, 190–93, 229
De la Motte-Fouqué, Friedrich von, 38
Derzhavin, Gavril Romanovich, 125
Deutsch-Französische Jahrbücher, 37–40, 56, 61, 78, 88
Deutsche Brüsseler Zeitung, 165, 167
Deutsche Jahrbücher, 32
Deutsche Revue, 12
Deutscher Musenalmanach, 51
Dickens, Charles, 44–45, 135–36, 231
Diderot, Denis, 102, 122–23, 134
Disraeli, Benjamin, 149
Dobrolyubov, Nikolai Aleksandrovich, 107, 125, 217
Döblin, Alfred, 209
Dostoevsky, Feodor Mikhailovich, 125, 136, 205, 217
Dreyfus, Alfred, 226
Droste-Hülshoff, Annette von, 15, 136

Echtermeyer, Theodor, 25–28
Eichhoff, F. G., 124, 125
Eliot, T. S., 223
Engels, Friedrich, v, 8, 9–33, 34–46, 47, 59, 60, 61, 64–69, 74–75, 78–80, 88, 90, 95, 96, 97, 104–5, 107–8, 110–15, 116–51, 153, 154, 157–59, 160, 162–65, 167–69, 170–71, 172, 173–77, 178, 179, 183–84, 185, 188, 189, 194, 209, 210, 219, 228–29, 232, 233, 236, 243 (n. 4), 246 (n. 109), 247 (n. 1) ; *Anti-Dühring*, 183; *Communist Manifesto*, 151, 170; *Deutsche Ideologie, Die*, 64–69, 73, 143, 150–51; *Dialektik und Natur*, 183; *Holy Family, The*, 105; "Letters from the Wuppertal," 9–10, 18; *Situation of the Working Classes in England, The*, 149
Engels, Friedrich (senior), 10, 11, 34

Ernst, Paul, 139, 140–41
Ewerbeck, August Hermann, 78–79

Fadeyev, Konstantin, 107
Fairley, Barker, 159
Feuerbach, Ludwig, 39–40, 59–60, 61–62, 63, 64, 65, 66, 82, 182, 228
Fichte, Johann Gottlieb, 28
Flaubert, Gustave, 205, 214, 226
Follen, Karl, 25
Fontane, Theodor, 136, 204, 223
Fourier, Charles, 104
Freiligrath, Ferdinand, 11, 42, 83–87, 90–101, 117
Freiligrath, Ida, 90
Friedrich II (king of Prussia), 186, 187
Friedrich Wilhelm IV (king of Prussia), 7, 24, 58, 77, 90, 92
Fuegen, H. F., 3

Gans, Eduard, 57
Gaskell, Elizabeth, 45
Gautier, Théophile, 104, 197
Geibel, Emmanuel, 49
George, Stefan, 201, 214
Gerstenberg, Heinrich Wilhelm von, 153
Gervinus, Georg Gottfried, 6–7
Goethe, Johann Wolfgang von, 1, 11, 16, 18, 23, 39, 41, 50, 51, 118, 119, 121, 123, 126, 127–28, 135, 153, 154, 159–69, 170, 205, 213, 217, 226; *Faust*, 56, 62, 118, 163, 165, 167, 213
Goetze, Peter Otto, 125
Gogol, Nikolai, 125
Gold, Michael, 230
Goldmann, Lucien, v, 181, 227, 233, 234, 236
Goncharov, Ivan Aleksandrovich, 107, 125, 136
Goncourt, Edmond-Louis, 76
Goncourt, Jules Alfred, 76
Gorky, Maxim, 197–98, 231
Gottsched, Johann Christoph, 134
Graeber, Friedrich Christian Ludwig, 14–15
Grib, Vladimir, 170
Grillparzer, Franz, 17, 56
Grimm, Jakob, 120
Grimm, Wilhelm, 120

Grün, Karl, 49, 160, 164–65
Gundolf, Friedrich, 154, 201, 214
Gutzkow, Karl, 6, 9–16, 29, 30–33, 35, 42, 75, 104, 128, 163, 169, 170, 171, 173, 214

Hall, Joseph, 134
Haller, Albrecht von, 253 (n. 25)
Hallische Jahrbücher, 7–8, 24–33, 42, 83
Hanka, Václav, 124–25
Hardenberg, Friedrich von, 204, 217
Harkness, Margret, 128, 130–33, 137–38, 139, 173, 175
Hauptmann, Gerhart, 208, 210–11, 226
Hegel, Georg Wilhelm Friedrich, 7, 12, 24–33, 36, 41, 45, 51–52, 56, 57–59, 60, 67, 69, 81, 98, 105, 111, 114–15, 121, 123, 130, 159, 179, 181, 184, 185, 191, 200, 201, 204, 206, 208, 209, 213, 215, 216, 219, 229, 232, 233; *Lectures on Aesthetics*, 26, 111, 153–54, 157, 209; *Phenomenology of the Mind*, 122, 213; *Philosophy of History*, 148; *Philosophy of Right*, 57, 75
Heidegger, Martin, 218
Heine, Heinrich, vi, 5, 6, 12, 18, 35, 50, 74–82, 87–88, 89, 161–63, 170, 176, 237 (n. 1)
Herder, Johann Gottfried, 5, 71, 121, 123, 133, 148, 153, 159, 186, 233
Herwegh, Georg, 82–90, 90–91
Hess, Moses, 34–35, 60–61, 62, 74, 156, 206, 228
Hetherington, Henry, 240 (n. 25)
Hippel, Theodor Gottlieb von, 52
Hitler, Adolf, 206, 227
Hölderlin, Friedrich, 213
Hölty, Ludwig Christoph Heinrich, 50
Hoffmann, Ernst Theodor Amadeus, 52, 171, 234
Hofmannsthal, Hugo von, 92, 215
Holthusen, Hans Egon, 223
Homer, 48, 50, 68, 69–70, 114, 118, 121–22, 202, 226
Horace, 3–4, 11, 79–80, 93
Horthy, Nikolaus von, 205
Houben, H. H., 15
Howe, Irving, 227
Hugo, Victor, 134
Humboldt, Alexander von, 90, 108, 135

Hutten, Ulrich von, 112
Hyman, Stanley Edgar, 242 (n. 81)

Ibsen, Henrik, 129
Iffland, August Wilhelm, 157
Immermann, Karl Leberecht, 14, 163–64

Jacoby, Johann, 181
Jahrbücher für wissenschaftliche Kritik, 24–26
James, Henry, 136
Janin, Jules, 122
Jaurès, Jean, 179
Jean Paul; *see* Richter, Jean Paul Friedrich
Johnson, Samuel, 154
Jones, Richard, 121
Joyce, James, 230, 235
Jung, Alexander, 31–33
Junges Deutschland; see Young Germany

Kafka, Franz, 92, 180, 218, 226, 227
Kant, Immanuel, 179, 183, 185, 188, 189, 192, 195–96, 198, 225–26, 229
Kapper, Siegfried, 125
Karadžić, Vuk Stefanović, 125
Karl August, Duke of Saxe-Weimar, 161
Kautsky, Karl, 72, 128, 151
Kautsky, Minna, 128–30, 139, 174, 247 (n. 1)
Keller, Gottfried, 136, 213–14
Khrushchev, Nikita, 200
Kinkel, Gottfried, 98, 99
Kinkel, Johanna, 98
Kipling, Rudyard, 231
Kleist, Heinrich von, 17
Koch, Hans, v
Kock, Paul de, 171
Kossuth, Louis, 124
Kotzebue, August, 2
Krummacher, Gottfried Daniel, 119
Kühne, Gustav, 13, 237 (n. 1)
Kugelmann, Ludwig, 126
Kun, Bela, 199

La Bruyère, Jean de, 134
La Rochefoucauld, Duc François de, 122–23

Lafargue, Paul, 154, 172, 210
Lamarque, General Maximilien, 175
Lassalle, Ferdinand, 107–15, 117, 130, 154, 157, 182, 186
Laube, Heinrich, 13, 30, 45
Lavrov, Pyotr, 183
Law, John; *see* Harkness, Margret
Lenin, Vladimir Ilyitch, 127, 174, 197, 198, 200, 206, 207, 220, 231, 232
Leon, Don Diego, 83
Lessing, Gotthold Ephraim, 57, 118, 134, 153, 159, 185–87, 224, 253 (n. 25)
Leupold, Heinrich, 11
Levidov, Mikhail, 231
Liebknecht, Karl, 56, 182
Lindau, Paul, 182
Liszt, Franz, 88
Lopatin, German Aleksandrovich, 125
Louis XIV (king of France), 197
Louis-Philippe (king of France), 175
Louise (queen of Prussia), 53
Lubbock, Percy, 201
Lucretius Carus, 223
Ludwig I (king of Bavaria), 78
Lukács, Georg, v, vi, 116, 127, 170, 180–81, 185, 199–227, 228, 229, 232, 234, 242 (n. 81), 246 (n. 109), 247 (n. 1); *Aesthetik*, 200, 218–27; *Historical Novel, The*, 212–14; *Realism in Our Time*, 218; *Soul and the Forms, The*, 201, 218; *Theory of the Novel*, 201–5, 214, 215, 216
Lunacharsky, Anatoly, 198, 231
Luther, Martin, 120
Luxemburg, Rosa, 182

MacCulloch, I. R., 61
Mach, Ernst, 207
MacNeice, Louis, 230
Maeterlinck, Maurice, 208
Malraux, André, 101
Mann, Thomas, 211, 218, 222, 227, 234
Marcuse, Ludwig, v, 78, 81, 114, 246 (n. 109)
Marholm, L., 140
Marinetti, Emilio Filippo Tomaso, 231
Marx, Heinrich, 48–49, 50, 51, 53, 57, 118
Marx, Jenny, 48, 50, 118, 138
Marx, Karl, v, 8, 36, 39, 45, 46, 47–73, 74–75, 77–82, 87–90, 90–91, 95–101,

102, 104–7, 107–8, 110–15, 116–19, 120–27, 128, 129, 138–39, 142, 145, 149, 150, 153, 154, 157–59, 160, 163–67, 170–74, 178, 181, 182, 183, 184, 185, 186, 188, 189, 191, 194, 214, 219, 228–29, 232, 233, 242 (n. 81), 246 (n. 109), 247 (n. 1); *Capital*, 121, 126, 138, 149, 171, 183; *Communist Manifesto*, 151, 170; *Critique of Political Economy*, 68–73, 110, 140, 142–44, 150; *Deutsche Ideologie, Die*, 64–69, 73, 143, 150–51; *Economic-Philosophical Manuscripts*, 61–64, 154–57, 166–67, 228–29, 236; *Holy Family, The*, 105; *On the Jewish Question*, 60, 156; "Oulanem," 53–57, 171, 172; "Skorpion und Felix," 52–53
Masaryk, Tomaš Garrigue, 124–25
Matthiessen, F. O., 230
Maturin, Charles Robert, 171
Maupassant, Guy de, 226
Mayer, Gustav, 237 (n. 4)
Mayer, Hans, v, 181, 233–34
Mehring, Franz, v, 146, 160, 179, 180, 181–89, 190, 192, 193, 195, 198, 206, 229, 236, 250 (n. 21)
Meinecke, Friedrich, 4
Melville, Herman, 37, 38, 226
Menzel, Wolfgang, 2–3, 5, 20–21, 160–61, 162
Metternich, Prince Klemens von, 1–2, 6, 12, 16
Michaelis, Johann David, 133
Michelet, Karl Ludwig, 25
Mikhailovsky, Nikolai Konstantinovich, 191
Milton, John, 213
Molière, Jean Baptiste, 189
Montesquieu, Charles de, 16, 161
Moore, Thomas, 161
Morgan, Lewis Henry, 194
Morrow, Donald, 152–53
Müllner, Adolf, 56
Münzer, Thomas, 112, 113
Mundt, Theodor, 13, 30

Nagy, Imre, 199, 218
Napoleon I, 16, 197
Napoleon III, 197
Narodnaya Volya, 125, 126
Narodniki, 125, 189

Neue Rheinische Zeitung, 96–98, 99, 100, 124
New American Cyclopedia, 58
New Masses, 230
New Moral World, 45
New York Daily Tribune, 45
Nibelungenlied, 120
Nicholas I, 197
Nietzsche, Friedrich, 201, 214
Nodier, Charles, 134
Novalis; *see* Hardenberg, Friedrich von
Nyugat, 201

Oken, Lorenz, 135
Ostrovsky, Aleksander Nikolaievich, 197
Overbury, Sir Thomas, 134
Ovid, 57
Owen, Robert, 45, 132

Palacký, František, 124
Pascal, Blaise, 234
Pfizer, Gustav, 163
Pissarev, Dmitri Ivanovich, 107, 125–26, 196, 216
Plato, 3–4, 41, 202, 204, 207, 227
Plekhanov, Georgi Valentinovich, v, 179, 180, 184, 189–98, 220, 228, 229, 230, 231, 232
Plievier, Theodor, 101
Plotinus, 64
Propertius, 50
Proudhon, Pierre-Joseph, 164
Proust, Marcel, 230–31
Prutz, Robert, 26, 45
Pückler-Muskau, Prince Hermann von, 20
Pushkin, Aleksander Sergeievich, 125, 197

Racine, Jean, 18, 234
Radcliffe, Ann, 103
Raumer, Friedrich von, 37
Razumovsky, Count Alexej Grigore-vich, 197
Regnier, Henri de, 215
Reimann, Paul, v
Reinhardt, Richard, 79
Rheinische Jahrbücher, 78
Rheinische Zeitung, 36, 83, 87, 91
Ricardo, David, 61
Richter, Jean Paul Friedrich, 52, 162

Rilke, Rainer Maria, 208, 226
Rimbaud, Arthur, 230
Robbe-Grillet, Alain, 226
Rosenkranz, Karl, 25, 26
Ruge, Arnold, 7–8, 25–31, 58, 82, 87–88, 117, 231 (n. 1)
Ruhmor, Carl Friedrich, 58
Ryazanov, D. B., 250 (n. 21)

Saint-Simon, Claude-Henri de Rou-vroy, Comte de, 104, 132
Sainte-Beauve, Charles-Augustin, 104, 123
Sand, George, 45, 104, 136–38
Say, Jean-Baptiste, 61
Schelling, Friedrich Wilhelm Joseph von, 24, 36, 42, 134, 162, 209
Scherer, Wilhelm, 186
Schiller, Friedrich von, 16, 23, 50, 51, 98, 110–11, 114, 118, 129, 135, 153–54, 157, 179, 185, 187–88, 202, 209, 213, 226
Schlegel, August Wilhelm, 18, 50
Schlegel, Friedrich von, 18, 42, 134
Schmidt, Conrad, 139–40, 145–46
Schmidt, Erich, 186–87
Schönberg, Arnold, 222
Schücking, Levin, 15
Schweizer Republikaner, 36, 37
Scott, Sir Walter, 213, 227
Semler, Christoph, 133
Seydelmann, Carl, 56, 118
Shaginian, Marietta, 159–60, 250 (n. 21)
Shakespeare, William, 18, 36, 48, 62, 68, 110–12, 118, 119, 126, 127–28, 152–59, 209, 212
Shaw, George Bernard, 179
Shelley, Percy Bysshe, 15, 44, 240 (n. 25)
Shklovsky, Victor, 201
Sickingen, Franz von, 112, 113
Sidney, Sir Philip, 4
Silone, Ignazio, 101
Simmel, Georg, 201, 214
Simmons, Ernest J., 232
Smirnov, A. A., 152–53
Solger, Karl Wilhelm Friedrich, 57
Song of Igor, 124
Sophocles, 47
Sorge, F. A., 138, 139
Spectator, The, 134

Spender, Stephen, 230
Staël-Holstein, Anne-Louise-Germaine de, 3, 5, 17, 233
Stahr, Adolf, 26, 29
Stahr, Carl, 87
Stalin, Josef, 180, 200, 217, 231, 232
Starkenburg, Hans, 139, 146–47, 194
Stein, Lorenz von, 61
Stendhal; *see* Beyle, Marie Henri
Sterne, Laurence, 52
Strauss, David Friedrich, 23–24, 25, 44
Strauss-Wohl, Jeanette; *see* Wohl, Jeanette
Strindberg, August, 130
Sue, Eugène, 45, 102–7
Svoboda, Václav, 124–25
Swift, Jonathan, 161
Szeliga; *see* Zychlin von Zychlinski, Franz

Taine, Hippolyte, 130, 134, 136, 146–50, 170, 171, 193–94, 195, 204, 234
Tatler, The, 134
Taylor, W. C., 149
Telegraph für Deutschland, 9–10, 12, 13, 14, 18, 21, 35
Thackeray, William Makepeace, 45
Theophrastus, 134
Tolstoy, Leo, 129, 174, 190, 213–14, 226, 227
Trémaux, P., 183
Trotsky, Leon, 231

Ulbricht, Walther, 188

Vatke, Wilhelm, 25
Vauvenargues, Luc de Clapiers, Marquis de, 134
Vergil, 202
Vico, Giovanni Battista, 4–5, 71, 121, 233
Villemain, Abel François, 171
Vischer, Friedrich Theodor, 26, 58, 206
Vizetelly, Henry, 175
Volk, Das, 82

Voltaire, François Arouet de, 161
Vorwärts, 78

Wagner, Richard, 120, 211
Waterloo, Battle of, 53
Weber, Max, 201
Weiss, Guido, 181
Welcker, Friedrich Gottlieb, 50
Wellek, René, vi
Werner, Zacharias, 56
Westminster Review, 41
Westphalen, Georg von, 48
Westphalen, Jenny von (mother of Ludwig von Westphalen), 48, 154
Westphalen, Jenny von (daughter of Ludwig von Westphalen); *see* Marx, Jenny
Westphalen, Ludwig von, 48, 50, 118, 154
Westphalen, Philipp, 48
Wienbarg, Ludolf, 6, 12, 13, 162–65, 167–69
Wilhelm II (emperor of Germany), 186
Wilson, Edmund, v, 230
Winckelmann, Johann Joachim, 5, 57, 121, 186, 201, 213, 233
Wishart, Jenny; *see* Westphalen, Jenny von (mother)
Wölfflin, Heinrich, 201
Wohl, Jeanette, 75
Wolfram von Eschenbach, 120
Wright, Richard, 101

Young Germany, 6, 7, 14–15, 18, 28–32, 35, 38, 44–45, 160, 162, 163, 169, 170, 228
Young Hegelians, 7–8, 23–33, 38, 44–45, 59, 64, 104, 105, 126, 160, 216, 228
Young Italy, 6

Zassulich, Vera, 126
Zeitlin (Russian critic), 231
Zhdanov, Andrei A., 218, 232
Zola, Émile, 104, 173, 174–75, 202, 208, 213, 226–27
Zychlin von Zychlinski, Franz, 105–6